To look for other titles in this series, visit www.tcpress.com

tinued)

D1453922

Courageous Leadership
in Early Childhood Education
Taking a Stand for Social Justice

EDITED BY

Susi Long

Mariana Souto-Manning

Vivian Maria Vasquez

Foreword by Sonia Nieto

TEACHERS COLLEGE PRESS

TEACHERS COLLEGE | COLUMBIA UNIVERSITY

NEW YORK AND LONDON

Published by Teachers College Press, 1234 Amsterdam Avenue, New York, NY 10027

Cover design by Dave Strauss. Photograph © 2015 Laura Dwight Photography. All Rights Reserved.

Library of Congress Cataloging-in-Publication Data

Names: Long, Susi, 1952- editor of compilation. | Souto-Manning, Mariana, editor of compilation. | Vasquez, Vivian Maria, editor of compilation.
Title: Courageous leadership in early childhood education : taking a stand for social justice / edited by Susi Long, Mariana Souto-Manning, Vivian Maria Vasquez ; foreword by Sonia Nieto.
Description: New York : Teachers College Press, 2016. | Series: Early childhood education series | Includes bibliographical references and index.
Identifiers: LCCN 2015035725 | ISBN 9780807757413 (pbk. : alk. paper) | ISBN 9780807774519 (ebook)
Subjects: LCSH: Early childhood education—United States. | Social justice—Study and teaching (Early childhood)—United States. | Educational equalization—United States.
Classification: LCC LB1139.25 .C69 2016 | DDC 372.21—dc23
LC record available at http://lccn.loc.gov/2015035725

ISBN 978-0-8077-5741-3 (paper)
ISBN 978-0-8077-7451-9 (ebook)

Printed on acid-free paper
Manufactured in the United States of America

*We dedicate this book to the incredible administrators we have come to love and admire through the years. Representing them, we honor **Jan Long** who, for 42 years, was an inspirational leader in the lives of children, teachers, and families. Teachers express admiration for his "nurturing style," "unassuming encouragement for innovations without taking them on as his own," "support for trying something difficult even if it might fail," and "living his belief that every child matters."*

To Jan and every administrator who works toward a more just tomorrow by engaging in the difficult conversations that lead us to take action for change, we dedicate this book to you.

Contents

Foreword

It is almost impossible nowadays to find a school or university that does not proclaim its support, even reverence, for social justice. But every time I hear these noble pronouncements, I recall the Spanish saying, *"Del dicho al hecho, hay gran trecho,"* which can translate as, "From saying to doing, there's a big gap," but in essence means, "Actions speak louder than words."

What does it mean for early childhood administrators to *really* support social justice in their schools? Look no further than this inspiring book. The vision of the 13 administrators featured herein is loud and clear. Their actions, not only their words, proclaim: "We are here for the children. We are working for a society where our children—*all* children—have the opportunity for a bright future and a consequential life." In these pages, you will read powerful examples of administrators "doing" social justice, not just saying they believe in it. From engaging in honest conversations about race and privilege, to insisting on respect for children's native languages and home cultures, to supporting teachers in their schools with respect for their intelligence and professionalism, the administrators in this volume "get it"; they know what the children, families, and their staff members need in order to succeed. That is why *Courageous Leadership in Early Childhood Education* is a welcome addition to the theory and practice of creating empowering learning spaces for young children.

Although a good number of books have focused on teachers breaking barriers of injustice for their students and for the profession—I have written several of these myself—very few have paid attention to the vision and the actions of school administrators. But teachers cannot do it all, no matter how hard they work or how honorable their intentions. Without the active support and blessing of administrators, precious little can get done in schools.

It is no secret that so-called educational reform is wreaking havoc on U.S. schools, particularly those that serve young children of Color who live in poverty. Indeed, it is often the case that these children, their parents, and their teachers are blamed for the brutal conditions in schools. High-stakes testing, the wholesale privatization of schools, and unfair evaluation of teachers are driving out good teachers and administrators alike. These conditions place our most vulnerable children at greatest risk. Yet even school leaders, who ostensibly hold the most power in their respective settings, are having a hard time putting their vision into action because all sorts of unreasonable mandates are getting in their way. Until administrators take the lead, this dismal situation will be hard to change.

Susi Long, Mariana Souto-Manning, and Vivian Maria Vasquez, scholars with stellar reputations in the fields of early childhood education, critical literacy, and social justice education, have combined their considerable talents to edit a book that will serve as a beacon of hope for administrators, policymakers, and educators at all levels of learning and teaching. Challenging deficit views and business-as-usual remedies, Long, Souto-Manning, Vasquez, and the other chapter authors of *Courageous Leadership in Early Childhood Education* have made it their goal to challenge power structures that dictate who is deserving of a high-quality and empowering education. In spite of the demands of the current reform movement, and at a time when all educators are struggling, the stories you are about to read will remind you what courageous leadership is about. The authors of these chapters write about administrators who not only work tirelessly to create loving schools for their young charges, but also take into account the richness of children's backgrounds and experiences, and the passion of their parents' dreams for their futures as a basis for true reform.

Lately, even early childhood settings have become bleak and dreary environments, rather than the lively and joyful places of learning they used to be. But preschools and schools do not have to be like this. I've often said that true reform (not what goes by the name of reform in schools today) is not easy; if it were, everyone would already be doing it. As you will see in the stories of visionary educators working for equity for our very youngest students, it takes hard work, persistence, and a dogged determination to put a social justice perspective into action. The educators featured in this book shine a light on the kinds of values and practices that can point the way to a more hopeful future.

—Sonia Nieto

Acknowledgments

Our deepest thanks go to the 13 leaders who are highlighted in this book because of the work they do every day to bring their social justice convictions to life. We are grateful that they opened their doors to the chapter authors so we can glimpse into and be inspired by their commitment to building the knowledge, strategic savvy, and courage necessary to identify injustices and work to overturn them.

Opportunities to learn from these 13 early childhood administrators would not be possible without the chapter authors who lovingly brought their stories to light. Because of their own convictions and backgrounds, these authors were able to capture and represent the work of courageous leaders in poignant and powerful ways. We thank them for their contributions to this book.

In support of the work that led us to this book and the collaboration that the three of us have enjoyed as thinking partners, we owe a huge debt of gratitude to teachers, students, and university colleagues from whom we learn every day and who communicated the urgent need for such a text to be written. We are also grateful to Sonia Nieto, who has been an inspiration to the three of us. We feel truly honored that she wrote the foreword for this book.

On a more personal note, we are more than grateful for our families, who supported us by engaging in dinner table and late night discussions about key issues and ideas, and who were exceptionally patient about the time required to develop this text. In particular, we lovingly thank Jan and Kelli Long; Dwight Manning, Lucas and Thomas Souto Manning; Andy Bilodeau and TJ Vasquez Bilodeau.

Finally, we acknowledge administrators everywhere who courageously take a stand for social justice. We hope that you will keep going in spite of challenges, reminded by the administrators in this book that *perceived barriers too often become excuses for not committing to work that matters.* These barriers are not insurmountable. We hope you will urge other administrators to live their social justice commitments and that you will support them in recognizing that our work to contradict racial, cultural, and social injustice continues to be one of the most urgent needs in schools and society.

Silence Is Not an Option

Susi Long, Mariana Souto-Manning, and Vivian Maria Vasquez

As this book goes to press, it is not an exaggeration to invoke words from James Baldwin's (1963) "A Talk to Teachers": "We are living through a very dangerous time." Across the United States and around the world, while many enjoy privileges afforded to dominant cultural, racial, social, and linguistic groups, educational potential continues to be denied, human beings are dehumanized, and lives are lost because of acknowledged and unacknowledged biases regarding race, ethnicity, language, income, religion, sexual orientation, and gender identification. These injustices manifest themselves in ways that are very visible, but they also operate insidiously under the radar of those who have not been their victims or who experience the privilege of not recognizing their existence. This reality is a bitter pill to swallow, particularly when we must acknowledge injustices in our own educational and societal backyards. But there is hope. As intentionally as injustices were put in place, they can be intentionally taken down. Recognizing them and taking responsibility for working to disrupt and dismantle them is a first step.

Early childhood educators, and early childhood leaders in particular, are perfectly positioned to take this step. In fact, we accept this responsibility when we choose to educate children who one day will make decisions that guide every institution and interaction in our society. Our enactment of that responsibility can lay a strong foundation for our young students and the adults they will become. Because of the moral, pedagogical, and systemic choices we make, the young children entrusted to our care will (or will not) build understandings that no race, ethnicity, language, religion, gender identification, economic situation, or sexual orientation holds more virtue or rightness than any other. They will (or will not) learn that their racial and ethnic histories, heritages, and languages hold great value in the world. They will (or will not) receive an education that recognizes their worth, ability, and potential, building on resources they bring to classrooms. They will (or will not) learn to recognize discrimination, silencing, and marginalization as well as strategies for working against these practices.

In this book we present the stories of 13 early childhood administrators who show the kind of courage leaders must possess if they are truly committed to building a more just society. These leaders do not merely stand by; they stand up to guide us through dangerous times. Their actions align with their belief that every child has the right to an equitable education and that such an education is the cornerstone of a democracy. For them, silence and inaction mean conforming to an unjust status quo. They choose neither.

READING THIS BOOK

We developed this book to share examples of courageous leaders in hopes that others might gain insights and courage to join them in standing up for change while continuously deepening their own insights and abilities. In Chapter 1, we introduce some of the key issues that will be addressed by leaders in subsequent chapters. We share historical information (and encourage educators to deepen learning about how schools and societies came to be inequitable in the first place) and explore reasons for tackling these issues as advocates for social justice in early childhood settings.

In each of chapters 2 through 14 we highlight the work of an early childhood administrator by focusing on day-to-day practices and strategic negotiations used to bring social justice convictions to life. The chapter authors—who are anchored in their own convictions about equity in early childhood—spent time with and interviewed the administrators as well as teachers, students, and family and community members. As a result, they provide vivid accounts of administrative practices in preschools, elementary schools, classrooms, and communities. Introduced briefly in the following paragraphs, the highlighted leaders reflect a range of settings: They direct preschools, Head Start programs, and public and private elementary schools in urban, suburban, and rural settings across four geographic regions in the United States.

The first highlighted administrator is Ms. Bessie Gray, introduced in Chapter 2 by her granddaughter, Marcelle M. Haddix. Setting the tone for the rest of the book, the chapter tells us about Ms. Gray, an early childhood education pioneer serving low-income, diverse communities through the development of Gray's Child Development Center, which provided quality child care in Milwaukee, WI, for more than 40 years. The voices of three generations of Black women educators (her granddaughter, daughter, and Ms. Gray) communicate Ms. Gray's resolve to address inequities. They describe the strategies Ms. Gray used to nurture children and their families, particularly those who were often marginalized in other settings. Hers is a legacy rooted in community, activism, and love.

In Chapter 3, Mariana Souto-Manning and Yandra Mordan-Delgadillo introduce Marilyn Barnwell, who has been the director of the Bloomingdale Head Start program in New York City for 35 years. In this chapter, we learn about Marilyn's leadership, vision, and commitment to the positive affordances of cultural and linguistic pluralism and how she makes it possible for young children to experience culturally relevant bilingual education. We learn how Marilyn positions parents to be critically aware of how schools continue to segregate children and compromise their futures. Marilyn facilitates a project whereby parents learn how to advocate for their children by refuting limitations imposed by inferior notions and deficit paradigms. We glimpse into these and other strategies she uses to position children as capable and worthy, and families as essential partners.

Chapter 4 focuses on Geralyn Sosinski, who leads a dual-language Head Start program in Kansas City, KS–El Centro Academy for Children. Authors Kindel Nash and Geralyn Sosinski focus on ways that Geralyn uses multilingualism as a resource to inform professional development, hiring practices, and curriculum in an environment that can be isolating when working to promote bi/multilingualism. In spite of commonly held English-only policies, Geralyn takes steps to nurture a preschool experience in which Latino/a linguistic resources and heritage are foundational centerpieces. The chapter describes how she works to develop the capacities of staff to address social justice issues, highlighting her ability to support and involve families as she leads from within.

In Chapter 5, Mariana Souto-Manning, Rebeca Madrigal, Karina Malik, and Jessica Martell introduce Dr. Victoria Hunt, founding principal of Dos Puentes Elementary School, a dual-language public school in New York City. The authors describe the philosophy and strategies Dr. Hunt uses to foster pedagogies that lead to academic success and to the maintenance of linguistic and cultural competence. To do so she invites teachers to problematize inequities that shape students' schooling and their lives. In Dr. Hunt's words: "You can't lead a school if all you are doing is reacting to mandates and compliance issues. You have to have a vision, a plan, and then assess how the mandates and compliance issues fit within your vision."

Chapter 6, written by Bilal Polson and Mónica Byrne-Jiménez, highlights Dr. Polson's commitment to replacing deficit views of students and families with a wealth mindset and a critical stance. Foundational to Dr. Polson's work is his refusal to adopt deficit views of teachers as he supports their positive engagement in home and community settings, leads them to identify out-of-school expertise, and helps them use that knowledge to recognize and transform inequitable teaching practices. This chapter describes Dr. Polson's move from a child-readiness approach to focusing on readying the school for all children, guiding teachers to recognize and overturn institutional and individual biases, involving families in leadership roles, and transforming curriculum to build from the expertise of young children.

In Chapter 7, Michele Myers describes her work as the principal of an elementary school with a predominantly African American population situated within a rural South Carolina community. The chapter builds from her concern that well-intentioned teachers can hold unrecognized biases about families and children that get in the way of equitable teaching practices. Dr. Myers shares strategies for creating a welcoming school by helping teachers identify those biases, hear and validate families' concerns, recognize the rich networks of support in homes and communities, and rebuild practices accordingly. Dr. Myers models critical reflection on her own practice and recognizes that the work is not just about her courage, but about the courage of teachers who step out of their learned experiences to seek new understandings.

In Chapter 8, Detra Price-Dennis introduces Mary Rykowski, a principal who spent 2 decades in Columbus, OH, working to overturn the stereotypes held about students from low-income communities as lacking in educational motivation and ability. Foundational was an unfaltering belief in the knowledge, skill, and ability of children and family members as she worked to counter the misperception that all was already lost for many of her students before they ever entered the school building. As Price-Dennis explains, "Mary put her career on the line many times to do what she believed was in the best interest of the students," facing district tensions and teacher bias as she insisted on equitable educational practices.

In Chapter 9, Julia López-Robertson and Mary Jade Haney describe ways that elementary school principal Parthenia Satterwhite passionately supports practices that utilize strengths of students from low-income, rural, African American, Mexican American, and White communities. Ms. Satterwhite insists on a multilingual, multicultural environment setting an important example by building her own genuine relationships with families *in* their communities. Lovingly subversive, she does not let mandates stop her but takes risks to support teachers in going beyond an unjust norm—*using* policy (that others may see as constraining) to support innovation that moves beyond a monocultural standard. At the core of her belief system is an understanding that the success of the school requires respect for and partnership with children, families, and teachers.

In Chapter 10, Alfredo Celedón Luján describes the work of Isabelle Sandoval, who spent her career advocating for excellence in the education of students in elementary schools in Española and Santa Fe, NM. The chapter shares strategies used by Dr. Sandoval to address injustices, including discrimination from those who considered her to be "too Hispanic" to lead the school and biased attitudes of teachers who chose not to acknowledge the expertise of their Latino/a and Native American students. Persevering, Dr. Sandoval sustained a commitment to never "breaking a child's spirit." Living her belief that no child is less than gifted, she worked tirelessly to preserve and promote multilingual communities by supporting teacher and student growth.

Chapter 11 focuses on administrator Jean Frey and her work in a culturally and linguistically diverse elementary school located near Washington, DC. Author Sarah Vander Zanden explains that a significant challenge Jean faced was that external accountability measures increasingly indicated that folks who pushed that agenda had little respect for the children, families, and teachers affected by those measures. Ms. Frey had the courage to take a very public stand against such injustices. The chapter also describes how she created spaces for teachers to engage in ongoing, self-directed, professional development that helped them utilize technologies to position critical literacies as foundational in early childhood classrooms in a time of restrictive mandates and standardized definitions of success.

In Chapter 12, Meir Muller takes us into the world of Dr. Sabina Mosso-Taylor, director of a public child development program serving children ages 3 through 5. The chapter showcases ways that she engaged faculty in studying issues of equity through a 3-year study group involving teachers in professional reading, home and community experiences, and curricular planning. The chapter identifies commitments guiding Dr. Mosso-Taylor's work to support teachers' understandings about race, language, privilege, and classroom practices. It discusses tensions she encountered and explains her negotiation of those tensions. The chapter also describes ways that Dr. Mosso-Taylor ensured a diverse student population, interrupted discriminatory actions, countered color-blind mentalities, and built supportive relationships with children, families, teachers, community members, and district administrators.

Chapter 13 highlights the work of Rabbi Meir Muller, director of the Cutler Jewish Day School in Columbia, SC. Chapter author Sabina Mosso-Taylor describes ways in which Dr. Muller commits to justice-based leadership by insisting on a diverse population with regard to secular and nonsecular orientations, race, ethnicity, ability, and gender identification, and how he establishes, nurtures, and maintains critically inclusive practices that support socially and culturally just educational experiences. The chapter showcases Rabbi Meir's belief that educators (and their students) have a significant role to play in dismantling injustices, drawing on stories from families and teachers to illustrate his work to help teachers and children understand that role and cultivate their ability to take action—leading by example.

In Chapter 14, authors Nathaniel Bryan, Lamar Johnson, Dywanna Smith, Brittany Garvin, and Anthony Broughton highlight the work of Ms. Cecelia Rogers, whose vision and voice led local officials to establish a public charter school in the heart of one of Charleston, SC's, public housing communities.

Ms. Rogers worked to counter stereotypes of violence and illegal drug activities through innovation, collaboration, and action as the school became a beacon of justice for those historically disenfranchised. The authors explain some of the strategies used by Ms. Rogers to address issues of disproportionality related to race, poverty, class, and in education, including the establishment of a collective vision, the activation of voice, and the execution of actions.

Chapter 15 concludes this volume by compiling the principles, goals, and strategies used by all 13 administrators and inviting other administrators to follow their lead. It provides possibilities, potential, encouragement, and support for those seeking tools for turning conviction into practice, and rhetoric into reality. Resources used by these administrators to further their own learning and that of their colleagues are embedded in the reference list at the end of the book.

AN INVITATION

With this introduction, we invite you into discussions of issues, ideas, and practices in the day-to-day lives of early childhood leaders. Through the voices of families, teachers, and the administrators themselves, we present their work to educate, enlighten, disrupt, and replace unjust practices with the purpose of attaining equity in the education of all children.

CHAPTER 1

Courageous Leaders

No Empty Platitudes

Susi Long, Mariana Souto-Manning, and Vivian Maria Vasquez

A school leader by definition has power and that power needs to be actively directed in providing the best for every child and family.

—Early childhood administrator Rabbi Meir Muller

Across the country, we see many educational leaders face or perceive constraints that keep them from using the power entrusted in them to challenge and change systems, practices, and dispositions that perpetuate educational privilege and inequity. At the same time, other administrators—facing similar challenges—find ways to alter unjust systems by working within and beyond curricular and testing mandates, funding crises, narrow ideologies, and discriminatory practices to effect substantive change. What is the difference? What principles, convictions, and strategies are common among administrators who use the privilege of their positions to address racial, linguistic, cultural, and social inequities in and beyond schools? What can be learned from them about developing and sustaining the knowledge, confidence, and courage to live our commitments to equity—to turn rhetoric into reality?

We (the coeditors of this book) are teacher educators. Our work focuses primarily on early language and literacy education in racially, culturally, and linguistically diverse contexts. At the core of that work is supporting educators in examining institutions, systems, and their own teaching, and learning to identify practices, policies, ideologies, histories, and dispositions that lead to educational inequity, then working to rethink curriculum and practice in empowering and transformative ways. Through this work, one of the most commonly voiced concerns we hear from teachers is that their hands are tied because of administrative dictates. At the same time, school administrators tell us about pressures that *they* feel from those in positions of power above them.

The tragic consequence of these layers of pressure is that too many educators stand by while programs, practices, and the ideologies that undergird them perpetuate success for a few while actively oppressing opportunities for children who are misrepresented, negatively profiled, and left out of or marginalized from the curriculum: often, children of Color, emergent bi/multilinguals, children from low-/no-income households, and lesbian, gay, bisexual, transgender, questioning, intersex, and asexual (LGBTQIA) children and families.

This book presents the stories of educational leaders who use the power entrusted in them to challenge and change systems of educational privilege and to create spaces where teachers are supported in building and using knowledge to (re)create practice. For them, *educating for social justice* is not an empty platitude. Their stories reveal not only their convictions, but also ways they work innovatively and strategically to transform educational institutions based on those convictions. Although geographically distant from one another, these leaders are joined by commitments to the following actions.

- They recognize that inequities and discriminatory acts continue to exist in schools and society; they refuse to settle for them.
- They consistently engage in critical institutional and self-examination informed by their study of equity issues and current research; they acknowledge biases and work to alter personal and institutional practices.
- They listen to teachers, families, and children and use insights to disrupt misperceptions and work toward institutional and pedagogical change.
- They work as partners with teachers to identify practices that privilege and those that oppress; they collaborate with teachers to transform dispositions, policies, and practices.
- They recognize and embrace families' expertise and knowledge; they understand that caring takes different forms across family contexts; they help teachers build similar insights.
- They serve as advocates with and for students' communities and are authentically present in the lives of children and families.
- They do not compromise or retreat from convictions with excuses or deflections, but promote innovation within existing systems while working to change systemic injustices.

The purpose of this chapter is to introduce particular issues that lie at the foundation of why these beliefs and actions are so important. These discussions are organized around topics we see as fundamental to engaging in the kind of honest talk that must occur within and beyond educational institutions if we are to move toward change. Although our discussions are introductory, we hope they will lead administrators and teachers to seek further knowledge as they deepen their abilities to understand, articulate, and respond to injustices. The chapter closes with a look at why these conversations, and the courageous leadership that initiates them, are particularly important in early childhood settings.

COURAGE

The leaders in this book bring social justice convictions to life through a range of informed, consistent, and deliberate actions. Because these actions often require administrators and those who work with them to examine, challenge, unlearn, and replace strongly held educational traditions and previously unquestioned truths, courage is required. In the following sections, we discuss five of many areas in which these administrators focus their actions: (1) challenging monocultural curricular models; (2) addressing the lack of equity-focused professional development; (3) dismantling deficit views and negative profiling of students and families by engaging in difficult talk about issues of race, ethnicity, social class, gender, and sexual orientation; (4) guiding teachers to value home knowledge and bi/multilingualism by addressing English-only mindsets; and (5) going beyond *verbalism*—talk without action (Freire, 1970)—by insisting on the work of justice as nonnegotiable in their educational spaces.

Monocultural Curricular Models

Monocultural models designed according to White, middle-class norms currently dominate early childhood curricula. While historical reasons for this are explored later in this chapter, the purpose of this section is to point out (a) that this is often connected to a misguided belief that dominant culture curricular models will lead to greater achievement and higher test scores, (b) the pressure felt by administrators to stick to those models, and (c) some of the obvious inequities that result.

The administrators in this book experience real fears and challenges regarding high-stakes test scores, scoring systems, and rating scales, particularly when testing systems are used to label preschools, elementary schools, classrooms, and students in very public and enduring ways. They are particularly incensed because they recognize that many of these so-called solutions to raising achievement and supporting children's growth *actually reduce prospects* for many students because they represent narrow cultural and linguistic models of teaching and assessment (Darling-Hammond, 2013; O. García & Kleifgen, 2010). These narrowly conceived models perpetuate educational privilege for students from dominant groups while continuing to underserve many students of Color, emergent bilinguals, students from low-/no-income homes and communities, and LG-BTQIA students and families (Blackburn, 2011; Ford, 2013; Howard, 2010).

Because these models often are mandated, the pressure is great to conform to practices that position many students away from educational opportunities (Delpit, 2012; Souto-Manning, 2013). In fact, administrators in schools with the lowest scores and the most diverse populations often feel the greatest pressure to participate in programs disconnected from cultural relevance (Darling-Hammond & Bransford, 2005; Perry, Moses, Wynne, Cortés, & Delpit, 2010). Instead of insisting on professional development to help educators recognize inequities and then transform teaching to broaden its cultural, linguistic, and social foundations, district, state, and federal efforts typically are doubled to focus on the very practices that marginalized and underserved students to begin with. As a result, instead of disrupting a cycle of miseducation (Woodson, 1933), inequitable practices endure.

Examples of ongoing inequities can be found as children of Color, emergent bilinguals, and students from low-income households continue to be sorted, labeled, and segregated into special education classrooms far more often than their White, English-only, middle-class, and affluent peers (Blanchett, Mumford, & Beachum, 2005). At the same time, more White, English-only, middle-class, and affluent students are referred to talented and gifted programs (Ford, 2013). In spite of the high quality of some special education programs, the very existence of this inequity imposes labels that follow students throughout their schooling, often becoming self-fulfilling prophecies as students' feelings of worth (or lack of worth) are internalized. As a result, the *education debt* (Ladson-Billings, 2006)—resulting from the "cumulative impact of centuries of educational inequities" (Castagno, 2014, p. 6)—owed to children of Color, emerging bi/multilinguals, and children from low-/no-income homes remains unpaid, and inequitable practices continue to favor those already privileged by the system.

This occurs in spite of decades of work that clearly indicates the success of culturally relevant, culturally sustaining, and humanizing pedagogies in promoting achievement and educational success (Boutte & Hill, 2006; Gay, 2010; Ladson-Billings, 1995a, 1995b; Paris, 2012; Woodson, 1933). Administrators in this book feel the very real need for these approaches to be understood and valued by district, state, and preschool/school-based administrators and teachers if we are to interrupt the cycles of inequity through which deficit images of children, families, and communities and discriminatory practices are established and reinforced. They stand against teaching that is dominated by narrow approaches that privilege and marginalize the same children year after year.

Lack of Opportunity for Equity-Focused Professional Development

The lack of opportunity for leaders to develop understandings about the damaging effects of monocultural approaches and then build knowledge about culturally relevant and humanizing alternatives is another constraint faced by educational administrators (Nieto, 1999). Rarely are leaders provided long-term, professional development that focuses on issues of race, ethnicity, language, religion, gender, sexual orientation, and class as those issues play out in schools and society. Nor do they have opportunities to learn deeply about transformative, fully inclusive, and humanizing pedagogies.

In addition, when leaders do build their own sociopolitical and pedagogical knowledge, they rarely have opportunities to learn strategies for guiding teachers through the same process. This includes the ability to lead educators to examine their own and others' assumptions about children and families and to identify the privileging of one cultural, racial, and/or linguistic group over others within systems that govern schools (assessment systems, systems for special education and gifted and talented identification, family support systems, instructional programs, school committee and advisory structures, etc.). Self-study and in-stitutional examination of this kind are critical if educators are to identify and problematize individual and structural biases that keep us from teaching every child well (Alexander, 2010; Noguera, 2009).

This void is reported not only in on-the-job professional development but also in programs of higher education from which many graduates leave unpre-pared to address negative student profiling, bias, and pedagogical and structural inequities they may encounter on the job (Boske, 2009; Shapon-Shevin, 2010). While many programs of educational leadership express commitments to social justice, in practice the in-depth study of justice/equity issues and how to address them rarely occurs (Beachum, White, FitzGerald, & Austin, 2013). And while there are examples of skilled social justice leaders in schools (Madhlangobe & Gordon, 2012; Theoharis, 2009), administrative challenges to the narrowly de-fined curricular status quo (Razfar & Gutiérrez, 2013) are not the norm across the nation. Consequently, injustices continue as students are failed by systems so normalized that educators often fail to recognize when students' histories are ignored or tokenized, languages are dismissed, expertise is discounted, and aca-demic marginalization is ensured (Delpit, 2012; Derman-Sparks & Edwards, 2012; O. García & Kleifgen, 2010).

The leaders featured in this book face these kinds of challenges every day. However, as their stories convey, they find ways to work within and beyond con-straints to ensure professional study and focused self-examination for themselves and the teachers with whom they work.

Challenging Deficit Views and Cultural/Social Rightness

A strong commonality across leaders in this book is their commitment to con-tradicting assumptions that undergird deficit views of children and families—the kind of biased commentary heard in teachers' lounges and hallways: "They live in the projects, nobody reads to them," "Nobody cares in that home," "They don't even speak English," "You can't get his parents in the school," "He won't sit still" (Long, Anderson, Clark, & McCraw, 2008). In addition to challenging commonly voiced deficit views about language, literacy, and physical behaviors, some chapters also describe early childhood administrators challenging the degradation and invisibility of LGBTQIA children and families and the marginalization of particular religious beliefs. Described in the following sections, these views of cultural, linguistic, and social rightness have deep roots in principles of appropriateness held dear by many early childhood educators. As a result, a kind of othering has seeped, unchecked, into the collective consciousness as a justified norm. This means that, when administrators work to change it, they have their work cut out for them.

Monocultural rightness and developmental appropriateness. To understand how deficit thinking has become normalized, it is important for educators to know that much of what guides this acceptance of appropriateness evolved from the belief that some families were not raising their children appropriately, that "the middle-class, typically White, community . . . knew best what young children require" (Goodwin, Cheruvu, & Genishi, 2008, p. 3), and that particular family structures (typically, married heterosexual parents, one male, one female) were the only effective families. This mentality survives because of messages permeating almost every aspect of U.S. society—sometimes visible and sometimes unrecognized, yet insidiously under the surface—perpetuating the belief that White, middle-class, heterosexual, Christian, English-only ways of parenting, caring, teaching, social development, and learning are *right* or *appropriate* (Derman-Sparks & Edwards, 2012; Miller, 2015; Souto-Manning, 2013). This rightness of Whiteness, middle classness, heterosexuality, gender binaries, and so on is so deeply embedded that many who are not its victims do not see it as other than normalcy. As a result, oppression and privilege persist as a status quo (Castagno, 2014).

Developmentally appropriate practice. In the late 1980s, the notion of monocultural appropriateness in early childhood education became reified in the concept of *developmentally appropriate practice* (DAP) (Bredekamp, 1987). This "framework of principles and guidelines for best practice in the care and education of young children" (www.naeyc.org/dap/faq) was held up as the definitive guide for early childhood educators. In subsequent years, the document was criticized for its narrow representation of developmental appropriateness as the actions and developmental markers of dominant groups were held up as standards often leading to assumptions of deficit about every other group (Cannella, 1997; Yelland, 2010).

Although each revision of DAP guidelines attempted to address these critiques (Bredekamp, 1987; Bredekamp & Copple, 1997; Copple & Bredekamp,

2009), interpretations of the work continue to perpetuate definitions of *best practice* as grounded in White, English-dominant, middle-class cultural norms. Even the most recent DAP publications (Copple, Bredekamp, Koralek, & Charner, 2013) do not specifically address the need for teachers and administrators to identify pedagogical, institutional, and personal biases. As a result, educators continue to interpret DAP through their own learned sense of cultural rightness, typically acquired as they were brought up in schools grounded in Eurocentric approaches (King & Swartz, 2014; Smith, 2012; Souto-Manning, 2010a). This is compounded when DAP recommendations for culturally relevant teaching focus primarily on building practice from students' expertise and interests and do not normalize or even address more complex understandings about cultural, linguistic, and social practices beyond the dominant norm. As a result, habits, ideologies, and beliefs anchored in monocultural perceptions of rightness go largely unrecognized and unquestioned (Gillborn, 2005), and many children and their families continue to be framed as deficient or deviant from an unjust and narrowly defined norm.

Recently, members of the National Association for the Education of Young Children (NAEYC) initiated a virtual forum, Diversity and Equity Education for Adults (DEEA), to provide a site for educators to "wrestle with social injustice within ourselves and between ourselves" (earlychildhoodequity.wordpress.com). The National Council of Teachers of English Early Childhood Education Assembly also developed a social justice website (www.earlychildhoodeducationassembly.com/social-justice-and-equity-in-early-childhood-education.html) with resources for teachers to use in developing knowledge about the injustices inherent in monocultural and normative models. These efforts are much-needed steps in the right direction. They can aid in the creation of robust dialogue *if* educators and educational leaders, such as those highlighted in this book, are willing to engage with colleagues in examining their own learned sense of morality and cultural rightness and their role in masking recognition of oppressive practices that establish and perpetuate monocultural and normative models in the first place (Castagno, 2014; Freire, 1970; Souto-Manning, 2013).

Knowing our past to inform our future. While understanding DAP's role in the history of cultural rightness is important, going back further we see a hierarchy of appropriateness derived from colonial powers imposing their ideas in order to establish their right to power (Bonilla-Silva, 2000; Jensen, 2005). In addition to acts of genocide killing millions of human beings on this Earth, colonizing powers committed cultural and linguistic genocide to establish the superiority of their own ways of being in the interest of power and control. Examples are seen in attempts to eradicate beliefs, traditions, languages, and cultural practices from the lives of indigenous peoples in Africa, Asia, and North and South America through colonization and enslavement (King, 2005; Fanon, 1952; Rodney, 1972; Smith, 2012). In the United States, Indian Boarding Schools provide one of many vivid examples of efforts with colonial movements. Developed as a mechanism to aggressively assimilate and oppress Native Americans (Leahy & Wilson, 2008), the schools worked to erase languages, parenting practices, and belief systems and replace them with European models (Giago & Giago, 2006). This was much like the government-sanctioned "re-education" of Indigenous Peoples in Australia leading to "stolen generations," which continued into the 1970s (Pilkington & Garimara, 2013), Canadian residential schools enforcing "Euro-Canadian and Christian ways of living" requiring young people to deny their heritage (First Nations Studies Program, 2009), and numerous other examples around the world as "indigenous societies . . . were not [deemed] civilized enough to have systems of order" (Smith, 2012, p. 29) nor to have worthy modes of thought, language, and literacy.

The enslavement of human beings was the most obvious act designed to ensure power through oppression (Jensen, 2005), as human beings were "ripped from their lands over several generations and shipped . . . [to] lands already taken from another group of indigenous peoples" (Smith, 2012, p. 28). Africans were enslaved and brought to the United States and many other countries because of *expertise* that would allow oppressors to amass great wealth. And yet control was assured by promoting the belief that Africans not only possessed less intellect but were commodities, not fully human.

Schooling and the reinscription of histories. Schooling across centuries reproduced these attempts to erase or render invisible the expansive contributions, heritage, intellect, and expertise of those who were enslaved or colonized (King & Swartz, 2014). Even today, "as soon as children enter school, their understandings of the past (and present) [continue to be] shaped by such narratives" (pp. 7–8). Thus, the impact of dehumanizing mentalities on the thinking of generation after generation is an important frame through which to understand the history of deficit frameworks. Understanding the intent to control with which these frameworks were initiated and how they became deeply held "truths" is essential to grasping the urgency of our work as social justice educators. We must challenge the tenacity of deficit views held today and their impact on our ability to teach every child well (Alexander, 2010; Howard, 2014).

One example of schooling and its reproduction of deficit thinking can be found in postdesegregation United States. While not discounting the importance of desegregation, a devastating outcome was that many African American educators were replaced by White teachers who had been schooled in the normalization (and hence, superiority) of White cultural traditions, language, and history (Siddle Walker, 1996). Thus, African American students were educated by teachers who had no knowledge of their families and communities; little (if any) knowledge about or appreciation for students' identities, histories, and capabilities; and little motivation to teach in culturally relevant and sustaining ways (King, 2005). At the same time, many remaining educators of Color were pressured to teach from a White normalcy/superiority stance, enculturating students into systems that effectively erased all but tokenized depictions of African and African American history, heritage, and global contributions from the curriculum.

All of this had a significant impact on students' and teachers' beliefs about the potential of children of Color. While it may be difficult for some to acknowledge, these beliefs affect educational practice to this day (Delpit, 2012; Razfar & Gutiérrez, 2013), as adults who learned deficit models through their own schooling (typically without realizing it was happening) become teachers who in turn reinscribe deficit ideologies that are embedded in their learned realities. In this way, the "created past [continues to be] given the authority of truth" (Smith, 2012, p. 70), an essential understanding if we are to "confront the tremendous injustice that has a deafening grip on our society and keeps us so far away from everything we know is right and fair and just" (Ladson-Billings, 2015).

Leaders challenging deficit realities. The leaders in this book are spotlighted because of their work to reverse these realities. They use specific strategies to help themselves and teachers grow in their understandings about the destructive effects of narrow definitions of "appropriate" and "normal" and how those definitions become mechanisms that keep educators from effecting change (Duncan-Andrade & Morrell, 2008; Tatum, 2009). They recognize that, hundreds of years after the country's constitutional commitment to equality, "America is still not an egalitarian society" (Alexander, 2010, p. 1). With that knowledge, they take on the responsibility of helping colleagues acknowledge and address the social conditioning that perpetuates the normalcy and supremacy of Whiteness (Sue, 2015) as they build educational settings where appropriateness is broadly conceived and diversity is the norm (Genishi & Dyson, 2009).

Valuing Bi/Multilingual Abilities

Another area in which the administrators in this book focus their actions is positioning linguistic pluralism as the norm. They do not dispute the need to ensure Academic English competence for children living in the United States, particularly given the fact that Academic English competence is currently a determining factor in measures of academic success. However, they do so with awareness that (a) the path to English expertise is not paved by eradicating students' existing languages; (b) Academic English expertise is supported when students' languages are integral to classroom learning; and (c) bi/multilingualism in the classroom benefits every child (Fu, 2009; Gutiérrez, Morales, & Martínez, 2009).

A common barrier to embracing bi/multilingualism in U.S. schools and preschools is the widespread misconception that children will learn English more easily if their academic lives are not complicated with other languages. Multilingualism is not, however, a complication. It enriches abilities to communicate, deepens intellect, and contributes to more complex cognitive functioning (Clyne, Isaakidis, Liem, & Rossi Hunt, 2004; Skutnabb-Kangas, 2002). In fact, it is a valued norm in almost every country in the world (Nieto, 1999). Ironically, the notion that bi/multilingualism should be discouraged in U.S. classrooms is not applied to nonimmigrant students who study languages in immersion and other language programs. However, acknowledgment of that expertise is regularly denied when children from immigrant backgrounds attempt to utilize multilingual abilities in schools and preschools and are met with responses such as "We speak English here" and "You won't learn English if you continue speaking Spanish." This occurs despite the fact that immigrant children often possess greater bi/multilingual knowledge and skill than do students attempting to learn languages in highly valued immersion programs (Nieto, 1999). Such attempts to shut down (and effectively eradicate) students' languages continue even though educators have access to a wide body of research describing classrooms in which multiple languages are normalized as assets (Coelho, 2004; Gregory, Long, & Volk, 2004; Laman, 2013; Martínez, 2010; Wheeler & Swords, 2004).

The forthcoming chapters describe ways in which educational leaders contest "structures that marginalize students' . . . linguistic capital" (Ntelioglou, Fannin, Montanera, & Cummins, 2014, p. 3) and support teachers in bringing students' bi/multilingual expertise into the classroom. Administrators' stories illustrate ways in which they provide professional development in support of multilingual classrooms, work within systems of monolingual testing and instruction to create more linguistically just practices, fight against language biases, work to learn languages themselves, and promote multilingualism for its potential to enhance learning for *all* students (Delpit, 2012; Zentella, 2005).

Beyond Verbalism: A Call to Action

One of the reasons we share the stories in this book is because we are concerned that *teaching for social justice* has become a rhetorical phrase in university, school, and district mission statements; course syllabi; professional development objectives; accreditation reports; and standards documents. It is regularly thrown around and yet rarely enacted in consistent and transformative ways. Freire (1970) named this kind talk without action *verbalism*.

The dominance of verbalism is clear when we consider the myriad of reasons given for not being able to challenge and change unjust practices. Deflection or avoidance strategies are heard everywhere: "My district won't," "The standards require," "Young children can't," "Time won't allow," "There is no money." This leads to one of the most important ways that administrators featured in this book demonstrate courage—through their commitment to transformative action without deflection. For them, social justice is not merely an objective; it is the foundation that propels every plan, program, interaction, and decision they make. From a social justice foundation, they educate themselves, hire faculty and staff, engage teachers in professional study, encourage the development of inclusive and equitable curricula, build relationships with families in their communities, and collaborate with families and teachers to make institutional decisions. They understand that we are cultural beings who have the power to perpetuate both privilege and oppression in our lives and teaching practice (Derman-Sparks & Ramsey, 2011; King, 2005), so they engage colleagues (and themselves) in the "constant process of self-examination and transformation" (Souto-Manning, 2013, p. 13). While taking action is never easy, they reject verbalism, accept the call to action, and extend it to everyone reading this book.

WHY EARLY CHILDHOOD LEADERS?

While the stories in this book hold insights for all leaders, we focus on those in early childhood settings because we believe that social justice begins with the education of our youngest children. More children than most educators realize enter formal schooling only to learn that who they are counts for little—in their classrooms and in the world. This occurs with the dominance of White, middle-class, heterosexual, English-only characters in classroom texts and materials; as they notice who among their peers go to special education classes and who are referred to talented and gifted programs; as they observe discipline strategies and overhear adult talk about children and families. Messages about self as less capable are quickly internalized. The negative impact of these insidious messages follows the children throughout their schooling.

At the same time, other children receive messages that they and their worlds matter more than others. These are children whose histories, people, and languages dominate curricula; who are assumed (often because of positive biases toward their race, ethnicity, socioeconomic class, and/or family structure) to have potential for success before they walk into the classroom; and whose families are seen to support academic success because they do so in ways largely defined by White, middle-class, English-only norms. These feelings of self-worth then translate into a confident foundation from which a cycle of educational privileging begins, following them throughout their schooling experiences.

Messages received in early childhood also impact how children see one another. From their earliest days, children can learn to value people from backgrounds different from their own or they can learn to enact negative biases.

Messages are delivered, received, and appropriated as young children listen, observe, and interact in faith-based settings, through extracurricular activities, at play, with social and print media, and in school (Miller, 2015). A well-known example of how early young children can internalize bias is found in Clark and Clark's 1947 Black doll–White doll research study. This well-known demonstration of children as young as 3 years of age choosing White dolls as preferable to Black dolls because of perceptions about beauty, intelligence, and goodness has been researched again and again over the past 70 years (Davis, 2007; Jordan & Hernandez-Reif, 2009). While these studies demonstrate learned racial bias, other work makes it clear that young children can develop similar perceptions regarding class, religion, gender, physical ability, size, sexual orientation, and family structure (Derman-Sparks & Edwards, 2012).

Because these biases filter into children's belief systems from an early age, early childhood educators have a tremendous responsibility. We can lay the groundwork from which children learn to recognize and act against injustice, or not. When early childhood leaders make the commitment to work with teachers to examine attitudes, assumptions, practices, and policies, they can begin to transform early childhood education to create a strong foundation of equity from which children will grow into adulthood.

With these thoughts in mind, we developed this book to support early childhood administrators who are ready to move beyond *talking* about educating every child to *taking action* for positive and transformative change. These 13 administrators "afford neither complacency nor despair" (Obama, 2015), but take action because the alternative is to settle for an inequitable status quo. While their experiences are not without tensions, setbacks, and frustrations, they persevere because they see solutions where others see constraints. They continue the work because they simply have no other choice. Using the words of Maya Angelou (1988), "Theirs is the kind of courage that makes it possible to practice every other virtue—kindness, truth, mercy, generosity, and honesty."

CHAPTER 2

The Courageous Leadership, Labor, and Love of Bessie Gray

Marcelle M. Haddix

It wasn't just a job; it was a passion to help children.

—Bessie Gray

My earliest school memories are from when I was a preschooler at Gray's Child Development Center in Milwaukee, WI, in the 1970s. My grandmother, Bessie Gray, was the director of the Center. I remember being part of a diverse, integrated classroom with African American teachers. This stands out for me because beyond my early childhood years, I never had a teacher of Color again. I also remember being taught from a curriculum model that I later would learn to characterize as culturally relevant (Ladson-Billings, 1995a, 1995b) and multicultural education (Banks, 1995). These memories are special because, in my role as teacher and teacher educator today, they represent that I belong to a legacy of educators dedicated to supporting and nurturing all children and their families, particularly those marginalized in schools and preschools. This is the legacy of my grandmother, Bessie Gray (Figure 2.1).

THREE GENERATIONS OF EDUCATORS

In this chapter, I reflect on my grandmother's courageous leadership as an early childhood administrator and present it as a model for educators and leaders who are committed to providing equitable educational environments for all children. I share the leadership of Bessie Gray from the perspectives of three generations of Black women educators—my grandmother (Figure 2.1), my mother, and me (Figure 2.2). All three of us embody a commitment to quality child care and early

**Figure 2.1. Ms. Bessie Gray, founder of Gray's Child Development
Center, Milwaukee, WI.**

**Figure 2.2. A legacy of educators: Ms. Bessie Gray's daughter,
Wanda Montgomery, and her granddaughter, Marcelle M.
Haddix (chapter author).**

childhood education, especially for underserved communities, that stems from the example set by my grandmother. Her courageous leadership is a reminder of the responsibility we must uphold if we intend to achieve the promise of educational excellence for all children and families.

Bessie Gray opened Gray's Child Development Center in Milwaukee, WI, in 1973. Gray's was a staple for quality child care and development in the Milwaukee area for 4 decades. This was in great part due to my grandmother's courageous leadership. As a pioneer in quality child care and development for diverse communities in the state of Wisconsin for more than 40 years, she was the founder, executive director, and president of the board of directors for the Center, the first Black-owned child-care center in Wisconsin to become accredited through the National Association for the Education of Young Children.

My mother, Wanda Montgomery, is a leader in child care and parent and community outreach and education in Milwaukee. She is a founding member and president of the local Milwaukee affiliate of the National Black Child Development Institute (NBCDI) and is the first vice chair on the organization's national board. At one time, she worked as director of development and executive director for Gray's Child Development Center.

My own experience includes work as an English language arts teacher, a writing instructor, a community educator and activist, a teacher educator, and a literacy researcher. I am an alumna of Gray's from the 1970s and, in my high school years, I worked at the Center after school assisting in the classroom and with administrative responsibilities. Without question, I know that my resolve to work for the betterment of teaching and learning experiences for all children is informed most by the leadership and commitment of my mother and grandmother. In this chapter, I weave together these three voices to provide a historical perspective and contemporary possibilities represented in the courage, legacy, and influence of Ms. Bessie Gray, a woman whose life's work is rooted in education, community, activism, and love.

RECOGNIZING INEQUITIES AND TAKING ACTION: ORIGINS OF GRAY'S CHILD DEVELOPMENT CENTER

I am convinced that, after 45 years of physical and emotional abuse, scrubbing floors for White folks on my knees at least 5 of those years, spending days and shifts in welfare lines for 13–15 years, "the will to do" is really within the individual. —Bessie Gray

Bessie Gray moved from Pine Bluff, AR, to Milwaukee, WI, in 1952 when her father brought her north to enroll in nursing school. Her plans were diverted when she met her husband, Percy Gray, and entered into a new phase of life—marriage and raising children. During a 10-year period from 1953 to 1963, her family grew and her attention was focused on home and raising her children. In 1966, however, Ms. Gray began her career as a Head Start volunteer. It was during this time that she noticed how desegregation meant that many teachers coming into the predominantly Black schools were not equipped to recognize the abilities possessed by the students. Too often, when the teachers saw poverty, they assumed inability or lack of intelligence. They defined children by poverty rather than by the attributes, knowledge, and potential they brought to the classroom. Ms. Gray knew that the children and families deserved much more from their educational environments:

> I saw the difference in how Black children were being taught in the public school system. [I] saw teachers teaching to an environment versus to the child. It was very obvious that we had a lot of suburban teachers that came into the Black community to teach in the Head Start program. And it was kind of like if you came from a poor family, there were certain things that you would not be able to grasp. That concerned me. Part of that was when I started sending my own children to suburban schools; it was surprising how different the environment was. . . . There was something wrong with this picture. That's why around 1971, I decided that there was something that I could do.

Ms. Gray's resolve to address inequities she observed working with Head Start was further strengthened in 1972, when she sought child care for her youngest child:

> That's how the Center started because at that time I couldn't find infant care. And if you could find it, it wasn't quality. Many centers did not deal with infant care at that time. So I thought, here's a way that I can start a business and can also stay at home with [my] baby.

From 1973 to 1981, Ms. Gray designed and operated Gray's Child Development Center, a licensed group child-care program, from her home in the inner city of Milwaukee. She recalls, "We chose not to name it day care; we chose child development. That was by design." She wanted to ensure that the name of the center communicated its pedagogical expertise and grounding in knowledge about the development and education of young children. Gray's was in an ideal location close to the downtown area, making the Center accessible for many working professionals.

Initially, the Center was licensed to serve 19 children and the enrollment represented children from multiple cultural and linguistic backgrounds. The curriculum put an emphasis on music, art, and foreign language. In the first years, the program was largely private pay, but its mission was to provide affordable, quality child care for low-income families in central Milwaukee. The popularity and visibility of Gray's Child Development Center grew quickly in the 1970s. People sought out Gray's because of its reputation and Ms. Gray's positive relationships with people from the Head Start field. Many university students conducted their fieldwork at Gray's. In the 1970s, there were few quality child-care programs in the city of Milwaukee. Word traveled quickly. When people heard of Gray's, they came.

EQUITY ACTIONS AS GRAY'S CHILD DEVELOPMENT CENTER GREW

As an organization that nurtures kids, we need to nurture adults as well. —Wanda Montgomery

Bessie Gray developed, nurtured, and grew the Child Development Center by focusing on children who were least well served by other centers or who had no access to excellence in early childhood education. The following sections describe the equity actions she took to develop Gray's Child Development Center into a place of the highest quality, a center educators continue to celebrate today.

Ensuring Equity in the Availability of Child Care

Gray's Child Development Center started as a for-profit business. Initially, income was generated primarily from families who could cover their own child-care costs. By the early 1980s, however, Ms. Gray began to get requests from families in crisis situations, including teen mothers and children who were abused. Instead of just focusing on private pays, Ms. Gray shifted to where the needs were:

> We made a decision to focus on especially those kids who were being abused. I was just shocked at the number of families who were in crisis situations. But, by doing so, we also became more involved with Milwaukee County. . . . As those private pays moved on, those slots were filled with children who had drastic needs.

At that point, Ms. Gray took steps to switch to nonprofit status and began to think about moving the program out of her home and expanding to multiple sites so the services would be closer to families in need. This led to a three-pronged approach: establishing neighborhood-centered locations, providing transportation for families, and continuing to support families who could bring their children to the Centers. With this expansion, Gray's added more staff, there was greater outreach to families, and Ms. Gray accessed grant programs to support the work and add more staff.

Grant programs allowed the Center to provide subsidized support for teen mothers so they did not have to drop out of school to care for their children. Additionally, parents in challenging circumstances—those who felt they were not equipped to care for their children—could get authorized, subsidized child care. My mother, Wanda Montgomery, explained:

> Gray's was not just [for people] going to work; [it gave some] parents respite during the day so that their children could be in a safe setting. There were many women who were at home or out in the streets all day; if they said, "I can't handle my kids during the day," . . . they got transportation and the children could be at the day care all day. It was a way of keeping the kids safe.

To ensure that these children had child care, Ms. Gray accessed government programs to fully cover their fees and transportation to the facility. There were only a few programs in the African American community that offered such care, so Gray's provided an important contribution and was one of the largest programs of its kind in the city. Ms. Gray's mission was to support families who were trying to transcend their circumstances. Ms. Montgomery explained that, although government subsidies were critical, the *real* support came through Bessie Gray's insight, sensitivity, courage, and action to care for children and families:

> There were people who came who couldn't afford to pay the cost. She would let them stay. From day one, she always supported families who were trying to do better. . . . Every year, she's written off what we call bad debt—people who couldn't pay the fees, but she knew they needed the care. So, she let the kids come and wrote it off.

Building Relationships as Foundational to Family Involvement

Gray's also sought to provide education and training for parents and families. Through some of the grant programs, they were able to order toys and books for classrooms as well as additional sets for parents to use at home. Ms. Gray also offered support services for parents. Her goal was to help parents think about the whole child: education, health, nutrition, and cultural traditions. For example, she explained how the Centers worked to preserve cultural values associated with food and family meals while advocating for holistic healthy lifestyles: "People would come in and say, 'Are you actually cooking greens and cornbread?' That was a big seller. We had chicken, pork chops—full-course meals."

Foundational to Ms. Gray's success with families was her commitment to developing genuine relationships by getting to know families in their communities and homes, sharing her own struggles and challenges as a parent and past welfare recipient, and teaching by example as she worked with children in the company of their families. She was not judgmental; she valued families for the love they brought to parenting, familial ties, and traditions. Through this example, the staff also developed a genuine interest in and love for the families. Families knew they were respected, not demeaned. Mutual learning about caring for and raising young children grew from that foundation. This was parent and teacher education at its highest level, a signature of Gray's program.

Committing to Success for Every Child

Gray's Child Development Center enrolled children from 6 weeks old to 12 years of age, with a focus on children with special needs. The enrollment process involved an initial assessment and a 2-week trial. Before the term "individualized education plan" was commonplace, Ms. Gray assessed each child to determine his or her social, emotional, and educational needs. With expertise in many different curricular models, she modified curricula to meet the needs of the children. Ms. Montgomery explained:

> For some, Gray's was the final option. I think there were people who came to Gray's because they had children who had been put out of other programs. And I don't know how the word got out, but people would say, "Take 'em to Ms. Gray; she can handle 'em." And so she had some challenging kids—Black and White—some of them had been put out of other programs. They came to Gray's and she was able to work with them. And they were successful [there]. . . . One thing Ms. Gray always said is, "We want to be able to meet the needs of these kids."

Actively Teaching in the Classroom as a Teacher Leader

Ms. Gray was not only an administrator; she was also a certified and qualified teacher, so it was not uncommon to find her in the classroom working with children. This was a strong component of her effectiveness as a leader:

> During a lot of that time I was still doing some teaching in the classroom because some things you can't put in a person. There were some things that I wanted to see happen, so to make it happen, I needed to do it myself. . . . Even with the teacher in the classroom, I would take out a group of students and go through basic concepts. Games and things that a lot of times I would make up. What's up? What's down? What's round? . . . I really enjoyed that.

Ms. Gray felt that to be good administrators, educators must have experienced teaching in the classroom. She explained that this gives them an essential appreciation for the role and challenges of teachers: "If you have not been in the classroom, you have no idea." The insights she gained from her experience in the classroom and the fact that she always stayed close to the classroom allowed her to engage in effective teacher education and development.

Hiring High-Quality Teachers

In terms of teacher recruitment and selection, Gray's reputation preceded itself. According to my mother, "People wanted to work there. They'd come there and they felt supported. Gray's paid a decent salary, had benefits, and provided training. People came there because it wasn't just the Gray family; it was an extended family." Eight of Ms. Gray's nine children worked there, and some of the employees had been with the Center for so long, they were considered part of the family.

Seeking passion. Ms. Gray had a knack for selecting and retaining effective teachers, which provided stability and consistency. She sought teachers who demonstrated convictions and passion similar to her own. For example, Dorothy McBride taught at Gray's for over 25 years. Many commented that she was "like another Ms. Gray." Ms. Dorothy was known for being able to work with any child. Within 3 to 6 months, there was typically a significant difference in the children she worked with. Parents often requested Ms. Dorothy. Ms. Montgomery explained: "Where someone else would have put their hands up and said, 'Just forget this child, there's no use,' she made the difference." During her years at Gray's, Ms. Dorothy earned her associate's degree and several teaching credentials through NAEYC's Academy for Child Development Associates (CDA). Ms. Gray described Dorothy's lasting impact: "A lot of the students now who have gone on to college, they'll come back to her because she [gave them] something over the years that they can come back to."

Going beyond the résumé. In hiring, Ms. Gray always looked beyond the résumé for an individual's strengths that might stand out. Applicants' reasons for working in child care were critical. Just saying, "I love children" was not good enough. She sought teachers who demonstrated a belief in the potential of every child and she observed applicants in action to determine that belief.

Ms. Gray did this by bringing potential teachers into the Center to work for 40 hours under her observation. She let them know that, at the end of the 40-hour period, she would decide whether they were a good fit for the Center. Ms. Gray felt that certain behaviors and characteristics would stand out during that first week. For example, she could easily identify someone who was impatient.

Ms. Gray recalled, "I terminated a young man because of his yelling. I said, 'You know you've got some issues. . . . You're dealing with [some] children who are in abusive situations; they hear enough yelling at home.' And so I say that's just not a fit for here."

Building from strengths. Once teachers were hired, Ms. Gray committed to helping them build on their strengths, thereby cultivating quality teachers. In this way, her vision for supporting educators was much like the vision she had for supporting children. When she saw strengths that she wanted for the Center, even if a prospective teacher had more learning to do, she supported the teacher in developing that expertise. As Ms. Montgomery said, "That's, in some respect, why I think a lot of people stayed—because they didn't have all the things that they needed but she would fill in the gap."

Encouraging and supporting further education for staff. Ms. Gray credits the ongoing success of Gray's to the superior teaching that was at the core of the institution. Throughout her career, she continued learning and made sure that her teaching staff received individualized training as well as tuition reimbursement to support their own educational pursuits. Working full time and taking classes part time for 10 years, Ms. Gray eventually earned her bachelor's degree in early childhood education from the University of Wisconsin, Milwaukee, and later earned her master's degree in educational administrative leadership from Marquette University. She was also a state-certified child-care trainer and, as a result, cultivated the professional careers of hundreds of successful early childhood teachers.

At one time, at least half of the staff at Gray's consisted of women who, like Ms. Gray, had been on welfare; many of them pursued degrees encouraged by Ms. Gray's example and supported by the opportunities for tuition assistance. Janice McGee, who was a teacher at Gray's for nearly 30 years, said that working for Gray's helped her uplift her own life. Ms. Gray takes pride in having helped so many women reject the stereotypical expectation that they have a "welfare mentality" and to be able say to the system: "Close my case!"

THE COURAGE TO FACE CHALLENGES

At its height, Gray's Child Development Center had grown from a home-based business to a million-dollar-a-year business with 65 employees and more than 600 children enrolled in its programs. It had moved to a 7-acre, campus-like site that stretched several city blocks. The property was a former convent given to Ms. Gray by the Order of the Sisters of the Sorrowful Mother. This allowed

Ms. Gray to combine her 14 child-care centers serving 500 children throughout the city into one campus. At that time, Gray's also provided evening child care at four community college locations. In spite of this success, the process was not without significant challenges. This is where the courage of Ms. Bessie Gray becomes most visible as she met and negotiated challenges in ways that hold lessons for leaders today.

Courage to Be Heard as a Black Woman: No Room for Doubt or Fear

Over the years, some people questioned the choices that Ms. Gray made, particularly as she set out to start her own business. She initiated the Center in the 1970s in an environment that was not very receptive to women and, in particular, to Black women. Ms. Montgomery described this challenge: "Even as she began to start and develop her business, there were meetings that she could not go to; she sent a man because women were not respected."

Although gender and racial equity issues have moved forward since then, inequities continue to exist for many women and women of Color, particularly in higher levels of administration. Ms. Gray successfully navigated these realities, working against gender and racial injustices by leveraging her self-confidence, knowledge, skill, and experience in the field of early childhood education. For her, there was no room for doubt or fear. She was driven by a desire to serve children and their families.

Courage to Believe in Every Child's Potential: "They *can* learn"

A hallmark characteristic of Ms. Gray's courageous stance is her insistence on maintaining belief in the brilliance of every child and refusing to accept stereotypes or perpetuate deficit views of children of Color and children from low-income households. She refused to blame the child and always sought solutions for reaching each child:

> This business that [children] cannot learn because of where they came from just does not make sense. They *can* learn. Many times the teachers are not teaching or they don't have the resources to teach. Therefore we have a lot of students, a lot of children, who have fallen by the wayside.

Courage to Persevere: A Selfless Act in a Selfless Life

Off and on through the years, Gray's faced many financial challenges and struggled to stay open. Even when she was not sure where the money would come from, Ms. Gray kept the Center open every day. Ms. Montgomery described the selflessness required for this kind of perseverance:

It's doing it when you don't know what the end result will be. Her mission and overall goal has been to make a difference in the lives of children and parents. It's been a selfless act and a selfless life. She's put other people's needs in front of hers. . . . I've seen Ms. Gray reinvest money that's made back into the program. I've seen where she's not taken a salary but she's at work every day, even Saturday and Sunday. Where other folks they're going to get paid before they pay their staff. She pays the staff before she takes a salary.

Even though there were many times when people told Ms. Gray that she could not do it or that her ideas would not work, she remained true to her mission. Many people would not have persevered, given the odds she faced. As Ms. Montgomery said, "It could be considered faith. It could be considered crazy. Some people say, 'I would have never done that.' But it is courage. It's stepping out of the box. It's doing something when you don't know what the end result will be."

LESSONS FROM BESSIE GRAY: STRATEGIES FOR CHANGE

Even today, the narrative of my grandmother's leadership provides concrete examples of ways for administrators to meet the needs of children, families, and communities by:

- *Disrupting and rejecting deficit framing of working-class communities of Color.* Ms. Gray was very aware of the existing inequities in policy and practice. Many of the same inequities continue to dominate policy and practice today. Intentionally contradicting deficit framing of communities of Color was key to her successful leadership and serves as a model for early childhood leaders today.
- *Working with and providing supports for parents and communities.* Courageous leadership requires rethinking the role of parents and community members, and building reciprocal relationships. Ms. Gray did this by building relationships and showing that she valued families, offering regular parenting workshops that conveyed *their* abilities to support their own children, connecting parents with financial resources, and advocating for parents' rights in their children's education.
- *Committing to innovative thinking to support ongoing teacher training and development.* A cornerstone of Ms. Gray's courageous leadership was her commitment to the development of highly skilled and committed teachers. Her teachers received ongoing on-the-job training, they were encouraged and funded to attend local and national conferences, and they were enrolled in associate's and bachelor's degree programs to continue their education supported by funds procured by Gray's. She

was innovative and creative in acquiring funds for these educational opportunities. The far reach of Ms. Gray's legacy is a result of her resolve to prioritize and support teachers' growth in spite of circumstances that posed barriers to the process.

THE LEGACY OF BESSIE GRAY

From the start to the expansion of Gray's Child Development Center, it took courage to stand firm, especially when others' directives contradicted the mission of the work. Ms. Gray's deep concern for children drove her courage. She said, "Maybe it's a kind of selfishness, but I was not going to give up in spite of the challenges. The thing that kept me going was the passion." Ms. Bessie Gray's legacy is certainly one of passionate commitment to quality education and care for thousands of young children. This is acknowledged far and wide. As a former student reported, "It is a badge of honor to say 'I went to Gray's.'"

Today, many of Ms. Gray's children and grandchildren follow her lead by working with children, families, and communities in some capacity. We carry her legacy forward through our commitment to challenging inequities. Although officially retired, Ms. Gray continues to prepare early childhood teachers and consult with administrators. She remains committed to addressing the needs of children, particularly those who continue to be marginalized, strong in both word and action as she declares, "In the current climate of child-care fraud and scams, with so many centers being closed, who's going to care for the Black child?"

With those words, my grandmother reminds me that she did not come this far for me or anyone else to give up on children, the system, or ourselves. Ms. Bessie Gray continues to fill gaps where there is a need as she guides us with passion, knowledge, dedication, perseverance, and courage.

CHAPTER 3

Humanizing Early Childhood Education

Courageously Caring Leadership in a Bilingual Head Start Program

Mariana Souto-Manning and Yandra Mordan-Delgadillo

At 9 A.M., Marilyn Barnwell walks into the Columbus Avenue site of the Bloomingdale Family Program, which serves young children predominantly from low-/no-income Latino/a and Afro-Latino/a immigrant families in Manhattan. The program is bilingual (Spanish/English), inclusive (serving children with and without disabilities), and community-based. It is clear that Marilyn knows parents and family members well. She smiles and greets them. She stops and asks the mother of a former student, "How did your interview go?" Upon hearing the woman's response, she says, "I have been thinking of you. Please let us know if we can help in any way."

This is how Marilyn is: caring, humble, and knowledgeable of the families that make up the Bloomingdale community. Pre-K teacher and parent of a child formerly at Bloomingdale, Yandra Mordan-Delgadillo describes her as "una joya," a jewel. Yandra continues:

> You know that she is primarily a human being, a person who deeply cares at the same time that she is an educator and director. . . . She treats everyone humanely. She is a person who cares about parents, children, teachers, students, and all people in general. She sees the best in everyone. . . . Marilyn, as a parent, makes you feel that your family is her family, which is top priority. She is always ready to listen, to give support when you need it, and to give you the advice you need.

Much of Marilyn's courageous approach to advocating for teachers and families is informed by her own experience as a single parent, and a woman of Color, who worked three jobs to support her children. For example, if Marilyn had accepted the options her daughter's school envisioned for her future, her daughter would never have attended college to become a Wesleyan and UCLA alumna. She had to be actively vigilant, advocating for her daughter in informed ways. Repeatedly, she saw how many educators regard children of Color as being inferior and deprived (Goodwin et al., 2008; Souto-Manning, 2010c). Her experiences illustrated that parents cannot blindly trust the system and led her to courageously advocate for and with parents, showing them that they have power.

According to Marilyn, many Latino/a parents trust teachers and schools to a fault. Eugene E. García (2012) noted that Latina mothers have consistently high aspirations for their children's future; 93% believe that education is the single most important factor contributing to their children's future. These mothers trust that their children's schools and teachers will positively contribute to a successful future. Marilyn has a different point of view. She wants parents to be critically aware of how schools continue to segregate children and compromise their futures. In order for this to happen, she wants them to get to know the system, remain vigilant, doubt everything, and actively advocate for their children's education and futures.

INTRODUCTION

Marilyn Barnwell (Figure 3.1) has been Bloomingdale's program director of education since 1980. She has over 50 years of experience in early education, including working as an early childhood teacher. She works closely with Bloomingdale's teachers, children, and their families. She attended community college in her 20s, then went on to earn a master's degree in education from Columbia University—after being told repeatedly that she wouldn't succeed in higher education. She defied the odds and made it her business to empower families who have been historically disempowered by schooling and society.

THE BLOOMINGDALE FAMILY PROGRAM

Since opening its doors in 1960, the Bloomingdale Family Program has continued to identify, advocate for, and address the evolving needs of the diverse community it serves. At Bloomingdale, families gain necessary experience to become both advocates for their children and partners in the educational experience.

Each year there are 150–180 children, ages 3 and 4, in Bloomingdale's Head Start and Universal Pre-Kindergarten (UPK) program classrooms. After "graduation," Bloomingdale continues to serve its graduates through activities such as

Figure 3.1. Marilyn Barnwell with children and families from the Bloomingdale Family Program.

after-school homework help programs for students and siblings in kindergarten through 3rd grade. Other outreach programs include education classes and advocacy support for parents and extended families. Leveraging resources, Bloomingdale partners with community organizations to help its students' families access the services and resources they need.

The Bloomingdale Family Program's history is unique, special, and intertwined with the history of Head Start. From their website we learn that in 1960:

A group of families from diverse ethnic, cultural, and socio-economic backgrounds came together because they shared a common purpose: the creation of a free, integrated preschool for their children in their upper Manhattan community. Their vision and commitment provided the foundation for what became known as The Bloomingdale Family Program.

For the first 5 years, workers from the Parks Department and Health Department assisted the parent volunteers in operating a free preschool for 70 children. The space was originally provided by the Children's Aid Society. In 1965 Bloomingdale received a grant from the Ford Foundation's Fund for the Advancement of Education to engage in a 3-year demonstration project "to develop, study, and document new ways of involving parents in the education of their children and in the life of the community." While this was happening, in Washington, DC, designs for Head Start had begun, and the Bloomingdale model was adopted as a framework for that program. The Washington planners were impressed with the involvement of Bloomingdale parents in their children's daily classroom life. They saw how working together in the program strengthened parenting skills and encouraged parents' growth toward self-sufficiency and community involvement.

Also in 1965, Bloomingdale began sponsoring a summer Head Start program, and in 1969, it began operating a year-round Head Start program. Since then, Bloomingdale has been regarded as a model and visited by educators from throughout the United States and abroad. Today, Bloomingdale focuses on fully inclusive, culturally and linguistically relevant early education for children from low-/no-income families. Foundation and other private funding enable Bloomingdale to provide children with early intervention services without attaching labels. The children at Bloomingdale receive services as needed, to fully develop socially, academically, and emotionally. These services are child-centered and enable Bloomingdale's alumni to enter schools and advance as successful learners.

ONE MODEL DOES NOT FIT ALL:
THE CASE OF BLOOMINGDALE

In 2015, Bloomingdale was in the midst of implementing UPK guidelines resulting from the New York City expansion of funding to UPK. Marilyn was learning to implement new assessments required by the city, which duplicated what was in place, adding a layer of bureaucratic work. She was undergoing training for the Classroom Assessment Scoring System (CLASS, a standardized observational tool to evaluate teachers), conducting evaluations using the Early

Childhood Environment Rating Scale-Revised (ECERS-R, a rating scale to assess group programs for preschool- to kindergarten-aged children—2 through 5 years of age), and entering information in a system called ASPIRE (a way of collecting information and staff credentials).

Marilyn supported Bloomingdale's teachers while they negotiated and adapted definitions of "best practices" as defined by the agencies overseeing UPK in New York and Head Start nationally. According to teacher Yandra Mordan-Delgadillo:

> As a director, she gave you the opportunity to grow without putting you down. She is always looking for articles and ideas that you can implement in the classroom. Marilyn always helps you to reflect on your practice, to be an intentional teacher.

Yet, she was being asked by Head Start to put aside her careful observation approach, developed and improved over time, and embrace CLASS.

Unlike CLASS, Marilyn's approach to observation is to expand what works and invite teachers to reflect on their own practice by watching videos of their teaching, interpreting what they see, and coming up with plans for improvement. This process of cultivating teacher learning and leadership is fostered individually and collectively.

The impetus for the implementation of standard measures of observation, student achievement, and teacher performance is directly linked to the increasing funding allocations for early education, such as UPK funding in NYC. Yet, there is little coordination among agencies, such as the NYC Department of Education, Administration for Children's Services (ACS), and Head Start, that oversee the implementation of different programs. Mixed funding streams, with different standards and accountability measures, are partly to blame here. Also to blame is the ever-rampant corporate discourse, which deprofessionalizes teachers, treats them as technicians, and issues them step-by-step guides of what to say and how students should respond.

Marilyn regards teachers as knowledgeable professionals, whereas the new assessment systems do not. While UPK in NYC brought additional funds, there are many added demands and many potential grounds for the program being out of compliance. Yet, the teachers consistently felt Marilyn's support, even as she negotiated these tensions and advocated for them on multiple levels. Mordan-Delgadillo explained:

> She is always on your side. . . . When we had visitors to observe the classroom, like UPK, ACS, federal review, and others, she always said to the staff: "Do not worry, you only need to be yourself. Do what you always do,

because you do the best for our children and families, which is the most important thing."

CULTURALLY RELEVANT LEADERSHIP IN PRACTICE

Marilyn brings culturally relevant leadership to life in a variety of ways (Ladson-Billings, 1995a, 1995b). She sees the best in everyone. Her approach to leadership includes what Eugene E. García (2012) calls "assets inventory," whereby she documents everyone's assets (experiences, practices, knowledge, and skills) as she fosters their growth. At the same time, she recognizes that a subtractive approach to the families and children with whom she works is common (Valenzuela, 1999).

Regarding teachers, children, and their families as capable, Marilyn enacts leadership that is at once caring, humane, and culturally relevant. In this chapter, we detail some of the courageous practices in which Marilyn engages and some of the challenges she has faced. We address how she facilitates teacher learning, fosters family leadership, embraces bi/multilingualism as a norm, implements inclusion from a racial justice stance, and fuels advocacy efforts.

Teacher Learning

Marilyn sends announcements to educational staff by email on Sunday evenings. This way, staff meetings are reserved for teacher learning and professional development. She frames the sessions with questions, which are introduced in her Sunday correspondence. These questions often emerge from the experiences and lives of teachers, children, and families at Bloomingdale.

As requested by the teachers, staff meetings take place at one of the three Bloomingdale locations on a rotating basis. Teachers are encouraged, but not mandated, to attend. Marilyn organizes meetings so the teachers facilitate the learning. Throughout, she regards her staff as capable and professional. She highlights powerful classroom practices—such as pictorial message boards, hands-on experiences emanating from children's play that encourage oral language use in authentic ways, intentional neighborhood walks, the use of storytelling in mathematics, and oral storytelling by family members—inviting teachers to share some of what they are doing with their coworkers. She positions herself as a participant and learns alongside her staff.

Marilyn recounted a professional development session when she explained how the new lesson plan format for UPK did not match with HighScope's—a well-known and widely adopted early childhood curriculum used by Head Start:

How can we comply with the expectations as a HighScope program? They [UPK consultants] said they would get back to me. They never did. So I posed this question to the teachers.

She went on to say:

I love our teachers. Their lesson plans are all different from each other just like the work of the children they teach is all different from each other's. But they figured out a way to highlight the areas of the curriculum related to compliance.

A Strengths-Based Approach to Home Visits

A hallmark of Head Start is the practice of home visits. At Bloomingdale, the first home visit takes place before the child enters the program. Marilyn approaches home visits from a strengths-based perspective. During home visits, teachers seek to foster relationships with families, develop trust, and learn about the child and the family. Teachers are then able to document family funds of knowledge (González, Moll, & Amanti, 2005) and connect them to teaching opportunities in culturally relevant ways (Ladson-Billings, 1995a). According to Marilyn, the purpose is:

to help teachers learn more about the child's background—who the child is—and his or her daily life, and needs. This is our first introduction to the child. So at the very least children will recognize a familiar face when they come to Bloomingdale. We also gather information and develop trusting and respectful relationships. It is not about judging, but about having a context to understand the child, his actions, his stories. The teachers don't go in to teach. They go in to learn.

Bloomingdale's education plan clearly states the reason behind home visits, which is "to take the first important step toward establishing a positive relationship with child and parent," and that teachers should "stress that we are there to help with any problem they may have; that you and all staff are always available to them. Emphasize our eagerness for their participation—working together." A resource offered by Marilyn is Bloomingdale's First Home Visit Guide (Figure 3.2).

Fostering Teacher Leadership

Marilyn keeps teacher leadership in mind as she faces mandates from agencies seeking to enforce new guidelines and define quality in their own terms. In addition to the tensions related to observing and offering feedback to teachers,

Figure 3.2. Marilyn Barnwell's Home Visit Guide.

First Home Visit Guide

Initiative

1. How does your child make choices (points, uses words)?
2. When your child has a problem with a material or toy, how does he/she solve it?
3. Does your child choose to play alone most of the time or with others?
4. Does your child have a daily routine? Can he/she follow it without help?

Social relations

1. Has your child ever been in school before?
2. How does your child play with other children (solitary, associative, cooperative)?
3. How does your child relate to adults?
4. When your child has a problem with another child, how does he/she solve it (physical, words)?
5. Can your child identify his/her feelings and how does he/she express them? Can he/she identify others' feelings?

Creative representation

1. Does he/she build or make things?
2. What is his/her favorite toy?
3. Does he/she like to draw or paint?
4. Does he/she like to pretend? What does he/she pretend to do?

Language and literacy

1. What language does your child speak at home? Any other languages?
2. What are your child's favorite books? Who reads with your child?
3. Does your child recognize his/her name and can he/she write it? Can he/she recognize any letter and/or numbers?

Music and movement

1. Does your child like to listen to music? What type of music does he/she like?
2. Does your child like to dance?
3. Does your child like to play outside? With what?
4. How are your child's self-help skills?

Logic and mathematics

1. Can your child count? Up to what number?
2. Does your child know his/her age?
3. Can your child recognize any numbers? Can your child write any of the numbers?

Is there anything else that's important about your child? (Prompt for allergies, fears, naptime, food issues, toilet training, religious observances, etc.)

Marilyn has also experienced a change in her role. Agencies now demand a director at each site. Since Bloomingdale has three sites, Marilyn now serves as supervisor for two other site directors. She turned what could have been a stressful situation into an opportunity to foster teacher leadership, promoting master teachers to site directors. She meets with these site directors regularly, mentoring them in the process—asking critical questions, modeling positive and constructive interactions, and offering resources.

Empowering Parents

One of the signatures of Marilyn's leadership is the empowerment of parents and families. Two major initiatives reposition parents: the employment practices at Bloomingdale and the Parent Leadership Project.

Employment practices committed to the community. Bloomingdale offers employment opportunities within the program, making it possible for talented and skilled parents to join the staff while at the same time furthering their education. This ensures that teachers are knowledgeable and representative of the community served by the program. Bloomingdale employs 51 staff members. The diversity of the staff reflects the cultural diversity of the program and its community. Two-thirds of the staff began their association with Bloomingdale as parents and were helped by Bloomingdale to acquire the credentials for the positions they now hold. Yandra Mordan-Delgadillo is a case in point. Marilyn underscores the importance of relationships and of diverse socioeconomic, racial, and linguistic representations. This is a systematic way to ensure that such representation happens in committed and respectful ways.

Parent Leadership Project. For the past 3 years, Marilyn has facilitated the Parent Leadership Project (PLP), a collaborative effort between Bloomingdale and the Center for Immigrant Families, helping Bloomingdale's families make the transition from Head Start and UPK to public schools. The PLP is informed by Marilyn's experiences as a mother and as a learner in the New York City educational system.

Every Wednesday morning at 8:30 in Bloomingdale's Parent Room, Marilyn participates in a Parent Leadership Project meeting, such as the one depicted in Figure 3.1. The PLP grew out of stories from parents who were dealing with discrimination in the school district. One of the things Marilyn learned while listening to the families is that some schools do not welcome parents and family members coming from low-/no-income backgrounds, as they are not seen as contributing members of the school. Bloomingdale families also shared stories of discrimination against them as Spanish-dominant people of Color, seen by many in terms of deficits instead of strengths (Goodwin et al., 2008). For example,

Bloomingdale parents encountered many schools that did not have school tours in Spanish, even when dual-language programs were in place for the children.

So PLP meetings help parents and family members know and understand their rights. Parents are informed of what schools can and cannot require. For example, they learn that schools cannot ask about their income or ask for their Social Security numbers. Parents then call schools, request bilingual tours, and visit schools as a group. "There is power in numbers," she explains. Parents are in a better situation to advocate for their children as they transition from Bloomingdale to kindergarten. According to Marilyn:

> Parents were used to looking at education in a different way. So whatever the school said, you believed it, because you respected the school and the teachers. But when parents see these discriminatory practices before they even enroll their children, they become aware that the school and the teachers may not have their child's best interest at heart. It is hard because it shatters their cultural expectations of schools and schooling. There are expectations about our parents before they ever set foot in schools—that they don't care, that they can't afford, that their kids need help, etc.

Reflecting on the PLP, Marilyn voiced:

> It is nice to watch, because parents come to the first meeting expecting us to give them a list of kindergartens to go to, and we do talk about that and we do take them on tours to see them. Our parents think that they are supposed to go to charter schools. In our area, there is heavy recruitment and marketing from charter schools. They come to think that's where the rigor and learning happens and that's where the children should go. And then the children get suspended. . . . And then they have to find a new school for their child. And they come here, to me. Because [the charter schools] don't want special education kids at all.

Marilyn explained further:

> Discrimination is rampant. Most of our children live in New York City's most segregated district. And this is saying a lot because New York City is the most segregated school system in the nation. . . . These parents experience discrimination when they try to go on tours and enroll their children. These are Spanish-speaking parents and the schools don't offer translation. These are schools, some of them, that have dual-language programs that suffer because they don't have Latinos in them.

She clarified this point with an illustration:

> My favorite story is of Jesus, who was in Yandra's classroom. He scored on the 99th percentile of the city's gifted and talented test. He was brilliant. Well, all of our children are gifted. And his parents knew about a [well-known gifted] program and went to put him there. . . . Then the parents came back and said: "They want to retest him." I said: "They better not. They better not. They are going to have to accept that they will have Jesus in their school."

In summarizing the Parent Leadership Project, Marilyn said, "This is a very strong advocacy group."

TEACHING YOUNG CHILDREN AS INTELLECTUAL WORK

Marilyn recognizes that teaching is intellectual work (Shulman, 2004)—a complex endeavor, being "perhaps the most complex, most challenging, and most demanding, subtle, nuanced, and frightening activity that our species has ever invented" (p. 504). This commitment to teaching and intellectual work extends to Marilyn's focus on bilingual and multicultural education and redefining inclusion from a racial justice stance.

Bilingual and Multicultural Early Education

Curriculum and teaching at Bloomingdale are multicultural and bilingual. Bloomingdale's *Education Plan* (Bloomingdale Family Program, 2013) states, "All services are offered in English and Spanish" (p. 4). This was a response to the community's languages—predominantly Spanish and English. Fifty to sixty percent of the children attending Bloomingdale are Spanish-dominant. Recognizing the importance of children seeing their teachers' linguistic identities mirror their own, half of the instructional staff hired at Bloomingdale is Spanish-dominant.

All teaching takes place bilingually and builds on community resources and home literacies. For example, stories and special practices from the children's homes are brought to the classroom. Bilingual teaching is also a way of engaging in culturally relevant teaching. As a proponent of multicultural and bilingual education, Marilyn acknowledges that efforts are always made to address multiple dialects, cultures, and languages. She also recognizes that the diverse cultural backgrounds of parents and staff are rich resources for multicultural teaching and learning.

Redefining Inclusion from a Racial Justice Stance

Marilyn is committed to inclusion from a racial justice stance. She knows that children may need services but wants to avoid stigmas often associated with special education labels. She redefines inclusion as a verb, "to fully include," as opposed to a place or label. She explained:

> I don't want them to think that any one racial group knows everything. If we are doing inclusion, we have to be inclusive of multiple experiences and stories, of multiple languages and cultures. Otherwise, it is not inclusion.

Services without labels. Marilyn knows that the children may need additional services, such as a bilingual speech program or play therapy, to succeed. She also acknowledges different developmental pathways as part of the learning process. As Genishi and Dyson (2012) wrote, critiquing the federal government initiative, Race to the Top, and the push-down of academics and standardized learning expectations:

> We imagine the classroom stage, not as a race, but as a dance hall, where teachers and children adapt to each other, even as they sometimes move to a rhythm all their own. The teacher responds, leads, and sometimes lets go to observe more carefully the rhythms of children in motion. (p. 20)

Marilyn believes that not attaching labels to children serves them well, as they receive the services needed without experiencing the stigmas often associated with such labels. For example, the Bloomingdale board and the director of development arranged for foundation money to cover play therapy and speech therapy so children could receive needed services more readily. Marilyn said:

> If they need early intervention, they receive it. They don't need to have a lifelong label to receive intervention. Most of the time they discontinue services because they no longer need them prior to entering kindergarten.

ADVOCATING FOR TEACHERS, CHILDREN, AND FAMILIES

Marilyn engages in advocacy to counter mandates that dehumanize education and threaten to compromise the mission and philosophy of powerful programs such as Bloomingdale's. She explained:

> These mandates are compromising the philosophy of our program. Now we are required to do developmental screening. But for many, many years, we

didn't do it, because we have an arm of the program that addressed disabilities in very holistic ways. We had therapists, play therapists, that served the children without the need for them to be labeled. . . . We addressed this by trying to find the least time-consuming, least invasive assessment.

Marilyn also explained how, at times, a seemingly good idea might negatively impact teaching. For example, Bloomingdale employs HighScope (it has several HighScope-certified teachers) and its assessment, Child Observation Record (COR). While COR provides valuable information, inputting all the information collected in the COR computerized system is overwhelming. She described how the system is unfair, how there are more and more demands being placed on teachers with little additional resources that value teachers:

COR provides us with a lot of good information about the children, but it takes time to implement. I just wish teachers were better paid and the work that they often do on their own time could be compensated in some way. But as a society we don't value early childhood teachers as much as we should.

Marilyn also explained how the systemic deprofessionalization of teachers can impact the quality of education children receive:

We used to be able to afford planning time. . . . Once a week, teachers could be out of the classroom together as a team. Our teachers plan every day. During naptime, they have conversations about children, they reflect on what happened today, and they plan for tomorrow. So that time that they had outside of the classroom, which I would at times scaffold, had to stop because of new regulations.

Marilyn questions standardized notions of quality, such as year-round education, which do not regard the history of practices in early educational sites or community needs:

Last year was the first year that we did not have August off. I have been here since 1980. They changed things. Vacations were happening all throughout the year, which meant that children were afraid that their teachers would be gone. This affected their relationships with teachers.

Marilyn described her advocacy on behalf of her teachers, children, and families:

I wrote a letter letting them know that this new schedule had negatively impacted our program, and most importantly, the children. I interviewed teachers about how the new schedule affected their teaching. I consulted with mental health providers about the effects of this new schedule on children. I even made the case that there was not enough time to make building repairs.

DEFENDING HUMANITY IN TEACHING:
MANDATES AND COMPLIANCE MEASURES

Don't try to keep fixing us. Learn from us. —Marilyn Barnwell

For Marilyn, high expectations do not justify standardization. In fact, standardization counters the kind of quality education that Marilyn supports: education that is culturally and linguistically relevant, contextually bound, grounded in the very lives of the children and families whom it serves. Yet, as more investments are made in early education, more control is taken away from individual centers. Nevertheless, Marilyn stated, "All this compliance talk doesn't define who we are and what we do." She explained:

> My biggest challenge is to help the outside world understand who we are, what we do, and appreciate our children. Because many times, when they hear we are a Head Start program, they immediately think, "Oh, those poor children," seeing them as deficits.

Marilyn challenges us to rethink what counts as quality:

> We have successful alumni. Patrick Gaspard, formerly Obama's National Political Director and Director of the White House Office of Political Affairs, is currently the United States Ambassador to South Africa. He is our alumnus. Our state's Deputy Commissioner of Instruction [Angelica Infante-Green] is our alumna. There are so many others. Again and again, our alumni have shown us that Bloomingdale's children will grow up to be leaders and not numbers in a jail cell.

All in all, Marilyn sees her function as advocating for teachers, families, and most of all, for children:

> I protect the teachers from turmoil; they already have too much to do and their focus is on the children and families. I feel very protective of what they do. . . . If we are out of compliance, so be it. Most importantly, we need to remember the power of our work and act knowing that we are the keepers of what we know.

CHAPTER 4

Leadership in a Dual-Language Community Preschool

SMALL STEPS TOWARD CREATING AN ASSETS-BASED PROGRAM

Kindel Nash and Geralyn Sosinski

A mother rings the buzzer outside El Centro Academy for Children. The school's director, Geralyn, seated at the front table, buzzes the parent in and greets the mother: "¡Hola! ¿Cómo estás?" Sign-in materials, newsletters, and community flyers printed in both Spanish and English line the front table. The mother signs in and walks down the bright hallway to retrieve her child. They soon reappear. "¡Hasta mañana!" Geralyn says, as the parent carries her smiling child out of the school.

Using multiple languages is a way of life at El Centro Academy for Children in Kansas City, KS. While it may seem like a simple accomplishment, many administrators have to fight in courageous and often isolating ways for the right to support linguistically plural environments in their schools.

Geralyn Sosinski (Figure 4.1) has been the director of El Centro Academy for 2 years. She has been involved with the Center in one capacity or another for 7 years. Her insight, willingness to learn and grow, and insistence on taking a stand about valuing multilingualism in the preschool are very important reasons why El Centro enjoys its dual-language status today. In spite of challenges posed by the English-only policies of most public schools in this region, Geralyn has courageously taken important steps to nurture a preschool program where Latino/a linguistic resources and heritages are centerpieces. Hers is an assets-based approach that goes beyond "individualistic approach[es] to understanding people" (Castagno, 2014, p. 9), taking care to highlight—not obscure—the inequities of monolingual models.

Figure 4.1. Geralyn Sosinski working with 4-year-olds from El Centro Academy for Children.

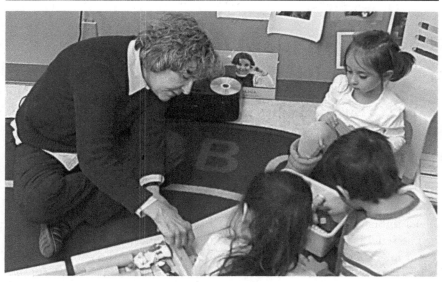

El Centro is a dual-language (Spanish/English) preschool and Head Start community partnership school for 2½- to 5-year-olds. It is tucked in a quiet community with a high number of Latino/a immigrants. Each day, Geralyn's job as director involves her with parents, children, teachers, and outside agencies to create liminal spaces that allow children to build and sustain identities connected to both Spanish- and English-speaking communities, fostering a breakdown of boundaries "between worlds" (Anzaldúa, 2002, p. 1).

At El Centro, Geralyn's daily work focuses on an additive approach (Tabors, 2008) to dual-language education. She guides teachers to see the process of language acquisition as additive, grounded in the understanding that home languages are the foundation of children's communicative expertise and that learning English means adding another language to children's existing repertoires rather than replacing home languages. To honor this knowledge, Geralyn (a) promotes a *both-and* approach to language instruction through which children are encouraged to use both languages at home and school in ways that support their communicative needs (Genishi & Dyson, 2009; Tabors, 2008), (b) helps members of the school community understand that being bilingual, biliterate, and bicultural is a valuable asset and that language cannot be considered apart from culture (González et al., 2005; Valdés, 2001), and (c) values the idea that learning two languages simultaneously builds proficiency in *both languages* and opens opportunities for richer communication now and later in life (Durán, Roseth, & Hoffman, 2010; Espinosa, 2008). This chapter shares stories that illuminate this work, highlighting specific strategies, practical steps, and tensions that Geralyn encounters in the process of standing up for and ensuring the normalization of bi/multilingual practices in her school.

EL CENTRO ACADEMY FOR CHILDREN

Housed in a redbrick, refurbished Catholic school, El Centro Academy for Children (El Centro) preschool is part of a larger community-based nonprofit organization whose overall mission is "to strengthen communities and improve lives of Latinos and others through educational, social, and economic opportunities" (www.elcentroinc.com). El Centro's mission and vision is to foster a research-based, dual-language preschool, building on the idea that being bilingual is an advantage (Valdés, 2001). At El Centro, where 70% of students are Latino/a emergent bilinguals (O. García & Kleifgen, 2010), that mission is enacted by promoting dual-language curriculum, instruction, and assessment, and by hiring Spanish- and English-speaking bilingual teachers and staff. Theresa Torres, a well-known advocate for Latino/as in the Kansas City community, described El Centro as a "wonderful social service agency with a good reputation and a director who is highly thought of."

Parents appreciate having their children at El Centro because of its dual-language mission. For example, at a family get-together at El Centro, a father shared:

> That's why I want Isabella [pseudonym] to come to El Centro, even though we live 30 minutes away. . . . I mean I lost my Spanish because my teachers did not want me to speak it in school, and my parents thought if I didn't speak Spanish then I'd learn English better. So now I can't speak it. I want Isabella to speak it.

Geralyn feels that, because of its clear mission and strong support, El Centro is "the only viable program in [this region] that really uses research to support kids who are dual-language learners." She is in the process of collecting assessment data to see whether, after attending El Centro, children's linguistic abilities reflect wider research findings about the positive impact of bilingual preschool programs on academic achievement in both Spanish and English (Durán et al., 2010; Espinosa, 2008).

TRANSFORMATIONAL LEADERSHIP AT EL CENTRO

Since Geralyn started working at El Centro, she has taken practical and measured steps to nurture a dual-language environment. These steps are discussed in the following sections as they relate to three elements of Geralyn's leadership: (1) standing up for her beliefs, (2) transforming thinking to promote dual-language education as an asset, and (3) negotiating tensions along the way. We offer them to provide insights as well as affirmation for other leaders involved in transformational work in support of dual-language early childhood education.

Standing Up for Beliefs

Geralyn began her early childhood career in a forward-thinking early childhood school program for teen mothers called Catholic Charities:

> It was an amazing place to work. . . . They were very innovative . . . and thought outside the box. They had all of the resources the mothers needed at the school, and they had a really high graduation rate. So I really, really benefited from being a part of that.

Starting her career in an innovative, before-its-time kind of school laid the foundation for the development of Geralyn's courageous approach. There, she was a part of program that valued the lives and parenting abilities of teen mothers when many other programs did not. It was one of the first experiences through which she learned what it means to stand up for your beliefs.

Geralyn first came to El Centro in 2006 as a Quality Rating Systems (QRS) (a rating system for child-care settings) coach funded by an Early Reading First grant from the U.S. Department of Education (2014). Geralyn knew right away that her assignment, to "coach teachers to implement a literacy curriculum written entirely in English," was problematic. The necessity of taking a stand for equitable dual-language practices became clear:

> When I got assigned to El Centro with Early Reading First, I was supposed to go in with this English-only approach, *to this bilingual program*. And I was there for just a very short period of time . . . and I was like, *it just wasn't going to work for so many reasons*. . . . So I went back to the Principal Investigator and we really started thinking about what we needed to do to change the way we were approaching this and to really tap into the language expertise that teachers and children had and use it.

As a result, Geralyn was able to implement dual-language curriculum and instruction within the confines of the Reading First framework, which recommended a scripted, one-size-fits-all approach. She explained her choice to push against structures that marginalized and failed to utilize home languages: "I just felt really strongly about really supporting kids who are dual-language learners." Specific practices illustrating her commitment to honoring families, children, and their home languages included:

- Creating dual-language classroom resources such as T-Charts for contrasting Spanish and English vocabulary and BINGO games using the English and Spanish alphabet
- Finding and using a Spanish version of the Scholastic© English curriculum package adopted by Early Reading First
- Conducting bilingual teacher professional development
- Forming bilingual parent/family groups
- Applying for sustained funding to support a schoolwide plan to sustain the dual-language curriculum

Geralyn soon discovered, however, that while some of these practices were useful, others were not. For example, the books used in the Scholastic program were mere translations of European American stories and, as Geralyn explained, did not "reflect the [cultural] experiences of most of the children." But this was the only Spanish/English literacy preschool curriculum that the Reading First grant would support, so they continued to use it. As explained later in this chapter, when Geralyn returned to the school as its director 6 years later, she was able to address this issue in concrete and lasting ways.

Articulating a clear mission and vision. Geralyn's return to El Centro in the role of director gave her the opportunity to build from her earlier experiences to establish a clear schoolwide mission and vision and then use that mission to develop and implement a plan for El Centro as a bi/multilingual preschool. Part of the reason Geralyn was able to stand up for her beliefs was this mission. It was rooted in additive and strengths-based thinking about dual-language education, focusing on adding English to children's already rich linguistic repertoires instead of replacing Spanish with English. The mission expressed the school's emphasis on *fostering a research-based, community-oriented, dual-language approach to early childhood education.* With this firm foundation, Geralyn was able to use the mission as a justification and a guide for professional development and curricular planning, and in her work with the leadership to advocate for continued funding to support dual-language approaches.

Developing a research–based, schoolwide plan. Informed by El Centro's mission and vision, Geralyn developed a plan with and for teachers, children, and families. They began by building knowledge:

We actually developed a plan, and consulted with Dr. Espinosa [then a professor at the University of Missouri] using her [2008] piece, *Challenging Common Myths About Young English Language Learners.* And then we used information from Tabors's [2008 book], *One Child, Two Languages.* We just did tons of research around the topic, so then we put together a kind of a plan for what bilingual curriculum, instruction, and assessment would look like here.

The plan involved small steps; these were practical strategies that Geralyn hoped would lead to a community-wide transformation in thinking about assets-based bilingual education. Involving a mind shift for some, this approach required the faculty and families to see the home languages as assets and not as obstacles or deficits. Geralyn explained:

> We were very intentional about how we approached our plan so that by the time children left we felt like they had a good command of their home language, but also had the English that they needed to be successful in school.

Transforming Thinking About Bilingual Education

In our Midwestern community, there has been significant growth in the number of immigrants from Spanish-speaking countries, yet English-only policies prevail in public schools. However, Geralyn's practical steps toward assets-based thinking have made El Centro feel like a haven where children's languages are safe and valued. Those steps focused on teachers, parents, assessment, and curriculum.

Teachers. El Centro Academy teachers historically recognized the significance of foregrounding Spanish by speaking, teaching, and labeling the classrooms in Spanish and by making a point of learning and correctly pronouncing children's given names. As one teacher explained:

> I like to be at El Centro because it is a place where we call children by their real names. I feel like if a child is named Laura, the teachers should pronounce her name the same way her parents do, not L-ah-ra, but L-ow-rra! That is why I wanted to teach here.

While this tone was set at El Centro before Geralyn's directorship, when she returned to the school in a leadership role, she involved teachers in deeper examinations of specific bilingual practices and the use of bilingual teaching materials (books, games, circle time) within a predictable daily schedule. She talked about how she "continually encouraged the teachers to write and visibly post bulletin boards, letters home, and lesson plans both in Spanish and in English." She worked with teachers to fill the classrooms with bilingual books, books-on-tape, and other classroom materials. This required spending "a lot of time in informal conversations with teachers during professional development sessions and in classrooms" to help them understand the importance of investing time in accessing and sometimes creating these materials.

In support of the teachers' growth and her own learning, Geralyn was instrumental in involving staff members in professional study. She recognized that, without understanding the research behind the practice, they would not be able to justify or sustain shifts in their teaching. This led to broadened thinking and affirmation of teachers' existing knowledge. One of the teachers explained, "I was learning about the research that backed up teaching that I already knew was the right thing to do."

Geralyn regularly reported on the impact of professional development on her own learning. For example, she reflected that, at one time, she thought that teachers' code-meshing of Spanish and English—combining two or more language systems "to effectively write and speak within the multiple domains of society" (Young, Barrett, Young-Rivera, & Lovejoy, 2013, p. 2)—was confusing for the children. She thought it could delay their proficiency in either language. However, through her study of language and observations of code-meshing in the classroom, Geralyn came to understand it as supportive of emerging bilinguals' ability to understand their own and other language structures (Durán et al., 2010; García & Frede, 2010). Geralyn spoke of how she and the teachers needed to continue this kind of learning:

[These understandings are] really complex, so [you and] your teachers need a high level of support. . . . That was one of the reasons why we brought Dr. Durán in to lay a good foundation in language acquisition. . . . We're still learning all the time [about] the research and how to take all of these things into consideration and try to make everything work in the classroom.

Another key element in Geralyn's work with teachers was changing the typical English-only delivery of professional development (PD). She discussed her work with teachers to set up bilingual study groups in support of their professional growth:

English- and Spanish-language small groups were set up. Teachers started working in the [language] group that they were the most comfortable with. We started bringing in interpreters for all of the PD so that . . . everything was being translated into Spanish. We also provided all of the professional development materials in Spanish.

Parents. Geralyn had long observed that some parents felt it was better not to speak Spanish at home or at school if their children were going to learn English: "Parents were really like, 'No, English, English, English only. English only. I want my child to speak English.'" Having internalized widely projected deficit views about their own languages and cultural practices, they felt anxiety about the dual-language approach. A teacher at El Centro explained, "The parents always think that if they speak Spanish with their children, they won't learn English." To provide a counterpoint to this belief and help families understand how children can develop expertise as simultaneous bilinguals, Geralyn led the school in hosting Parent Groups and Family Nights:

> We started holding parent meetings. We had interpreters for that. And some of the first meetings that we had, we used Dr. Espinosa's *Challenging Common Myths About Young English Language Learners* to really . . . say, "Yes, we *want you* to speak to your child in Spanish at home."

Through these Family Nights, Geralyn was committed to helping parents understand "why we're doing what we're doing and sharing some of the research." The first evening began with a tour of the facility to show families the presence of both English and Spanish throughout the school.

Other useful strategies that helped parents appreciate the dual-language program were: (a) ordering bilingual children's books and making them available for families, (b) designing and administering "family home language surveys" (adapted from Durán et al., 2010) to learn about languages used at home so teachers could gain insights about each child's language assets and incorporate them in the classroom, and (c) providing bilingual forms and flyers printed in Spanish with translations in English (Figure 4.2). In these ways, Spanish was privileged in spaces where English traditionally had been foregrounded, sending an important message about how much the school valued the home language of its students.

These strategies were each important in the process of countering dominant messages that degraded or devalued languages other than English. Geralyn described this as a balancing act: "ensuring that parents get what they want for their children [while staying true to] the dual-language approach." Her main purpose was to emphasize—to children, families, and teachers—that home languages were to be valued, utilized, and normalized in and out of school.

Assessment. Geralyn considers the implementation of a family home language survey a crucial step in the process of moving toward more equitable assessment. Providing an overview of it, she explained:

> It's pretty detailed and it starts with, "When the child first started speaking, what language were they using?" and then it looks at the course of the day, so, "In the morning what language does the child hear?" and "What language does the child hear throughout the day?" and then, "What language does the child hear in the evening?"

Figure 4.2. Spanish-first format: Privileging home languages.

Understanding how and in what contexts children used language(s) at home, Geralyn guided teachers to identify children's linguistic assets/strengths. This proved to be important contextual information necessary for countering the results of more formal assessments (Test de Vocabulario en Imagenes Peabody; Pre-school Assessment of Literacy Skills Español; Language Assessment Screening Español; and Test of Preschool Early Literacy). These assessments, even when administered in Spanish, continue to hold significant cultural biases (Haitana, Pitama, & Rucklidge, 2010), often masking children's language strengths.

Geralyn and the El Centro teachers discussed how the survey, in conjunction with informal, day-to-day, conversational assessments, provided a more "well-rounded picture of [their] language acquisition in both [Spanish and English]." She felt that the complexities of children's language abilities could be better understood in these informal ways:

If you give them a formal test it's only going to give you a small picture of their language abilities, and you know are you talking about their receptive language only, or you know their expressive language too . . . it [is] very complex.

In addition to skewed and limited information obtained through the formal assessments, teachers found them to be "frustrating" and time-consuming—"one more thing on my plate." Through Geralyn's leadership, they were able to re-evaluate and reposition formal assessments, validating their insights that informal assessments were much more valuable in helping them support children as emergent bilinguals.

Curriculum. As mentioned earlier, the Scholastic curriculum—still in use when Geralyn took on the role as the school's director—was rife with issues related to cultural irrelevance, in spite of its availability in both Spanish and English. To counter these tensions, Geralyn led the staff in supplementing the materials and practices in culturally relevant ways. The teachers created class-made books with photos of the children reflective of their everyday stories. They taught children nursery rhymes in Spanish and English, not merely translations but rhymes from their communities' cultural traditions. In addition, teachers alternated the languages used to conduct circle time: one day in Spanish and the next in English. Geralyn described this all-out effort to ensure a dual-language curriculum:

Spanish [language] nursery rhymes were used as a counterpoint to the ones being used for English. And we taught the Spanish alphabet. We encouraged children to write in Spanish. Not just speaking in Spanish, listening to Spanish, but then they would also write in Spanish. So we had all that in place. . . . Everything was in English and Spanish. All the games that they used in the classroom. So no matter what we did in English, we had the equal opportunity then for . . . the Spanish version.

Negotiating Tensions and Challenges

Geralyn used her role as leader to cultivate spaces where Spanish and English were both valued, but the process was not without persistent tensions and challenges, such as: (a) working within developmentally appropriate and best practice ideologies, (b) English-only granting agencies, (c) English-only assessments, and (d) teachers' time.

Developmentally appropriate and best practice ideologies. A primary challenge was the dominance of "developmentally appropriate" practices as the standards for good teaching. Although this was the prevalent early childhood model, Geralyn felt strongly that such standards did not validate ways of parenting, teaching, and learning beyond those of the White, English-only middle class. Similarly, Geralyn worried about prevailing views of *best practice* as based on a narrow perception of what counts culturally and linguistically. Because these widely accepted norms can lead to assumptions about English language learners as "inferior" or "deprived" (Goodwin et al., 2008; Souto-Manning, 2010c), Geralyn worked to change these views through the professional development opportunities she provided for teachers at El Centro.

English-only granting agencies. Despite efforts to ground El Centro's policies and practices in current understandings about simultaneous bilingualism, the school's reliance on community-based grant funding made bilingual education "really, really difficult." Geralyn explained:

> [The work] remains challenging in that [granting agencies] who come in from the outside are English-speaking and so just helping them be aware of what we're trying to accomplish and not throwing everything that we're trying to do out the window when this person is here [is important].

One of the El Centro teachers also described this challenge, saying: "They come in here and they want you to do this, and do that, all for their grant. How does it help the children?" In one example, a funding agency was providing professional development for teachers focusing on setting up the preschool for "family-style dining." Geralyn tried to talk with the project organizers to tell them that their monocultural interpretation of "family-style dining" privileged one norm for dining over others:

> I let the person know that we preferred not to use the term "family style" because that leaves a connotation that all families dine a certain way and we know that all families are different and do not dine the same way. So, we like to call it "group-style dining" and . . . I sent her some information. But when the presentation was actually done, it was [still] referred to as "family-style dining."

English-only assessments. Another challenge had to do with the monolingual strings attached to funding that supplied preschool measures and assessments. Geralyn explained that, using these assessments, teachers often were directed to read from scripts requiring them to shut down children's attempts to use Spanish: "If a child starts to answer you in Spanish, you are supposed to say, 'I need you to tell me that in English.'"

The challenge of assessments available only in English and the requirement to dissuade children from using their home language led Geralyn to seek funding agencies that supported bilingual assessment. News of dual-language assessments came as a relief to parents who saw that their children would be more fairly evaluated in their home languages. They were coming to appreciate the maintenance of home languages in the classroom. When Geralyn asked parents for permission to conduct assessments in Spanish, she said, "[They] were like, 'Wow! That is so great!' They were really excited about that. [So it seems that a] good part of what we're doing is valuing their language and they're seeing it."

Teachers' time. Geralyn also acknowledged the time-consuming nature of building and sustaining a dual-language curriculum: "It is difficult for teachers to try and put all of these things in place because it takes more time and effort to [create curriculum and lessons] in English and Spanish." However, she felt strongly about the powerful impact that a dual-language environment can have on the learning of children and teachers, and on creating a welcoming space for families. So she worked to create time within the school day and support for teachers to do the work. Geralyn explained that when teachers do make the effort to plan for and teach in both languages, "It's huge! It may not seem important, [but it] is *so* important."

CONCLUSION

Geralyn's courageous leadership involves creating a liminal space at El Centro, a space for commitment to an equitable education for children and families whose heritage languages often are pushed to the margins because of the dominance of English-only perspectives, assessments, and curricula. Although her leadership has not been without challenges, she continuously demonstrates the ability to put rhetoric into action by leading the school's community to deeper understandings about dual-language preschool education.

CHAPTER 5

Bridging Languages, Cultures, and Worlds Through Culturally Relevant Leadership

Mariana Souto-Manning, Rebeca Madrigal,
Karina Malik, and Jessica Martell

It's 8:15 A.M. on a Thursday in October. As she does every day, Dr. Tori Hunt opens the door of Dos Puentes Elementary School and greets students and families by name in their preferred language.

"I can see you are tired. Did you have something special happening last night?" she asks a student whose baby sibling was born the night before. The girl grins and nods affirmatively. Then Dr. Hunt greets a parent and excitedly asks, "Are you coming tomorrow? I can't wait for us to meet and talk about your daughter."

After welcoming students and their families, Dr. Hunt returns to the office to meet with the mother of a student. At the mother's request, they are meeting to ensure that the child's needs are being met. A student with identified (dis)abilities, the child has not been reevaluated for 4 years. Dr. Hunt quickly develops rapport, facilitating the entire meeting in Spanish, even though Spanish is not her dominant language. Upon hearing the mother's request for a reevaluation, she pauses the meeting to call the district, advocating for the mother. After getting off the phone, she shares additional community resources and reassures the mother that the child will indeed be reevaluated. At the conclusion of the meeting, the mother smiles and says: "Ella es excelente. Estoy tan agradecida."

Within minutes, a Department of Education employee who has heard the conversation steps into the office and says, "You will be out of compliance." She explains that if the child is reevaluated, the school will be cited for being out of compliance with district regulations. Dr. Hunt calmly says, "This child needs to be reevaluated. . . . We need to know what other services he needs. This is worth being out of compliance for."

Later, Dr. Hunt explains: "You can't lead a school if all you are doing is reacting to mandates and compliance issues. You have to have a vision, a plan and then assess how the mandates and compliance issues fit within your vision, your mission." She will not compromise her vision for every child to be regarded as capable, for English and Spanish to be valued equally, for partnerships to enrich children's experiences in the school, and for families to be central partners in the growth and education process. This vision is at the core of Dr. Hunt's courageous leadership.

INTRODUCTION

Dr. Tori Hunt (Figure 5.1) is the founding principal of Dos Puentes Elementary School, a public school (P.S. 103) in Manhattan's Washington Heights neighborhood. This area of New York City is home to a large number of Dominican Americans and Dominican immigrants, and more recently Mexican Americans and Mexican immigrants.

The genesis for the vision of the school came when Dr. Hunt critically reflected on an experience she had as an undergraduate student living in Peru, South America. She recounted, "I was unable to make much sense in Spanish, yet they saw me as capable." Experiencing firsthand the power of a strengths-based approach to learning and to bilingualism/biliteracy, she was shocked when she started teaching in Texas and was introduced to immigrant children and their families in terms of deficits, what they could not do. As an immigrant in Peru she was conceptualized as capable, unlike immigrant families in Texas who were conceptualized as incapable. She quickly recognized this injustice. This led her to learn about ways of giving Latino/a immigrant children in the United States the advantage of being seen as capable and worthy.

Dr. Hunt joined a Master of Arts program in Bilingual/Bicultural Studies at Teachers College, Columbia University, and worked for 10 years as a primary-grades teacher at P.S. 165, a New York City public school with a robust dual-language program. Then she became the assistant principal for primary grades at P.S. 75, directing the dual-language program. Her leadership is connected to her extensive classroom experience teaching bilingual and multilingual children in Peru and in the United States (Texas, Washington, DC, and New York).

While at P.S. 165 and P.S. 75, Dr. Hunt pursued a doctorate at Columbia University. Her dissertation, in which she analyzed different dual-language

Figure 5.1. Dr. Tori Hunt.

programs in New York City, received the American Educational Research Association (AERA) Dissertation Award in Bilingual Education Research. It served as a foundation for the Dos Puentes Elementary School proposal, which was coauthored with former colleagues from P.S. 165 (including current Dos Puentes teachers Alcira Jaar and Rebeca Madrigal).

Dos Puentes Elementary School opened its doors in September 2013 with three kindergarten classes. The plan is to add one grade level each year until the school has three classes in each grade, K–5. Prior to the official opening of the school, Dr. Hunt conveyed: "The goal of our school is really to promote bilingualism and biliteracy. . . . We are in a Latino neighborhood. The majority of students have come from Spanish-speaking homes and we see that as a gift. We want to build on that."

In this chapter, we describe some facets of Dr. Hunt's courageous leadership—courageous because it stands for valuing children's resources, even as 100% of students at Dos Puentes qualify for free or reduced-price lunch, and courageous because it focuses on bilingualism and multiculturalism during a time of high-stakes test scores and teacher evaluations that overprivilege English language teaching and learning. While this chapter does not encompass everything that Dr. Hunt does, we aim to highlight some of the powerful practices in which she engages. Our hope is that her approach to early childhood education leadership will provide possible pathways for engaging in culturally relevant leadership and inspire others to value bilingualism, honor families, foster partnerships that impact educational success, and develop linguistically and culturally relevant and just visions for educational leadership.

DOS PUENTES ELEMENTARY SCHOOL

At Dos Puentes (Two Bridges) Elementary School all students learn in two languages: Spanish and English. All teachers and staff members are bilingual, and most are first- and second-generation immigrants. All Dos Puentes teachers are state-certified in bilingual education and in early childhood education, special education, and/or elementary education. Dr. Hunt deliberately hires highly qualified teachers who reflect the demographics of the students at Dos Puentes (Derman-Sparks, LeeKeenan, & Nimmo, 2015). This is a courageous stance because it counters the mismatch between children of Color and White teachers in U.S. public schools (Cheruvu, Souto-Manning, Lencl, & Chin-Calubaquib, 2014). Dr. Hunt recognizes the need for immigrant and bilingual children to see themselves in their teachers. Contrary to national statistics that document the racial and ethnic mismatch between students and teachers, at Dos Puentes over 80% of both the students and instructional staff are Latino/a.

Student work displayed throughout the school illustrates Dr. Hunt's commitment to valuing both languages equally. Labels in the classrooms are in both languages, with Spanish often positioned above English—a subtle yet important act. The school's office has tables for meetings and is filled with baskets of Spanish-language books. The school days alternate between instruction in English and in Spanish. Spanish is Dr. Hunt's second language, and it is common to see her interacting with students and families in Spanish.

The motto of Dos Puentes Elementary School, developed by Dr. Hunt in collaboration with a teacher team, is "bridges between languages, cultures, and worlds." This motto frames the mission of the school, which rests on four pillars well known in early childhood education: (1) bilingual/biliterate and multicultural education, (2) partnership with families, (3) hands-on experiences and inquiry-based learning, and (4) university partnerships (with CUNY's City College and Columbia University's Teachers College). These pillars include factors that Dr. Hunt sees as essential to fostering equitable education. They are present in school actions and visible on school walls.

The culture of the school is welcoming and warm. Positive language is employed to describe teachers, families, and students. Children are valued as capable and unique members of the school community. There is a strengths-based approach to everything. In problem solving, members of the school community often ask questions along the lines of, "How can we build on his/her strengths?" instead of, "How can I fix him/her?"

Dr. Hunt has created many opportunities for families to engage in the school. The school sets the tone with home visits and hosts a variety of family-focused events after hours when the whole school community comes together. Twice a month, families are formally welcomed to their children's classrooms to engage in hands-on inquiry with the children. Dr. Hunt explains: "All Family Fridays are in Spanish so that families can see that we have very high expectations for their children in Spanish. We are not a language-enrichment program. Spanish is as important as English in our school." This is courageous because schools are rated based on English-language test scores.

CULTURALLY RELEVANT LEADERSHIP PRACTICES IN ACTION

Dr. Hunt's leadership stems from "a pedagogy that empowers students intellectually, socially, emotionally, and politically by using cultural referents to impart knowledge, skills, and attitudes" (Ladson-Billings, 1994, pp. 17–18). Fostering culturally relevant teaching requires that teachers create bridges between students' homes and school lives, while still meeting the expectations of district and state curricular requirements. Culturally relevant teaching utilizes the backgrounds, knowledge, and experiences of the students to inform teaching and learning. Culturally relevant pedagogy rests on three propositions:

1. Students must experience academic success.
2. Students must develop and/or maintain cultural competence.
3. Students must develop a critical consciousness. (Ladson-Billings, 1995a, p. 160)

Dr. Hunt puts these principles into practice through her leadership. There are high expectations for students to succeed academically in both English and Spanish, and reminders of these are displayed throughout the school. In addition, there are three ongoing weekly professional development sessions in which the school comes together as a critical professional learning community (Souto-Manning, 2010b). At these sessions, the teachers and Dr. Hunt critically discuss readings about teaching and learning and analyze students' work, interactions, and understandings, focusing on teaching practices that are child-centered while at the same time helping children advance academically. Other action steps taken by Tori Hunt, which are foundational to her approach to leadership include: (1) developing an equity-based school philosophy, (2) encouraging home visits by teachers, (3) listening to and validating families, (4) insisting on language equity, (5) supporting nontraditional measures of growth, (6) re-envisioning teacher evaluation, and (7) providing time for professional study and planning. Each of these is described below.

Developing a School Philosophy

Dr. Hunt developed the school's philosophy in collaboration with teachers. In it, they included key aspects of social justice education, providing a blueprint with components that may be helpful to other school leaders. The philosophy of Dos Puentes Elementary School is visible, accessible, clearly stated, and posted in English and Spanish, at the school entrance and on posters around the school:

> Dos Puentes Elementary is based on the philosophy that bilingualism, biliteracy, and multicultural understandings are essential elements in achieving academic success in the 21st century. All students are given opportunities to build from the languages and cultures of their families as they gain full bilingualism and biliteracy in Spanish and English. The school takes the approach that high academic achievement is obtained through close collaboration between the school and the family. Hands-on learning experiences support deep academic understanding and linguistic development. Further, university partnerships provide opportunities for the school to continually engage in academic inquiry to provide multiple entry points for diverse learners to engage in rigorous work. The school serves all students, including emergent bilingual students with disabilities, to achieve success through a bilingual curriculum that supports high academic standards.

Home Visits

At Dos Puentes, there is a focus on students maintaining cultural competence: being able to fully and effectively function in their culture(s) of origin (Ladson-Billings, 1995a, 1995b). This starts during home visits before students enter the school. Dr. Hunt is a big proponent of home visits, as she believes that they can serve as countertexts to how society and, often, teachers think of students from nondominant backgrounds—in terms of deficits. She also sees home visits as important learning spaces and thus designed the home visits so that information learned from the families can transform teaching and learning. Because she sees great promise and possibility in home visits, she established them as a foundational practice at Dos Puentes.

During the visits, teachers ask families about their history and the history of their child's name and seek to identify family funds of knowledge (González et al., 2005). These visits allow teachers to begin to know who their students are as cultural beings and as members of caring families and communities. The information learned from families during home visits is essential to building bridges between their funds of knowledge (identified during home visits) and the school curriculum, positioning families as essential members of the classroom and school communities and expanding the curriculum in culturally relevant ways. Pictures from family visits are displayed on the school walls, clearly communicating that children and their families are all essential members of the school community.

Listening to Families

Another strength of Dr. Hunt's leadership is her commitment to the critical role of families in the life of the school and her focus on making sure they feel valued and heard. One way she does this is by challenging the larger discourse (common in New York City schools) that makes it difficult for families to spend time in school buildings due to (supposed) safety concerns. Countering that ideology, Dr. Hunt invites families into the school on a daily basis.

Similarly, Dr. Hunt regularly invites the views of family and community members and validates and acts on their concerns. One example relates to the issue of school uniforms. Dr. Hunt had not planned for the school to have uniforms; however, in listening to members of the Latino/a community, she heard their preference for uniforms as something they were culturally accustomed to and that would make dressing for school more economically viable and equitable. Thus, after discussions with all concerned, uniforms were ultimately adopted.

In this and many other ways, Dr. Hunt demonstrates her commitment to fostering a culture of authentic and critical dialogue with children, families, and community members—not in a rhetorical fashion but to deepen her insights and inform her actions. It is a commitment that begins as she makes a point of getting to know each and every member of the Dos Puentes Elementary School community and continues as she supports them, builds on their strengths, and learns with and from them.

Insisting on Language Equity

Dr. Hunt takes a strong stance toward language equity. Not doing so would continue to condone the overprivileging of English, which she knows is problematic not only in the education of the children in her school but in preparing them for life in a pluralistic society. At Dos Puentes Elementary School, bilingualism, biliteracy, and multiculturalism are instantiated in everyday teaching and learning. Students learn in Spanish 50% of the time and in English 50% of the time. In addition, all communication between the school and families is in both languages.

Dr. Hunt first recognized how easily multiple languages could be valued when she was traveling in Peru. Even though English was her dominant language and she was not yet "making [much] meaning in Spanish," she was framed as capable. In contrast, when she taught in a public school in Texas, Mexican immigrant students and families were seen as less capable than speakers of English the language of power in the U.S. (Delpit, 1988). It was then that she saw the need for bilingualism to be (re)framed as a valuable resource. At Dos Puentes, Dr. Hunt seeks to (re)frame bilingualism as a resource (Ruiz, 1984) through her everyday practices. Although, she recognizes that "there are external structures that differentiate the significance of acquiring a second language. . . . For minority children, the acquisition of English is expected. For mainstream children, the acquisition of a non-English language is enthusiastically applauded" (Valdés, 1997, p. 417). As a result, she leads a critical professional learning community that challenges dominant-language hierarchies as an essential stance (Souto-Manning, 2010b). At Dos Puentes everyone is worthy and expected to teach, learn, and inquire in two languages.

Supporting Nontraditional Measures of Growth

While it is too early in the history of Dos Puentes Elementary School to examine academic growth in the traditional sense (test scores), teachers see the impact of their dual-language teaching environment as they formatively assess the children. Dr. Hunt encourages this kind of assessment embedded in classrooms where pedagogical and curricular decisions are based on informal yet systematic analysis of student work. She knows that the city- and statewide standardized tests will only partially determine academic progress because they are conducted only in English. This is a tension Dr. Hunt negotiates daily in courageous and culturally relevant ways as she recognizes that teachers can gain more accurate insights about children's abilities when they interact, teach, and learn with them in both English and Spanish:

> We are putting in practice what we know about bilingual education. We are balancing languages; we are giving them access to learning in two languages. . . . We don't have test data yet . . . but I can tell that the children have made a lot of progress [and] we continue to regard all of our students as capable, having high expectations for them in both languages.

Re-envisioning Teacher Evaluation

Responding to required formal teacher evaluation practices by re-envisioning them in more productive and humane ways is another hallmark of Tori Hunt's leadership. Instead of relying on the system's teacher evaluation program in a summative and high-stakes way, she observes all teachers regularly and uses observations as opportunities to support, cultivate, and develop teachers and their teaching.

She observes all teachers in the school twice a month. Each time, she gives them constructive feedback and supports their needs, helping them to grow as teachers and improve their practice. She writes down what teachers and students say and do and how their words relate to learning goals, and offers suggestions for teachers to delve deeper in their interactions, expanding students' understandings. In between observations, she has 10-minute meetings with teachers to give them feedback and identify additional supports to help them hone their craft. "Here are some of my noticings," she might say, after which she highlights positive practices connected to specific rationales, with comments such as, "This is excellent, because you are holding them accountable and you provided them much-needed time to think."

Dr. Hunt also makes teaching suggestions. She builds on strengths with comments such as "Exactly! Build on what you've already done. Make connections." She asks teachers to take responsibility for employing her suggestions, saying, "Next time I come, I will look for that." As one teacher reflected, her evaluations are not focused on a numerical rating but "to help us grow." In doing so, Dr. Hunt challenges punitive evaluation approaches so common in an educational reform movement that seeks to identify and blame "bad teachers" (Kumashiro, 2012).

An important part of Dr. Hunt's teacher evaluations is her connection with the children (Figure 5.1). This not only supports her ability to understand the teacher, but also helps her build relationships with the children. For example, as she entered Ms. Jaar's science classroom for a teaching evaluation, a child asked her how to spell a word. Her response to the child gave her an opportunity to hear about the impact of Ms. Jaar's teaching:

> I can't wait to hear what you are going to write about. Can you tell me what you learned today? And then can you tell me what you are going to write? Then we can think about the spelling.

Throughout her time in the classroom that day, Dr. Hunt listened to the children and asked questions that stretched and deepened their thinking. When Ms. Jaar called the children to the meeting area, Dr. Hunt joined them on the floor (Figure 5.2), a demonstration of how she seamlessly merges teacher observations with a commitment to being a part of the classroom, informing her ability to fully represent teachers' talents in their evaluations and a common practice for Dr. Hunt.

Foundational to positive change fostered by Dr. Hunt regarding teacher evaluations was the way she addressed the challenge of New York State Education Department (NYSED) teacher evaluations. Rather than putting teachers and children in competition with one another (which can be the result of the state's growth model, which compares students across schools), she instituted a goal-setting model allowing teachers to set goals for the growth of individual children. Requiring teachers to know their students deeply, instead of using punitive

Figure 5.2. Dr. Hunt, positioned with the children, as she observes teacher Alcira Jaar.

evaluations, is more likely to lead to pedagogical reflection and, ultimately, stronger pedagogical practices.

Teachers are unfaltering in their appreciation for Dr. Hunt's approach to teaching evaluations. They know her as a knowledgeable and caring supporter as well as a critical cheerleader and protector. As teacher Rebeca Madrigal explained:

> She knows who we are; she knows what goes on in our classrooms. She doesn't need to wait for official evaluations to give us feedback. She supports us and pushes us always. Also, she protects us. I know there are many things we don't get to know because our focus is the students, the classroom, you know?

Providing Time

One of the biggest challenges identified by Dr. Hunt was time: time to bring to life her vision for the school, time for teachers to plan in English and in Spanish, and time to remain focused on the children in light of multiple mandates and compliance deadlines. She recognizes that while bilingualism and biliteracy are key to the philosophy of the school, it takes more time for teachers to plan, teach, and assess in two languages. She also recognizes that this mission results in extra work for the office staff, as every piece of communication from the school must be written in both English and Spanish. When asked how this challenge is addressed, she stated that it is addressed first by building the teachers' commitment to and knowledge about bilingual education, and then by administratively allocating extra planning time. She recognizes: "There ought to be systemic support or you can burn out people."

One of the supports in place is the school-based option to engage in professional development three times a week from 2:50 to 4:00 P.M. On Tuesdays, the focus is on families (including the planning of Family Fridays and the more integral positioning of family funds of knowledge in teaching and learning). On Wednesdays, the focus is on languages and literacies. On Thursdays, the focus is on mathematics and the development of academic language in English and Spanish. This time allows teachers to learn and plan collaboratively.

Another support Dr. Hunt put in place required applying for and being selected to participate in a districtwide learning partnership program launched by NYC Department of Education Chancellor Carmen Fariña to pair schools with similar aims, programs, and populations in hopes that their collaboration would lift school quality. Dr. Hunt received additional funds to pursue collaboration with two other dual-language schools serving similar populations in NYC.

The challenge of time is also related to the enforcement of state-mandated assessments, which need to be administered by the teachers. Dr. Hunt immediately acknowledges how such tasks add to the teachers' workloads. She tries to support them by providing extra planning time and administrative assistance.

CLOSING THOUGHTS

Dr. Tori Hunt sees possibility where others see constraints. She reconceptualizes challenges as valuable opportunities for teaching, learning, and growing. Her leadership is defined by *respeto* (Valdés, 1996), responsiveness, responsibility (high expectations), resourcefulness (E. E. García & E. H. García, 2012), and humility (recognizing that no one knows it all). Each element is anchored in authentic relationships—caring about and being very respectful of teachers, students, and families. She also knows that to be responsive, she has to understand issues of language and culture so that she can lead teachers in building on the assets of all those who make up the Dos Puentes community. She is responsible for fostering humane and informative assessments of children and for building an atmosphere that encompasses high expectations and plentiful support. She is resourceful and committed to the investment of time and work that it takes to ensure cultural and linguistic empowerment as the norm.

Dr. Hunt supports teachers so that they can support the children. She coordinates the priorities of teachers in light of district mandates. She fosters their development in critical ways. She regards them as co-learners along with her and allocates time for collaboration. Dr. Hunt communicates and advocates on behalf of families. She listens, seeking to understand their situations and perspectives. She identifies needed resources and joins families in doing what is best for their children. Dr. Hunt supports bilingualism and positions herself in linguistically vulnerable ways by speaking in her second language much of her day.

At the heart of Dr. Hunt's leadership is her recognition of unjust systemic issues and her ongoing actions to disrupt them, repaying the "education debt" (Ladson-Billings, 2006). Dr. Hunt refuses to embrace practices that position students in terms of deficits; she gets to know students and families beyond labels and stereotypes, finding ways to help them succeed by getting to know them as unique and worthy human beings and by building on their strengths. And while some principals fall into the role of colonizer/dictator when faced with mandates and compliance issues, Dr. Hunt constantly finds ways of re-envisioning and appropriating them to benefit teachers, students, and families.

At the end of the school day, when Dr. Hunt dismisses the students and closes the school door, she does so with confidence that she has listened to, learned from, and respected those around her. In turn, families, teachers, and students trust and respect her. They know she is someone who is there to help them build bridges between languages, cultures, and worlds as she does so herself. They know that Dr. Hunt is a leader who engages in culturally relevant leadership each and every day.

CHAPTER 6

Developing a Wealth Mindset and a Critical Stance

COLLABORATIVE INQUIRY AS A PATH TO SOCIAL JUSTICE

Bilal Polson and Mónica Byrne-Jiménez

MONICA BYRNE-JIMÉNEZ:
INTRODUCING A COURAGEOUS LEADER

Dr. Bilal Polson walks into a room and it lights up. His infectious smile and high energy are hard to ignore as he makes every visitor, student, and teacher feel at home and valued. However, the smiles and energy should not be mistaken for mere hospitality. Dr. Polson's demeanor is deeply tied to his convictions about change that needs to happen in schools and society, something he personifies with a sense of seriousness *and* joy in the work. He embodies Milner's (2015) credo that "complacency is unacceptable if educators are committed to improving education for all. . . . Educators are either fighting for equitable education for all students or they are fighting against it" (p. 11). He engages in this work using keen insights, breadth of knowledge, and deep commitment to children to "support practices that build beyond good intentions" (p. 143). Dr. Polson guides teachers in examining self, society, and institutions of education; he makes you believe that anything is possible. Then he joins you in making it happen.

Dr. Polson's commitment to addressing inequities is grounded in his observations as an elementary school administrator and in memories of being negatively profiled and misjudged in his own schooling experiences. Much like well-documented occurrences of the persistent negative profiling of Black males in and out of schools (Fergus, Noguera, & Martin, 2014; Howard, 2014; Kirkland, 2013), Dr. Polson's energy and precociousness as a student were regularly interpreted as disruptive. He describes being ignored or seen as a behavior problem when his teachers could have used his kinesthetic, artistic, and visual expertise to celebrate and support him as a learner.

Dr. Polson's commitment also derives from memories of support provided by adults who were insightful enough to recognize systemic inequities that did not seek or acknowledge his strengths, so they took extra steps to build on them. He describes a team of educators—his physical education teacher, a dance instructor, and the school's principal—who recognized his talents and created an educational program that used those gifts to build an important foundation for learning and for life. Offering a counternarrative to stereotypes often portrayed about families of Color, Dr. Polson's parents saw his struggles in the classroom and provided additional support to "develop resilience and promote academic success" (Fergus et al., 2014, p. 53). They sought activities outside of school to capture and build his knowledge and skill (dance, theater, sports, music) as well as an array of mentors who helped Dr. Polson integrate out-of-school learning with learning expected *in* school. Each player in Dr. Polson's support system demonstrated caring "through high expectations, . . . connection of content to out-of-school experiences, . . . and being demanding, yet nurturing" (Howard, 2014, p. 14). As he became more adept at connecting home and school, Dr. Polson began to achieve at higher levels.

My name is Mónica Byrne-Jiménez. As a professor in the educational leadership doctoral program at Hofstra University, I met Dr. Polson early in his studies. When he walked into my class as a first-year doctoral student, we did not know each other's stories. By the time I worked with him again as a third-year doctoral student, he had traveled many miles in his academic and leadership journey and had developed an interest in improving the learning experiences of children by seeking and building on their expertise. It was no surprise to me that his earlier interest in supporting young children's school readiness had evolved into a more critical focus on *making schools ready for students*. Dr. Polson had developed an interest in engaging teachers in exploring students' literacy lives outside of school, valuing those literacies as educational resources, examining their own assumptions by taking a critical stance toward teaching and learning, and ultimately changing practices that perpetuated educational inequities. This led to an action research project conducted in collaboration with teachers working to transform deficit assumptions, identify and challenge inequitable practices, and promote student success.

Because of his own experiences, Dr. Polson recognized the importance of being valued for his "funds of knowledge" (Moll, Amanti, Neff, & González, 1992) and was keenly aware of how easily injustices can occur (and be sustained) in systems that reify funds of knowledge from dominant cultural groups. Witnessing the prevalence of such practices, he developed a commitment to helping teachers work to change them. In doing so, Dr. Polson refused to adopt a deficit view of teachers. Rather than blame them for an inability to see children's out-of-school expertise, he worked with teachers to develop awareness and necessary skills. His courageous leadership, therefore, grows out of his own history in conjunction with engaging in his own and teachers' transformation.

Dr. Polson has been the assistant principal at Northern Parkway Elementary School (NPS) in Uniondale, NY, for 7 years. Uniondale is a first-tier suburb approximately 30 miles from New York City. Like other first-tier suburbs, Uniondale has seen recent growth in the English language learner (ELL) population. The school district has approximately 6,400 students. NPS is one of five elementary schools in the district. There are 782 students in grades K–5. The student population is approximately 57% Latino/a, 40% African American, 1% White, and 2% Asian. Twenty-two percent are emergent bi/multilinguals who come to school speaking Spanish or Haitian Creole. Almost 80% of the students receive free or reduced-price lunch. NPS is unique in that the leadership team, one principal and two assistant principals, represent the community racially and ethnically. Over the past 7 years, Dr. Polson has carefully cultivated relationships with teachers, parents, and other community members. Despite being encouraged to seek a leadership position elsewhere, he has chosen to stay. He challenges unjust systems through collaborative work in the interest of building a better educational environment for students (Figure 6.1). This is the work of a courageous leader.

In this chapter, Dr. Polson shares leadership lessons learned as he and NPS teachers engaged in a collaborative action research project taking them into children's homes and communities. The work is particularly important if we consider the prevalence of negativity about students' homes and communities voiced in schools (Howard, 2014; Irvine, 2003; Ladson-Billings, 2009) and the surprising regularity with which many principals discourage teachers from spending time with families in their communities (López-Robertson, Long, & Turner-Nash, 2010). At the same time, research in the field of education tells us that one key to altering an unjust status quo is for teachers to come to know students as collaborators, learning firsthand about the assets that students bring to the classroom and their networks of support beyond schools (Milner, 2015).

The purpose of Dr. Polson's project was to support teachers in acknowledging and overturning institutional and individual biases as they developed deeper relationships with families and more equitable classroom practices. His stories describe changes in his own thinking and the process and outcomes of collaborative efforts with teachers and families. Through his leadership, Dr. Polson continues to courageously engage with educators, parents, and community to ensure that NPS is ready for all children.

Figure 6.1. Dr. Bilal Polson and students from Northern Parkway Elementary School.

BILAL POLSON: MY LEADERSHIP JOURNEY, SHIFTS IN MY OWN THINKING

My name is Bilal Polson. I am a parent of young children, an elementary school administrator, and an educational researcher. In this chapter, I share one of many journeys taken as I work to grow as an administrator while supporting the growth of teachers in my school. This journey is specifically related to an action research project in which I engaged with six teachers. The idea for the project evolved from my personal experience and my doctoral studies, which I entered into with an interest in school readiness. At that time, I assumed that children and families needed to engage in particular practices at home in order to be ready for school. However, as I engaged further in doctoral studies, my thinking started to shift. I began to realize that every child comes to school reading and writing in some form and ready to learn more. I built a strong conviction that schools, teachers, and administrators are where the readiness lies: *They* need to be ready to receive students by first acknowledging inequitable practices and then learning about and utilizing the knowledge and experiences children bring to the classroom so they can construct new, more equitable practices. Consequently, my focus, research agenda, and leadership approach shifted from a mindset that views some children and their families as *not* possessing useful school knowledge toward a *wealth mindset* that sees children and families as possessing tremendous amounts of cultural, social, and academic knowledge. As I continued the work, I ultimately was able to support teachers in identifying underlying equity issues that lead to the dominance of one group's knowledge over that of others, a critical stance necessary if a wealth mindset is to be fully embraced and sustained (Castagno, 2014).

Forming an Action Research Team

In 2010, I conducted a pilot study in my school to learn more about what teachers knew about their students' literacy lives. One problem I identified was a disconnect between home and school literacies in kindergarten through 2nd grade, manifested in academic underachievement in grades 3 through 5. I also found that teachers' own educational experiences shaped their attitudes toward their students' literacy lives. Because they had been schooled to see legitimacy primarily in literacies defined by the dominant culture, they often had deficit views of children from backgrounds different from what was normalized as the mainstream.

However, when teachers learned about knowledge that exists abundantly in homes and communities, their views often changed. Data indicated that teachers knew the importance of the home–school connection but were not proficient in gathering data effectively and consistently enough to impact teaching. They wanted to learn more about how to identify the literacies in students' home lives and use that knowledge to inform their teaching. So, in 2012, six early childhood teachers and I formed an action research team (Figure 6.2) to continue our investigations of students' home literacies.

Home visits. The foundation of our work was spending time in students' homes and communities. Our shared understanding was to approach the home visits as learners (not as evaluators), to learn about the expertise used by children and their families outside of school. We agreed that this project was to learn about the wealth of knowledge in children's homes and use it to inform classroom practice.

Because the home visit idea was new to the teachers, some of them raised concerns about personal safety. These concerns highlighted teachers' limited experiences with families outside of school and assumptions held about students' home lives as potentially dangerous or threatening. They asked questions and made comments such as: What is the school policy with home visits? What if something happens while we are conducting the home visit? My husband says we should never travel alone. This gave me the opportunity to stress that, as uneasy

Figure. 6.2. The action research team including family member, Ms. Hernandez; the teacher/co-researchers; Dr. Polson; and social worker, Dr. Douglas.

as they might have felt, families might feel even more uncomfortable with teachers coming into their homes.

Ultimately, most teachers visited families in pairs, choosing partners for different reasons: support with language translation, grade-level similarities, and curricular interests. We discussed the importance of protocols (how to approach home visits as relationship-building rather than potentially threatening experiences), invitation design, and methods of communication. This conversation was important to our growth as a team. As one teacher said, "I guess this is what you were meaning when you suggested that we work on this project as co-researchers. We all get to participate in the decision making."

Discussion-group meetings. Before the home visits, we began meeting as a professional discussion group. Initially, we met during lunch or after school. We formalized the group as an action research team working to understand the impact that home visits might have on our understanding of a *wealth model* and on our teaching. At the end of each meeting, we established goals and an agenda for the next meeting.

Outcomes

Through the home visits and our group discussions, we learned about the rich contexts students inhabited and how those contexts were literacy- and knowledge-filled. We identified ways to more successfully support children by using their "funds of knowledge" (Moll et al., 1992) to shape curriculum and inform teaching practices. A range of outcomes defined our work: (a) altered attitudes about families, (b) more responsive teaching, (c) teachers' ownership of the process, (d) a new sense of collegiality, (e) establishing more trusting relationships with families, and (f) families taking leadership roles.

Altered attitudes about families. The teachers were surprised and humbled with the way they felt welcomed into homes, contradicting initial fears and concerns. They shared ways that new connections to families were forged as they shared life experiences with each other, finding commonalities:

> [When] we mentioned that we were the first-generation immigrants . . . we could see the parents became more relaxed. When we shared that we spoke Portuguese and Greek, the parents really became excited. They shared that their family was from El Salvador.

The students and families welcomed teachers by giving guided tours of their homes and inviting them to sit at their tables:

> When I arrived . . . everyone was seated at the dining room table. The dining room was symbolic as a place for family discussions. When I was invited to the table I felt like I was invited to join the family conversation. [My student] Max gave me his seat.

The reception that the teachers received from the families during the home visits influenced their approach to teaching and encouraged them to question prior assumptions in ways they were not expecting. An important aspect of altered attitudes was coming to appreciate the educational aspirations held by families and the academic support they provided. For example, during one home visit, a pair of co-researchers and I met a child's grandmother and learned how she used her electronic tablet to develop vocabulary lessons for her grandchild: "[His] grandma was very technologically savvy. What I learned was that she had her own academic agenda for Henry to increase his vocabulary and enhance his learning experience."

This experience and others are significant because a prior assumption about many of the families was that there was little or no support for education in the children's homes. The biases driving that assumption were acknowledged in discussions after many home visits. Teachers began to recognize their complete misinterpretation of what was actually occurring at home.

More responsive teaching. As a result of the home visits and our collaborative reflections, the teachers began teaching differently. Instructionally, the co-researchers became more responsive to student interests, expanded the resources they used, and developed more interactive teaching styles. The teachers also felt greater autonomy in their classroom decisions and were able to move away from scripted curricula to embrace practices more congruent with the students' interests and backgrounds.

Use of more culturally relevant literature. One specific instructional difference was that the teachers increased the use of literature that reflected the students' identities and lives. This, in turn, motivated students as readers. For example, during a home visit, one of the teachers learned about a particular student's love for particular books. The teacher, in turn, surveyed all of her students and built her classroom library according to their interests. She also began providing opportunities for students to demonstrate their expertise by sharing favorite books, and she utilized those books for reading instruction. Another teacher found out during a home visit that one of her students had a love of farm animals and buildings. So she expanded her classroom library to reflect those interests.

Decreased dependence on scripted programs. The impact of the home visits and group discussions on instructional practice was also evidenced as teachers began to decrease dependence on scripted programs and build curriculum from students' strengths. For example, after learning about one child's interest in construction, his teacher, Silva, reduced reliance on the scripted math curriculum by developing a geometry lesson around block structures. In another example, Silva used her knowledge of a child's interest in climbing trees to encourage him to participate in ways he had never participated before. Although an interest in tree-climbing may seem trivial to some, it was in fact pivotal in bringing Max into the lesson. A teaching colleague who observed the lesson commented:

> [Silva] decided to focus on the trees based on what we learned about Max's interest from the home visit. . . . As the children contributed to the word web, Max . . . wanted to share his interest and knowledge about trees. He is a shy boy but he raised his hand and talked about his ability to climb trees.

In a similar example, one of the teachers shared that a student (Katharine) was having difficulty with word problems in mathematics. Rather than continue with problems as they were written in the mathematics textbook, I asked the teaching team to find out about Katharine's strengths and passions and develop lessons based on those interests. As a result, a series of word problems were developed based on Katherine's favorite novella, *Porque El Amor Manda.* This inspired her to create her own word problems, which led to her re-enfranchisement in the curriculum and ability to see herself as a mathematician. The experience affirmed the importance of (re)positioning students' strengths instructionally and reinforced the importance of moving outside traditional approaches to envision new curricular practices.

Teachers' ownership of the process. Important to the success of our work was the transition from my facilitation of the project to our roles as co-researchers who took ownership of the work together. When our project began, we agreed that I would serve as facilitator of our meetings. However, as teachers gained experience and expertise and saw student responses to new practices, they developed a sense of empowerment. As a result, they began to bring ideas to our group that became the focus of discussions and to take leadership roles in the collection of data and direction and facilitation of the work.

A new sense of collegiality. A new sense of collegiality emerged from our work. One of the practices that led to this was observing in one another's classrooms, then giving one another feedback. This allowed teachers to gain the comfort necessary to offer suggestions for further connections between home visits and classroom applications. Initially, the teachers felt awkward, nervous, and uncomfortable when observing their peers. But, through opportunities to debrief together, they began supporting one another with new eyes. This enhanced their professional relationships and contributed to their increased confidence.

This also contributed to teachers' reduced dependence on me. They began to rely more on their classroom colleagues for recommendations, feedback, and support. With this empowerment came greater investment in the work, and the project increased as a priority in their professional lives. They worked together in more collegial ways, explaining how important it was to be able to "hold each other accountable . . . [and] count on each other."

Establishing more trusting relationships with families. While the action research project clearly had an impact on us as teachers and co-researchers, we were not sure about the effect the visits would have on the families. However, families appreciated being able to share their homes, lives, and values with the teachers. Some expressed that the home visits helped them feel more supported by the school. For many, it was the first time that a teacher made the effort to visit and, as one parent described, it brought joy as well as validation:

> I [am] happy that the teacher called and said she was coming to my home. . . . She was the first teacher to make a visit to my home. [My son] was so happy that she came because his teacher helped and now my son helps me and his brother.

Another parent explained how the home visit helped her child build confidence:

> My son gave them a tour of the house and the yard. He showed them his special climbing tree and it helped to build his confidence in school to know that his teachers and one of his principals came to his home.

The home visits led some parents to feel more at ease advocating for their children: "After establishing the home–school connection I feel more comfortable sharing with the school my issues and concerns." Another parent appreciated that home visits fostered new insights for teachers:

> Sometimes assumptions are made about homes and children. . . . [The] home–school connection is . . . a resource for how we can help each other, for how I can help you get to know my child as a person.

Families taking leadership roles. Because of relationships built through the home visits, some family members took on leadership roles in the school, suggesting and implementing various projects. One of the grandparents, Ms. Hernandez, was very interested in continuing the work to connect families and the school. She approached Dr. Sean Douglas (the school social worker) and me about starting a mentoring program for 2nd-grade boys. We responded immediately and attended meetings with Ms. Hernandez taking the lead as she worked to gain funding from local merchants and clergy. Following her vision and leadership, we identified six 2nd-grade boys in need of support and matched them with 5th-grade peer mentors. The mentors were students who achieved well academically and previously had shifted their own behaviors from being unproductive and disruptive to being excellent examples of leadership.

With the money raised by Ms. Hernandez, the school was able to purchase board games, books, and video game consoles. Together the boys played games that enhanced critical thinking and problem-solving skills, and the older boys provided academic tutoring. Within weeks, the instances of behavioral infractions from the 2nd-grade boys dropped 80% and they sustained that level of improvement throughout the remainder of the year. In addition, within 2 months, the boys' schoolwork completion increased by 75% and, 3 months later, by 90%.

Leadership, Power, and Responsibility

My role as administrator/facilitator is multidimensional and does not remain static. Through this project, and as I live my life daily, it evolves from initiating ideas to supporting, participating in, and contributing to decisions determined by teachers with whom I work. The project reinforced the importance of my role as an instructional leader working in tandem with teachers *in the classroom* and *in the community*. I learned that it was important for me to have a clear vision for the work while being willing to adapt to the process in flexible, collaborative, and responsive ways (Byrne-Jiménez & Orr, 2007). I learned that, as a school leader, I was in a position of power and therefore had a responsibility to model my own self-directed learning (Heron, 2008).

Ultimately, it was important to ensure an environment where the teachers/co-researchers and family members felt empowered to carry on the work without the direct support of a facilitator. This meant that also foundational to my role was my commitment to creating conditions that supported teachers in "turn[ing] their learning into action" (Byrne-Jiménez & Orr, 2007, p. 84) so they could develop into leaders themselves.

MONICA BYRNE-JIMÉNEZ: REFLECTING ON DR. POLSON'S COURAGEOUS LEADERSHIP

In August 1967, Reverend Dr. Martin Luther King Jr., spoke to the Christian Leadership Conference using the words, "The arc of the moral universe is long, but it bends towards justice." The quote hints that the work of justice is a long journey that requires painstaking care and commitment. For educational leaders, it means engaging in the daily—and often invisible—work of challenging teaching practices, fostering the adoption of equity-oriented values, reaching out to families in culturally responsive and respectful ways, and acknowledging the importance of an expansive and inclusive community of learners. Through his stories, Dr. Polson demonstrates the work of social justice leadership in education. In many respects, this requires being prepared to move from tensions to learning, from messy problems to multiple solutions—making oneself vulnerable as a learner and activist.

The social justice path is unpredictable, bumpy, and full of surprises. It is populated by children, families, and educators who believe that a better world is possible. A tremendous strength of Dr. Polson's work is his use of a powerful position to empower others as leaders who carry the work forward. This is done through leadership that breeds trust, is mutually educative, and is not judgmental but also not compromising in the deliberate move toward change.

As Dr. Polson continues this work, it is difficult not to appreciate the ways in which his courageous leadership is anchored in his childhood experiences. His convictions about the importance of a wealth mindset and a critical stance are unwavering. At the heart of it all, Dr. Polson recognizes and acknowledges that educational injustices are more pervasive than many educators have been encouraged to admit, so he is steadfast in his commitment to join others working to "rearrange our world"; "to make it better . . . to get the job done" (Walker, 2006, p. 28).

CHAPTER 7

Understanding Family Involvement

RACE, CLASS, SCHOOLING, AND FAMILY LIFE IN A RURAL BLACK COMMUNITY

Michele Myers

Dr. Myers, I can't put up with this, I tried calling his mom. . . . I can't deal with her. I can't deal with him. They don't want to do better.

His mom never darkened these doors to even come and check on Devonte. That's why he is getting all Fs. I don't think the woman even cares. . . . His dad is missing in action; he lives in the projects; they never come to the school when you call.

Have you ever heard well-intentioned teachers talk about their students and students' families in ways that robbed those human beings of their humanity? During my first year as an administrator of an elementary school in rural South Carolina, I began hearing comments such as those that open this chapter. I noticed the subtle and not-so-subtle ways that some teachers—White and African American—spoke negatively about the families and the students from the African American, low-income, rural population we served. While feeling dedicated to all children, their own middle-class experiences sometimes led to biases revealed in the ways they talked about, interacted with, and taught our students.

Concerned about the comments, I also realized that my lack of response to them made me complicit in perpetuating views that were racist and classist (Castagno, 2014). I knew that addressing this would be difficult, but by allowing the comments to pass unexamined, I was doing what Kohli (2009) warned us about: sustaining a culture that perpetuated views of Black and low-income families as uncaring and unsupportive of their children's academic lives, and of Black students as disinvested in their own education (Edwards, McMillon, & Turner, 2010). I knew better.

My own parents cared deeply about and supported my education, but I have little recollection of them ever coming to my school when I was a child. One of the few memories I have of a parent coming to school was when my brother was in 1st grade. During the middle of the year, his teacher sent a notice informing my parents of her plans to retain him. According to the teacher, Michael was a nonreader and needed to repeat 1st grade. She insinuated that my mother did not support him as a reader. This is the same mother who, every Thursday, took my brother and me to visit the bookmobile that came through our small town in rural South Carolina. Our mother was deeply involved in our academic development outside of school. She took us to the local museum, zoos, and historic parks. She reveled in our accomplishments and always talked with us about the importance of an education. She taught us that, as Black students, we would have to be cleaner, smarter, better prepared, and more courteous than other children because assumptions would be made about us, assumptions deeply embedded and largely unexamined in the culture of the world beyond our community.

In these ways, my mother and other relatives and community members formed the network of support that set my feet on the path to college and a career in education. They equipped me with what I needed to know. However, many educators in my life often failed to recognize the roles that my family and community played, because my mother was not a regular presence in our school or in our classrooms.

Since my childhood, I have heard many teachers misperceive a child's home experiences as lacking in care, concern, and family involvement, because they view parental support only through their own cultural lens. As a result, they often detail a litany of pathologies and deficits that are narrowly defined, presumptuous, and judgmental (Dantas & Manyak, 2010). I know the role such views can play in keeping children from reaching and exceeding their potential.

As an elementary school administrator, I knew that something had to be done. I needed to be courageous enough to address the discourse that had become so commonplace at my school and that, if left unchecked, would continue to perpetuate academic success for some children and marginalization for others. This chapter describes my work to support teachers in recognizing and countering deficit views, to build home–school relationships and thereby recognize the networks of family support too often hidden by those who define parent involvement in singular ways.

EVERY SCHOOL HAS A STORY TO TELL

My story is from Riverside Elementary School, a small Title I school nestled on the outskirts of a rural town in the southeastern United States. When I was principal at Riverside Elementary, the school enrolled approximately 250 students:

98% Black, 1% White, and 1% Latino/a. The faculty was 68% Black and 32% White, with varying levels of academic degrees. I succeeded a much-loved former principal who had been affectionately referred to by the staff as "Momma." I knew that it would be hard to fill her shoes; therefore, I told the faculty that I would not undo anything that was working well but would address issues that did not actualize the vision we would develop together for the school.

INVITING PERSPECTIVES: HOW IS IT GOING?

When I became principal, it was important to begin by developing shared goals for the school with staff, students, families, and community. I began by interviewing families, students, teachers, and community members, asking two questions:

1. What is working well at Riverside Elementary?
2. What changes are needed to make Riverside Elementary better?

Concerns were expressed about student achievement, curriculum and instruction, assessments, and the handling of discipline issues, but families communicated the greatest concerns. Many of them felt disenfranchised and misunderstood by the school. They felt they had little voice in its inner workings. Family members felt that assumptions were made about them that caused some teachers to have low expectations for their children. One grandmother talked about the importance of helping teachers change their perceptions:

We have to talk to these teachers. We have to get them to see the picture as it is and not what they think it is. Yes, because they will draw their own conclusions, and they'll treat your kids according to what their conclusion is, and that is sometimes totally different.

In particular, some parents felt that assumptions made by teachers about their children were informed by negative stereotypes about African Americans. One mother shared an example that occurred when she was a few minutes late bringing her child to school and took her to the cafeteria for breakfast. She was told that breakfast was over but she could run up the street to get the child breakfast "since she had nothing else to do." Insulted by the insinuation that she did not have a job or other obligations, the mother said:

You know I am not that parent who just sits home all day. I got to go to work. . . . How do you just automatically assume that I don't have somewhere to be also? . . . I come in here every day dressed up . . . [and they] automatically assume that I am going back home to relax for the rest of the day.

Bearing this in mind, the staff and I developed several goals, the most important of which was to deepen teachers' understandings about children's homes and families by developing better home–school relationships. This chapter focuses on that goal.

MOVING FORWARD: YOU CAN'T BE HELD ACCOUNTABLE FOR WHAT YOU DON'T YET KNOW

Working toward our goal, I began to think about how to help the faculty develop a deeper understanding of children and families. Recognizing that they could not be held accountable for what they did not yet know and that short-term experiences do not always shift perspectives (Donnelly et al., 2005), I utilized a range of ongoing strategies so that we could learn with, from, and about students and their families.

Book Clubs

My first action was to secure resources to provide site-based professional development throughout the year, focusing on issues related to home–school connections, culturally relevant pedagogy, and antiracist education. The ongoing format afforded teachers time to read, reflect, and begin to consider that home–school relationship problems might originate in our attitudes and assumptions.

For our book club discussions, I selected readings that focused on topics such as home–school partnerships (Allen, 2007, 2010; Hoover-Dempsey & Sandler, 2005; López-Robertson, Long, Turner-Nash, 2010; Myers, 2013), culturally relevant pedagogy (Edwards et al., 2010; Gay, 2011; Ladson-Billings, 2009; Nieto & Bode, 2011), and antiracist education (Hayes & Juárez, 2012; Lewis, 2001; Lynn & Parker, 2006; Milner, 2008). Book clubs replaced our faculty meetings and were facilitated each week by one of the teachers. This gave faculty members opportunities to hone leadership skills, and it afforded me the opportunity to take the stance of learner alongside the staff.

Each Tuesday was early release day for the students (school dismissed at 1:30 p.m. instead of 3:00 p.m.). This gave us the opportunity to engage in book clubs from 2:00 until 4:00. We always began with an entrance slip on which teachers reflected about their current thinking related to the reading for that week. This was followed by a discussion of key points, anomalies, and new ideas to explore. We ended each session with reflective exit slips in which teachers detailed current thinking, new questions, and connections made as a result of that day's session (Figure 7.1).

As teachers reflected on their beliefs, dramatic shifts were often the result. For example, during one session, we discussed African American Language (AAL)

Figure 7.1. Dr. Michele Myers and the faculty book club.

as an important linguistic, historic, and social structure, and a language spoken by many of our students and their families. One of the teachers wrote, "I don't understand why students have to bring the way they talk at home and in the streets to school and [don't] think it is appropriate. They need to learn how to talk right." This let me know that I should share resources to support the development of teachers' knowledge about the legitimacy of AAL and ways they could use that knowledge to appreciate students' bilingual abilities and teach students to code-switch across contexts. We read and discussed an article by Boutte and Johnson (2013) focusing on AAL and biliteracy, and watched Jamila Lyiscott's TED Talk (2014) about identity and language. Discussing carefully selected texts such as these, teachers began to consider aspects of family culture in new and more appreciative ways, laying the groundwork for building better home–school relationships. As one teacher wrote, "I didn't realize how much of a student's identity is found in his language, and that language is his family's heritage. By dishonoring his language, I dishonor him and his family."

Home Visits

One of the most important things we learned was that parents often felt that teachers did not know them as individuals. A grandmother explained the need for mutual respect as a responsibility of families and of teachers, again referring to the bias that some families felt because of assumptions made about Black children:

> [You have to] show [teachers] you are not who they think you are so that your child will be respected. It's about respect. Children deserve respect, and parents deserve respect. Okay. It's not a one-sided thing.

To address this need, I encouraged teachers to visit families regularly in their homes and communities. These visits were designed to build relationships so teachers could begin understanding families as partners, and to help teachers better understand the range of possibilities for parenting and family involvement in students' educational lives. The teachers and I took the stance of learners and developed questions to ask informally, such as:

- Tell me about you and your family.
- What do you want most for your child?
- What are your biggest fears?
- In what ways can schools and families work together?

Using time differently. In order for teachers to visit students' homes without spending personal time to do so, I encouraged them to use professional development days and planning periods for home visits. To be respectful of families' time and schedules, we worked with them to ensure that days and times for our visits would be convenient for them.

Getting fears out in the open. Some teachers were fearful about visiting families in neighborhoods that they saw as unsafe. Recognizing that fear often comes from learned misperceptions, I talked with them about why they were fearful and was able to dispel some of those notions. Sometimes the school's Care Director (who assists students with class assignments and in-class behavioral issues), the Parent Liaison, or I would visit homes with the teachers. The Care Director, Mr. Blake, was invaluable because he lived in the community and was well-respected there. As we discussed teachers' discomforts, he urged us to turn the tables to consider how uncomfortable and fearful families might feel anticipating visits from teachers, helping us understand the experience from families' points of view.

Positive Communication

I also encouraged positive communication via phone calls and notes sent home. The need for this was clear in parent responses to our surveys and interviews. One parent explained that most of the phone calls she received from teachers were when she was at work and that those calls typically communicated that her child had done something wrong: "They never call to say he is doing good." In contrast, another parent talked about the impact of a postcard her sister received from her child's teacher:

[The teacher] said she just wanted to commend [my niece] for the great work she is doing in [her] class. . . . And my sister was sitting there crying like you had a million-dollar check.

Once we discussed this issue as a faculty, teachers began focusing on letting families know when children had a particularly wonderful day or accomplished something large or small. The results were overwhelmingly positive when teachers did not contact families exclusively when problems arose.

Participation in Community Events

Because many faculty members at Riverside Elementary resided outside the community, impromptu meetings with families at local venues were rare (that is, they did not run into each other at local grocery stores, markets, or doctors' offices). So I encouraged the staff to attend community-sponsored events such as the County Fair, the Festival of Roses, dance performances, sporting events, and so on. Actively participating in community events helped the teachers become more familiar with students and their families and led to casual conversations about day-to-day life, in contrast to the more formal, academically focused interactions that tended to occur at school. As a result, stereotypes and fears held by some teachers began to dissipate.

CREATING A MORE WELCOMING SCHOOL

During my first year as principal, it became clear that many families rarely attended the regularly scheduled monthly meetings or other school-sponsored events. I soon realized that the ways we informed families about such events were ineffective. The staff and I came to see that we had been exacerbating families' discomfort and uneasiness by putting up barriers (intentionally and unintentionally) that confronted families when they came into the school.

To address these issues, I looked at how the school had been communicating with families. I realized that we relied heavily on written documents sent home with the children. For a variety of reasons, these documents did not always reach family members. Another problem was that our communication efforts were unidirectional: We sent information home, but rarely solicited families' opinions or suggestions. Further, despite the fact that we had a growing Latino/a population, most of our correspondence was written in English, rendering the information inaccessible to many families. As a result of these reflections, we implemented a range of strategies to ensure better and more reliable communication and a more welcoming school (Allen, 2007). Following are descriptions of these strategies.

Thursday Express and Classroom Websites

One strategy used to better communicate with families was to designate a particular day (Thursday) each week for sending information. This way, families knew when to expect correspondence. The *Thursday Express* was sent home in brightly colored folders that included feedback forms with questions such as: With what areas of the school are you most pleased? What areas of the school could use improvement? What other concerns, questions, or issues would you like to share? The same information also was posted on the classroom website for families who preferred to access it via the Internet. Families also received computer-generated phone calls with the information in both English and Spanish.

On Fridays, when students returned their *Thursday Express* folders, teachers collected the feedback forms and sent them to the front office. The assistant principal and I compiled the data, which were then sent to the leadership team (grade-level teacher leaders, media specialist, guidance counselor, assistant principal, principal, a parent), who used the feedback in their monthly meetings to develop plans of action.

Feedback Box

Sometimes family members wanted to share feedback anonymously, so we positioned a feedback box near the entrance to the school. Next to the box, we kept a large supply of feedback forms for families to use so they did not have to request one from the office staff. The feedback box afforded families a safe place to share ideas about initiatives and changes that they wanted to see in the school. It gave them a space to share thoughts about what was going well, as well as a place to express disagreement and concern.

Surveys

We also used electronic surveys to solicit feedback from families. Using the free Internet resource SurveyMonkey, we asked families for their views about particular policies, practices, testing issues, school events, and so on. The information that families shared through these surveys helped to guide our planning of events as well as our ability to communicate information.

Valuing Multiple Languages

The literature is clear about the importance of valuing students' home languages in support of learning in school contexts (Laman, 2013; Nieto, 1999). However, attitudes in schools are often antithetical to this understanding, particularly when educators have little knowledge about effective practice in multilingual contexts. Once we realized how frustrating and potentially frightening a monolingual environment could be for many families, we made some important changes.

I began by ensuring that interpreters were always available for families and for children. One of the faculty members was fluent in Spanish, as was the TESOL (Teachers of English to Speakers of Other Languages) teacher assigned to our school. I provided support by covering classes or providing release time so that these teacher-translators could attend meetings and develop written translations when necessary. Ultimately, all documents sent from the school were written in both Spanish and English. In the process, the teachers and I learned more about Spanish and gained an appreciation that allowed us to value the students' linguistic repertoires.

Creating an On-Site Family Room

Through the use of a survey, we learned that families would appreciate a space where they could meet with one another, so, with family members, we developed a family resource room. It was designed with comfortable seating and appliances such as a television, microwave, coffeepot, and refrigerator. We stocked the room with resources and information for parents in both Spanish and English. Teachers made a variety of teaching demonstration videos available for parents to view there or to check out and take home.

The school-based parent liaison met with families in this room regularly and brought in community members to support families with activities such as applying for jobs and/or social benefits. Our goal was to provide parents with a nonthreatening space where they could meet, socialize with one another and the staff, and share and receive information.

Reducing Wait Time

Surveys also showed us that families often had to wait for long periods of time before seeing anyone when they visited the school. It was important to change this highly disrespectful situation. We developed an open-door policy so that family members were always welcomed and served, with or without appointments. We ensured that enough staff were always available (or reachable) so that family members did not have to wait before they could speak with someone.

In total, these strategies led to more and more engagement of families within the school walls. Our actions let them know that we were sincere when we said, "We want you here. Come often." And they did.

ALTERING VIEWS ABOUT FAMILY SUPPORT

Prior to our systematic attempts to build a more welcoming school, many of the teachers viewed family involvement through their own middle-class experiences. Through our work together, they came to recognize the myriad ways that familial support exists. This included reading to and with children, rewarding good work, stressing the importance of getting good grades, teaching the importance of showing respect for teachers, telling stories to emphasize the importance of doing well, and creating college- or career-bound cultures. More important, teachers also learned about the depth and breadth of support not typically recognized or validated by teachers from middle-class (and often White) backgrounds.

The first acknowledgment was that effective home support comes not just from parents but also from extended family and community members. Teachers began to see how families drew on the collective resources of many members of their various networks (family, neighborhood, church) to sustain the academic, emotional, physical, psychological, and cognitive well-being of their children. In one of many examples, a grandmother explained how she accessed help with homework from her family network—folks living nearby and in other states: "I get on the phone and I will call up my niece [or] I call my grandchildren in Georgia or wherever to get the help I need."

Second, teachers learned about the ways through which family members carefully and knowledgeably prepared their children to successfully interact within classroom environments. Family members felt that these environments, albeit educational, perpetuated negative stereotypes about Black children from low-income households. Because of families' own school histories, they were well aware of how such attitudes can impact teachers' expectations of children and, consequently, their ability to teach. To address this, families supported their children by ensuring that their actions, dress, and demeanor would contradict any negative ideologies that might exist. Intentionally, families went to extra lengths to prepare their children in ways that would dismantle the belief that poor children are dirty and unkempt and that parents do not care.

In addition, some parents explicitly taught their children the strategy of avoiding confrontation so they could survive in classrooms where teachers' biases might lead them to misinterpret children's behaviors. Like many parents of Color bringing up children in rural and/or low-income communities, they were well aware of how their children's actions might be perceived differently than the same actions by White middle-class children. It was a reality that they had come to expect and an element of school support not recognized by many teachers. To recognize and validate these supportive moves by family members, teachers had to begin considering the racist, classist realities that led to the need for them. As Coates (2015) wrote, these realities were very different from those faced by middle-class White students: "No one told little white children . . . [that they must] be twice as good" (p. 91) if they were to be successful in schools.

CHALLENGES AND COLLECTIVE COURAGE

Recognizing the deficit nature of discourse at my school and confronting the fact that I had not supported teachers in understanding biases at play led me to work toward new approaches. This required leading faculty in identifying and critically examining practices that were dishonoring families. In doing so, we began challenging deficit orientations that positioned students and families as uncaring and incapable. We started down the road toward building more productive and honest relationships.

In the process, the most difficult challenge I faced was raising issues of racial and class bias that lay beneath the deficit views we worked to contradict. Initially, several White staff members were uncomfortable with discussions about race and averred a neutral or color-blind disposition (believing that we are a postracial society, seeing all kids as the same "color"). Some felt that I was bringing up issues of race because I was a Black principal with a chip on my shoulder.

As we read and discussed together, however, we were able to begin examining the fallacies of color-blind approaches as disavowing the very characteristics that give us the rich heritage we seek to bring into classrooms. We also began to explore how color-blindness means avoiding talk about the ongoing existence of racism, an issue necessary to examine if we are to understand how deficit views originate and are sustained, and if we are to overturn them.

Where did I find the courage to continue? I had no choice when I saw the marginalization, bias, and even fearfulness felt by families and students. It was my responsibility to engage staff in conversations through which we could begin to understand and address the covert and overt ways that Black students from low-income households and their families were being disadvantaged in our school. But it is important to emphasize that, while the work required courage on my part, it also required courage from the teachers. They had to be brave enough to step out of their learned experiences and seek the perspectives of families and community members, listen, validate others' accounts, and use what they heard to join me in interrogating ourselves and our practices. It was our collective courage that held the potential to turn rhetoric into reality as we worked toward the equitable education of all students.

CHAPTER 8

Determined to Make a Difference

Becoming a Culturally Responsive Administrator

Detra Price-Dennis

I was sitting at my desk after school working on plans for a unit of study. My principal, Mary Rykowski, walked into the room, pulled up a chair, and sat beside me. Mary was concerned about Janet, a student who was not succeeding academically. Mary wanted to be sure she did not slip through the cracks, worried that, because of assumptions often made about children from Janet's community (frequently defined only by poverty and crime), her intellect, kindness, and inquisitiveness might be overlooked. Two weeks later, Mary showed up again in my classroom to say she had arranged for us to visit Janet and her grandmother at their home. She wanted us to get to know Janet's grandmother and convey our belief in her granddaughter. I gathered my things, hopped in the car, and we drove to Janet's home, where her grandmother greeted us at the door and invited us inside.

In the next hour, I watched the foundation for a trusting relationship grow as Mary conveyed a sense of belief in Janet and in her grandmother's wisdom. We learned that Janet's grandmother was also concerned. She was relieved that the school recognized Janet's potential. In the first few moments, I learned something very important from my principal. In spite of the wider community's portrait of people from Janet's neighborhood as lacking in educational motivation and potential, Mary knew that much knowledge, expertise, *and* family support for education existed there. She believed in Janet and in Janet's caring grandmother.

By encouraging me to visit Janet's home, initiating the visit, accompanying me, and providing a model for genuine and respectful interaction, Mary exemplified the notion that meaningful relationships require our full presence and commitment in each student's life and our genuine belief in children and their families. Both Mary and Janet's grandmother taught me not to buy into misperceptions and stereotypes that too easily lead teachers to expect little of their students. Within these pages, I thank Mary for these lessons by sharing stories from her career. I do so to give other administrators the courage to foster the same spirit in teachers by doing what it takes to keep the success of every student at the forefront of the mission that guides our work.

MEET MS. RYKOWSKI

You have to step up to the plate and do what's best for the children.
—Mary Rykowski

I met Mary Rykowski when I was a teacher at Indianola Informal Elementary School in Columbus, OH. As my administrator, she shaped my practice—then as a classroom teacher and now as a university professor preparing new teachers. An extraordinary principal, Mary has spent the past 2 decades positively impacting the lives of children, families, and teachers in central Ohio. Her work exemplifies tenets of culturally responsive leadership. Her ideology and life experiences have informed a career spent cultivating inclusive learning environments for all children.

Mary entered the teaching profession with a passion for ensuring that students of Color and students from low-income households, many of whom were relegated to the margins, would find confidence, purpose, and success. As a classroom teacher and then a principal, Mary worked in a variety of contexts, accumulating a wealth of experiences with students and families from urban and suburban settings.

Mary began her career as an elementary school teacher in a small Catholic school where she sought ways to involve all of her students in learning. She drew upon their cultural resources to help them make sense of the content she was teaching. Her firm belief was that all children are capable learners. After several years, she moved to a large urban public school system where she completed her administrative credentials and became the principal at an urban elementary school.

To date, Mary has provided leadership at four elementary schools, two urban and two suburban. With each move, she incorporated lessons learned along the way from teachers, children, and families with whom she worked over the years. Her foundational beliefs in the potential of every student and the supportive intentions of family members guided her teaching decisions and daily interactions with students, families, and colleagues. As described in the following pages, she took (and continues to take) a stand in a variety of ways to challenge systems that sustain an unacceptable and deficit-laden status quo.

A FRAMEWORK FOR LEADERSHIP TYPIFIED BY ACTION

The framework for Mary's leadership is grounded in the idea that culturally responsive teaching is constructed on the premise that teachers should:

a. Know their students and acknowledge their background as rich in academic, social, and cultural resources
b. Critique pedagogies for the cultural, academic, and social voices that are too often devalued or silenced
c. Create collaborative learning spaces grounded in a critical consciousness, identifying and bringing missing or devalued voices, knowledge, and resources into the norm
d. Encourage students to communicate across cultural backgrounds and linguistic repertoires (Gay, 2010; Ladson-Billings, 1994)

This framework not only requires teachers to draw on students' cultural ways of being as important resources but insists that teachers take action to overturn the sociopolitical factors that create inequitable learning environments, such as these:

- Over-referral of students of Color to special education programs and their under-referral to gifted and talented programs
- Insistence on English-only curricula (keeping many students from full participation and hiding the linguistic and cognitive skills, abilities, and knowledge of emerging bi/multilinguals)
- Assumption that children from low-income households are less capable and/or come to school with less language or less worthy knowledge

Locating Mary's administrative approach within this framework is an important step in understanding the courage she embodied as she transformed schools into supportive, validating spaces. Although some in the educational community may attribute her success simply to good leadership, I contend there is a clear distinction between "good leadership" and Mary's courageous approach to the culturally responsive guidance she provided. The distinction lies in her insight and involvement in daily practices that make systemic change possible and sustainable —defying the status quo to insist on changes in attitudes, assumptions, and practice. In this way, Mary's leadership is typified not by rhetoric, but by action as she consistently takes a stand for children, families, communities, and teachers.

Taking a Stand for Multilingualism as a Resource

As the daughter of second-generation Italian immigrants, Mary grew up hearing stories of how her parents spent their first years of school hoping that the teachers in their schools would not notice that they were just beginning to learn to speak English. As emergent bilinguals, her parents continually faced negative stereotypes and deficit models. Their experiences motivated Mary to become an educator who would work against practices that marginalize and degrade students with cultural and linguistic resources beyond the dominant norm. She explained:

> I think my background informs a lot of what I do. It is where I get my passion. Both of my parents spoke Italian, but they didn't speak in school. My mom told me this story where she would copy off of someone else's paper because she didn't even know what it was she was supposed to do, and somehow she figured out a way to learn. She just had to get by, that's what she did.

Remembering the degradation faced by her parents when their home language and culture were erased in the school context placed Mary in a unique position to understand why schools needed (and still need) to change. She was painfully aware that her parents had possessed great knowledge and linguistic skill that was hidden from teachers when they ignored or silenced her parents' abilities.

As Mary entered the teaching profession and became an administrator, these stories shaped her pedagogy and leadership style. Mary was adamant that, of all the lessons to be learned about working with bi/multilingual children, teachers needed to realize that students walk in the door every day with knowledge and resources that are rich in potential for their own and others' learning. They come to us already knowledgeable and successful and, therefore, on the road to further success. She elaborated on this point by sharing her experiences as an administrator:

> I brought that knowledge [about my parents learning English] and when a teacher would say, "What am I supposed to do with this student?" I would help them understand that the student knows way more than what we can assess. I would also think, "What if that child was my mom? What would I want someone to do for her in that situation?"

Drawing on her family's experiences, Mary was able to support teachers in valuing the intelligence and skill required to add English to existing language repertoires. This type of leadership was bold, gutsy, and at times difficult. Each exchange with teachers and administrative colleagues required Mary to be courageous in her approach, knowing that it could create tensions with those who maintained an English-only approach and did not yet appreciate the linguistic resources that children bring to the classroom.

Taking a Stand for the Brilliance of Children

Because of the No Child Left Behind legacy, phrases like "all children can learn" morphed into empty mantras. However, one only has to visit a building where Mary Rykowski is an administrator to see this mantra in action as her high regard for and belief in the academic potential of every student are evident.

"They are crazy smart! They are amazing!" she exclaimed, exuding admiration for the young learners with whom she has worked over the years. This message is clarified as Mary continues to work with children in a variety of ways (Figure 8.1): tutoring them during lunch, working on projects during an after-school program, or offering sensory breaks for children in her office.

Karen, a teacher who worked with Mary for 4 years at Jonesville Elementary School, also shared this sentiment, saying, "I really think that while Mary was at Jonesville, many of the children took pride in their work. They knew that Ms. Rykowski cared." The hours she spent each week before and after school talking with children and families to find out what they needed to feel confident as learners demonstrated her commitment to uncovering gems of brilliance in all children (and families) and making sure that each student's knowledge was accounted for in meaningful ways.

This belief in the brilliance of children as a clear pattern in Mary's leadership style spans demographics. When I last talked to Mary, she was working in an affluent area in a school that was privileged in many ways:

> **Detra:** From where I sit, it doesn't seem to matter where you go, urban or suburban; you make sure kids are successful. You exude this intrinsic belief that children are going to be successful and it is your job to figure out how to get them to that point. That is so different from, "There are too many mandates in the way" or, "Those kids just can't perform at a high level"; the status quo does not seem to deter you. Why?
>
> **Mary:** I don't think I know what the status quo means. Here we are in a very affluent building, and I have to use the neighboring art center for two of our classrooms because we don't have enough space. I have learned that it can't just be the status quo. I sit here at this high-achieving school . . . but I'm always saying how can I do it better? How can we push our students who are excelling? The status quo just cannot exist for children. . . . I don't believe in the status quo.

Figure 8.1. Mary Rykowski.

Whether she is documenting a child's achievement, handing out an award for hard work on a project, or trying to understand how a child with special needs experiences different classroom environments, Mary always strives to make sure children know that they are contributing to the school environment. She also ensures that teachers, families, and the wider community recognize every child's brilliance as well.

Taking a Stand for the Potential of Teachers

I asked Mary whether it has been difficult helping teachers shift their perspectives about students' potential for achievement when working with traditionally marginalized populations, and she replied:

> It is difficult to do when there is more diversity [in a school] because [many teachers] just don't know [what to do]. Teachers go to college, but they are not taught how to work with children who have been in this country for 2 weeks. At first I thought it was [the teachers'] attitude. Then I thought, maybe they just don't have the tools.

Of course, the tools that Mary talks about have everything to do with attitude shifts, but her comment reveals that she begins by believing in the good intentions of teachers. Then, recognizing that good intentions are not enough, she helps teachers develop "tools": a belief in children's potential; confronting and tearing down biases that lead to stereotypes, discriminatory practices, and low expectations; and the ability to value and access home and community knowledge in the classroom.

Thus, Mary does not spend time labeling teachers or making quick judgments about their ability. She visits their classrooms, talks with their students, and meets with them to find out what they need in order to do a better job.

Taking a Stand to Develop a More Welcoming Environment

Another facet of Mary's work as an effective leader is her ability to engage families in collaborating with the school to develop a more inclusive and welcoming environment. Engaging families collaboratively allowed Mary to learn *from* them rather than merely make assumptions about initiatives that might or might not address their needs and concerns. Such conversations produced initiatives such as a parent welcome committee, before-school programs, restructuring the ESL program, a math and science club for girls, Open House presentations specifically focusing on honoring and supporting linguistically diverse families, PTA meeting times to meet the needs of families, funding for translators, and providing transportation for families to attend after-school events.

Once she set the tone, everyone else wanted to do as much as possible to make school a welcoming place. For example, she explained how a gym teacher provided a before-school fitness club because so many students arrived early to school; "this way they could still arrive early, but were given fitness-related activities." As a result, instead of viewing families negatively because of the early hour their children arrived at school, Mary and the gym teacher found a way to fund a program to support students. Such innovative ideas allowed the school to function as a community space that blurred the traditional boundaries between school and community/neighborhood.

After meeting with several teachers who worked with Mary at Jonesville Elementary School, I realized how much they admired and respected the work she put into building a welcoming environment. Michelle, a primary-grades teacher, shared:

> Mary made sure that she was visible during recess, lunch, and in the halls. The kids knew Ms. Rykowski and felt comfortable with her presence. Mary also knew that some of the families came from backgrounds where school had not been a pleasant experience. She made sure that all the families felt that they were an important component of the [school's] community. Mary encouraged meetings that families could attend with their children, knowing that if parents didn't have child care (and most couldn't afford it) they wouldn't [be able to] attend these meetings.

Taking a Stand as a Community Presence and Advocate

Mary was deeply committed to connecting with children and families outside
of school, particularly when families may have had marginalizing experiences in
their own schooling and were reticent to approach the school.

In her administrative position at Jonesville, Mary frequently stopped by the
community housing that bordered her school. She did not do this to evaluate or
check *up* on families but to check *in* with them, to build relationships. As a former classroom teacher who worked with Mary for several years, I witnessed her
make countless home visits, phone calls, and the occasional morning pick-ups or
afternoon drop-offs for families who might have needed help with transportation
on a particular day. Michelle relayed similar stories about Mary and added that
she "knew every child's name, attended community events for children, signed
every report card. . . . She always went above and beyond to be an integral part
of the whole child."

Mary's community presence constitutes an approach for caring about the
needs of children that reaches far beyond academics but is foundational to them.
She shared:

> When I was working in Jonesville, there was housing within walking distance
> of my school. . . . I would always drive over there . . . and the kids would sur-
> round my car and say, "Ms. Rykowski! Ms. Rykowski!" Some mornings the
> children would just get up and come to school on their own for breakfast.
> They knew there would be breakfast and they would just walk over on their
> own. Sometimes when a child did not come to school, I would drive over
> there and knock at the door [and find out that] they overslept and did not
> hear the alarm. I would just put them in my car and come to school.

Mary also made frequent trips with the school counselor to local shops to
purchase basic school supplies. She had a knack for finding funding agencies or
places that would donate goods—United Way, Goodwill, and community agencies—and she encouraged classroom teachers to apply for grants and other funding sources to support the needs of students in their classrooms.

Expanding her role as administrator to include community advocacy led to
further school initiatives. For example, when Mary and the kindergarten teachers
realized that half-day kindergarten was not providing the time to meet the needs
all children, Mary, with the approval of the district superintendent, adjusted the
budget to support the idea of full-day kindergarten. Because of the relationships
she built in the community, the parents trusted Mary and therefore the program. They felt confident that their children were receiving a rigorous education

designed to make sure they had the academic experiences necessary to be successful in school in the future.

Taking a Stand to Cultivate Professional Learning Communities

Many successful leaders attribute their accomplishments to having incredible teams supporting their vision. Mary Rykowski is one such leader. Reflecting on how teachers may view her as an educational leader who values collaboration, Mary shared:

> I think teachers appreciated the work we did because we did it together. I rolled up my sleeves and worked with them. The teachers thought of [many of the great programs] and I just worked it out.

Establishing a community where teachers would feel comfortable coming together to work on issues that impacted the school's learning environment was very important to Mary. For example, when I worked with her at Indianola Informal Elementary School, she found funding for monthly all-day team planning sessions. Each month our grade level and the Arts team would meet for 3 to 4 hours during the school day to work on collaborative units of study. Mary would pop in and out of these sessions, checking in and offering important feedback.

When I was a teacher in Mary's building, I felt a collaborative spirit as a member of a team focused on designing, planning, enacting, and evaluating curricula that promoted inquiry and engagement for our students. Mary's leadership made those professional learning spaces possible, and her mentorship cultivated a community where raising questions about how to best meet the needs of all students was at the heart of our discussions. Michelle and Jennifer, two teachers from Jonesville Elementary, expressed a similar view:

> Mary was our leader! She didn't make all the decisions, we all had a say, but she supported us in those decisions and guided us in a different direction when she felt our vision needed [to be] refocused. There was constant communication.

Tina (who taught with Mary in two schools) also supported this sentiment, saying, "You can survey any teacher who worked with Mary at Jonesville and they will tell you she was one of the best leaders we ever had." Jennifer concurred and added that, in Mary's schools, there was no pecking order or hierarchy that determined who could participate. Mary's willingness to redefine the role of leader created space for cohesive learning communities to form and thrive.

CHALLENGES

Through the years, Mary has encountered her share of challenges and disappointments. One of the biggest challenges has been to get all of her teachers to believe that every child has the right to the best possible education. It was not unusual for her to encounter biases against children of Color, recent immigrants, and children from low-income homes. She worked to overcome those biases by encouraging her staff to design lessons that showcased the students' talents and academic abilities; extending invitations to locally and nationally known educators to visit her schools and talk with students and teachers; and supporting teachers as they engaged in research with university faculty or developed inquiries into their own practice that could showcase the potential of project-based learning in a diverse environment.

District officials did not always embrace Mary's advocacy for families and communities. This caused tension between the school and the district administration. Mary put her career on the line many times to do what she believed was in the best interest of the students. Her ability to back up her approach with statistics about the need for change was instrumental in her success with district officials. This type of courageous leadership exemplifies a humanistic approach.

Another challenge Mary encountered was the punitive nature of testing under federal and state mandates. Mary welcomed accountability and the use of assessment to document growth and inform instruction, but she witnessed the system perpetuate inexcusable and degrading practices in the name of rigor and accountability. She explained:

> As an administrator in a building with children from other countries who speak different languages, testing is very frustrating. I want to be held accountable, and I can guarantee that the child is going to be learning from the moment they step into the building. But, are they going to be [considered] proficient . . . on the test? The child is so much more than a test.

An example Mary shared comes from a student named Saal who recently had arrived in the United States as a fluent Arabic speaker. Saal was still required to take the state achievement test in English. Mary took action by using school funds to hire an Arabic interpreter at an hourly rate to translate the exam for the child. She recounted the experience:

> Saal worked and worked on the test and wasn't finished before lunch. So, we sent him to lunch and then he came back and worked until 2:00 on a math achievement test that I knew he didn't pass. And some of the words on the test, the interpreter didn't even know. . . . I thought: Why are we doing this

to him? I could never go to Palestine and [successfully] take a test in Arabic after being there for 3 months.

Mary went on to question not only the language disparities, but the amount of time that students spent suffering through the tests and said, "It took the whole day. I don't even think the bar exam takes that long!"

LEARNING FROM MARY

Given the experiences Mary has accumulated as an educator and administrator, she has the following words of advice to pass along to new administrators:

Get to know the culture of your building [and your school's community]. Ask yourself, what do the parents value? What do teachers value? Don't just come in and change things and say, "Well, this is what I value." 'Cause it's not about you. It's about them.

Mary takes insights from families and teachers and meshes them with her own knowledge and convictions to create a supportive environment for all learners. As a principal Mary sees her work tied to daily teaching and learning in and outside of the classroom and feels "blessed" to have been given the opportunity to work in so many diverse settings. As a result, she has developed an inclusive leadership philosophy that honors students, teachers, and families. When I asked her, "Why do you invest so much time into this?" she responded:

I believe we do what's best for kids no matter what. Some will think that means we are catering to them. But in the end, I hope they respect that's just how I am. I just try to lead by example. I hope people will say, Wow! She really does care about children and will put in the time. I will always do whatever it takes.

CHAPTER 9

Making It Happen

Risk-Taking and Relevance in a Rural Elementary School

Julia López-Robertson and Mary Jade Haney

It's a part of the package; you have to be a risk-taker [if you are going to] make a difference in the lives of children.

—Parthenia Satterwhite

It is a Saturday afternoon in mid-October. Elementary school principal Parthenia Satterwhite is sitting front and center, ready to enjoy a performance at the University of South Carolina's Latino Children's Literature Conference. Soon to perform is the Drama Team from Horrell Hill Elementary School. They will share their Literacy Alive Flash Mob Advocacy production. The Drama Team is a group of 30 kindergarten through 5th-grade students from Ms. Satterwhite's school in Hopkins, SC.

The Flash Mob grew from an intervention designed by teachers, using students' cultural, linguistic, and social strengths as a way to engage children in small-group reading instruction. Unlike practices in boxed curricula and scripted programs, the teachers identified the texts/topics/issues that were relevant to the students and engaged them in reading, learning, and performing poetry and songs selected to represent those topics. The positive response (by teachers and families) to the children's performance encouraged them to perform at larger venues (the university, the state capitol steps). Their performances focused on historical issues that continue to have importance today. An example of a signature performance is their rendition of the R&B song "Wake Up Everybody" (Whitehead, McFadden, & Carstarphen, 1975). Together, students and teachers turned their performance of this R&B classic into a Flash Mob event. Because the song asks everyone to take a close look at the world, notice the need for change, and become agents of change, the Flash Mob was a way for teachers to engage students in a powerful and emancipatory literacy practice (Fisher, 2007). Not only were the words to the song issue-oriented and the Flash Mob genre more "aggressive and 'in your face' than more traditional forms of poetry" (North, 2008), but the students' deeper engagement in literacy because of the experience was emancipatory in itself. At the center of this event, was the courage of a school leader who created an ethos that made this kind of out-of-the-box thinking not only possible but essential to better serving students too often disenfranchised from school.

LOVINGLY SUBVERSIVE: THE REAL DEAL

Seated with family members who had accompanied the children on the bus to the Flash Mob performance, Ms. Satterwhite beamed with absolute pride. She knew the whole story. Preparing for the performance, the students had examined the lyrics, the language, the message, the song's structure. They were engaged because of their teachers' efforts to select texts that were powerful and personally meaningful. As one student exclaimed, "My granddaddy plays that song in his truck!" Prior to and through the performances, teachers helped students build reading fluency using the lyrics. In contrast to scripted assessments that required teachers to check off correctly pronounced words and conduct timed oral reading of irrelevant texts, the Flash Mob lyrics drew students into the literacy experience purposefully and deeply. They engaged students in using literacy as it is supposed to be used—to impact who they are, who they can become, and what they can do to effect change in the world.

Fast forward a few years and again we are at the University of South Carolina, this time on a sunny spring morning. Ms. Satterwhite has come with Horrell Hill students, teachers, and families to offer a special performance of the Flash Mob for a long-time collaborator who was moving to a new institution. Ms. Satterwhite felt it crucial to thank this person for all of the years of service he gave to Horrell Hill. In her eyes, the most special gift is the voice of the very children he helped serve. A small crowd gathered outside as the performance began and, again, sitting front and center was Ms. Satterwhite, this time mouthing the words as the children performed "Wake Up Everybody." She had seen the performance many times, yet she could not help but be moved by the words once more.

This is Parthenia Satterwhite, an administrator who is gentle in her demeanor but impassioned about changes that must occur if we are to educate all students equitably. In a profession where rhetoric regarding commitments to *diversity* abounds, Ms. Satterwhite is the real deal. Concerned that too many students are disenfranchised from learning because curricula fail to capitalize on their strengths and knowledge, and worried about narrow curricular models and student labels that send indelibly destructive messages about self-worth and capability, Ms. Satterwhite encourages teachers to go beyond the norm. Then she helps them figure out ways to make innovation possible within perceived constraints. While these attributes may seem to be the work of good administrators in general, in a climate that often suppresses efforts outside of narrow curricular and cultural models, it is courageous. We call her lovingly subversive.

GUIDING PRINCIPLES

For the past 25 years, Ms. Satterwhite has been the leader at Horrell Hill Elementary School. It is a rural school with a student population of African American, Latino/a immigrant, and White students, many from low-income households. Ms. Satterwhite wants students to become strong and confident and be placed "at the center of schooling [so they are enabled] not only to acquire skills but to use those skills to become effective agents for social change" (Banks & Banks, 1995, p. 157). As she explains, "Children must be educated but not only in the textbook information, also . . . [to become] well-grounded citizens. Because we have them for a tremendous amount of time, 7 years, we can accomplish that." Ms. Satterwhite knows that, to do this, teachers must grow and be empowered to make decisions that may fall outside scripted programs and other mandates. In the interest of those goals, she is guided by five pillars or principles:

1. Value voice
2. Love
3. Learn
4. Know the policy, then take the risk
5. Encourage autonomy

While each of these principles addresses a different aspect of Ms. Satterwhite's approach to leadership, they are undergirded by beliefs that education is a civil right and that, because this right is not always upheld, actions need to be taken day-to-day in schools and classrooms.

Value Voice

Ms. Satterwhite is staunch in her belief that equity in education means that the voices of children, their families, and teachers need to be brought to the forefront, heard, and validated. The few examples provided below illustrate ways that she lives her advocacy for the right to voice.

Family voice. Ms. Satterwhite stresses to teachers that equity means that children's learning must be relevant to them and that they must be valued for the cultural and linguistic resources they bring to the classroom. For this to occur, Ms. Satterwhite knows that teachers first must value the voices and experiences of families, which often requires teachers to expand their views of communities beyond their own.

Ms. Satterwhite sets the standard for broadening these lenses and listening to the voices of families. For example, when a new population of Latino/a children (predominantly Mexican immigrants) came to Horrell Hill, she made it her business to get to know their families in genuine ways, as a regular participant in the community—attending weddings, funerals, dance recitals, plays, sporting and church events. As a result, Ms. Satterwhite learned firsthand about the issues they faced and the cultural misinterpretations and microaggressions they experienced. For example, anti-immigrant comments frequently were made directly to them in local businesses. In previous schools, some students experienced lowered academic expectations. Parents were keenly aware of deficit assumptions about their parental knowledge and abilities; they often felt invisible in other schools, their home languages rarely embraced and often ridiculed.

Ms. Satterwhite uses insights gained from families to build a more welcoming school. She begins by letting teachers know how much she values the cultural and linguistic contributions that *familias Latinas* (Latino/a families) bring, recognizing that without her advocacy teachers might not give as much validity to their voices. In addition, she enthusiastically supported a university faculty member who organized a Latina mothers' club that met regularly at the school. This was particularly courageous given the larger context in which anti-immigrant messages are common and *familias Latinas* often are viewed through deficit lenses. Ms. Satterwhite also created a position for a bilingual Spanish/English-speaking staff member to serve as the school's official Latino/a Advocate. Both actions were instrumental in helping families feel more welcomed and comfortable in the school (Allen, 2007) and sent a strong message to teachers and other families about how much she valued family involvement. Ms. Satterwhite was committed to taking steps needed to ensure it.

Student voice. Ms. Satterwhite also is committed to helping children find their voice and use it with confidence. She knows that many of her students will face biases that have the potential to be internalized and limit possibilities for further learning. Thus, a strong element in her commitment to equity is her desire to help students gain confidence and knowledge in the early years so that they are able to stand up and speak up. She explained:

I want the children to know that they do have a voice in society and that they matter. When we can instill in children the importance and necessity of making connections between education and using their voices to demand that they be at the center of school, we have done our job.

Over the years, Ms. Satterwhite has worked hard to create an atmosphere where children learn about the need for change and use particular skills "to become effective agents for social change" (Banks & Banks, 1995, p. 152), and, as she says, "to demand that they be at the center of school." The Flash Mob is one of many examples of a program through which children learned that they could use their voices.

Love

Discussing Freire's notion of a pedagogy of love, Darder (2015) wrote, "Love constitutes an intentional spiritual act of consciousness that emerges and matures through our social and material practices, as we work to live, learn and labor together . . . as we seek new possibilities for transformation" (p. 49). Ms. Satterwhite embodies this kind of spiritual consciousness as she comes to school each year eager for the possibilities ahead of her: the transformations that will occur as she works with children, teachers, families, and the community. Ms. Satterwhite lives this kind of love every day as she seeks the strengths of children, respects and builds trusting relationships with families, and focuses on raising children up rather than breaking them down.

Love is seeking strengths. Ms. Satterwhite recognizes that there are challenges in leading and teaching in a rural school and that these challenges are not exclusive to Horrell Hill. At the same time, she knows that focusing solely on challenges means that teachers miss the richness from the students' communities. For example, because the children are recent immigrants learning English, come from low-income homes, and/or are being raised predominantly by grandparents, negative assumptions about them often lead to lowered expectations, marginalization, and eventually miseducation (Woodson, 1933). Ms. Satterwhite's love says otherwise. So while she does not ignore the very real challenges faced by families, she identifies and celebrates the strengths that home experiences build in children's lives: their ability to interact within and across multiple cultural and linguistic contexts, their knowledge of family and cultural heritage, and their love of family near and far.

Love is respect. Recognizing that many families are profiled negatively, Ms. Satterwhite sees it as her responsibility to discourage judgment and build respectful relationships. As she interacts with family members and children, she looks into their eyes and listens with full presence. This is respectful love. She refuses to buy into the notion that parental lack of presence in the school means that parents are not interested in supporting their children.

Ms. Satterwhite's love and respect also allow her to help families understand and negotiate the system so that they gain the same cultural capital as other parents. For example, she helps them understand the nuances of Individual Education Plans (IEPs) and how to negotiate entry into advanced placement programs. This is one way that she demonstrates her respect for families: giving them keys to the insiders' club that is typically populated by parents who, privileged by the system, have developed the savvy necessary to succeed within it.

Love is trust. Ms. Satterwhite focuses on developing the school and community as her extended family. She knows that this requires trust that cannot be assumed but must be built over time. Every story told in this chapter captures how Ms. Satterwhite invests time in building strong and lasting relationships with families, teachers, and children. Trust grows from these relationships, not because of a leadership strategy, but because her love is genuine. As a result, she gains families' critical insights that inform her ability to lead the school and she gains an extended family that connects to the school across generations because of her love:

> I guess it was maybe about 5 years ago when I first had an opportunity to have the second generation of one particular family [enroll at the school] and the parent was like, "Wow, you know, I've been here and now I'm enrolling my children." I think of them as my grandchildren.

The bottom line is that families trust Ms. Satterwhite because they know she has their back—not merely in words but in actions. She demonstrates that she can be trusted with their vulnerabilities as well as their expertise. Recently, the Latina mothers' group honored Ms. Satterwhite with a surprise birthday party and a poem, a true testament to the love and trust she engenders.

Love is not breaking children down. Ms. Satterwhite is also intentional in the manner in which she demonstrates love for the children (Darder, 2015). She regularly creates spaces where children can see themselves as capable, loved, and supported. For example, she conducts goal-setting meetings with individual children to communicate that they "hold promise within." Even though she has many other demands, Ms. Satterwhite makes these kinds of moments a priority. She explains that some children are simply hurting, and that their hurt comes out in all kinds of ways. She worries that, without early support that gives them a belief in themselves, they will be lost to labeling, medication, and ultimately disenfranchisement. So she does not send them away or isolate them; she addresses that hurt with compassion and time.

One example, in particular, demonstrates this kind of supportive love. One late afternoon, Ms. Satterwhite was in her office sitting behind a pile of books flipping pages and pulling more books from her bookcase. When asked what she was doing, she replied that she was searching through her books for "just the right poem" for a particular group of African American male students. She was concerned that the group was internalizing stereotypical beliefs about Black males as uncooperative, less intelligent, uncaring, and disruptive (Howard, 2014), and that the boys were living out those beliefs through their classroom behaviors.

Because of these concerns, Ms. Satterwhite created a weekly meeting with the boys and engaged them in discussions of poetry and books written by African American authors. Her purpose was to create bonds and also to help them understand the legacy they represented. Ms. Satterwhite recognized that this heritage rarely was discussed in classrooms, and, as a result, a sense of pride in self and heritage remained largely untapped.

The memory most vivid to Ms. Satterwhite from that day is the way the boys looked at her, deep in thought, as they discussed their rich literary heritage. It is likely that no one had ever sat down to have this kind of conversation with them before. Instead of breaking them down, Ms. Satterwhite built them up, essentially saying, "I am your principal and I believe in you. I need you to believe in yourself." That is love.

Learn

When considering the influences that led to Ms. Satterwhite's leadership approach, it is important to share her experiences as a John Goodlad Scholar. Through that program, she learned about educational renewal through which schools would become genuine places of democracy and would privilege students' investigation of ideas over a primary focus on standardized tests (Goodlad, 2004). This approach deeply influenced Ms. Satterwhite as she participated in leadership training, educational inquiry groups, and research teams with administrators from across the country. This gave her the opportunity to develop a broader lens from which to view education as she learned from other administrators who created spaces for innovation even when mandated curricula seem to dictate otherwise. Through these experiences, Ms. Satterwhite gained the confidence to embrace innovation, understanding that it did not mean bucking the system altogether but doing what it takes to ensure that each child's needs were met: "It's not . . . going against the policies, but it is adding what you feel is necessary for *this* child to move forward."

Know the Policy, Then Take the Risk

Like every other administrator, Ms. Satterwhite's world is not without policies and mandates. While she is careful to follow established policies, she does not use them as an excuse for inaction. Ms. Satterwhite explains that her philosophy is to "follow the frameworks of the mandates, stay within that framework, but be a risk-taker and tweak what I feel is in the best interest of that child."

To do this, Ms. Satterwhite has a solid plan of action. She reads and rereads policies to be sure she understands them thoroughly, recognizing that if you do not know the policy behind the mandates, you cannot figure out ways to support innovative work while addressing those mandates. She is not influenced by hearsay among other administrators, knowing that it often can reflect inaccurate interpretations of policies or mere mythology. Because she knows policies well, Ms. Satterwhite usually can find "'wiggle room' [for innovation] linking what has to be done with what should be done" (Siegel & Lukas, 2008, p. 34). Thus, she is able to protect as well as support and inform teachers as they venture into new curricular territory.

One impactful example is the Latina mothers' group mentioned earlier. Because Ms. Satterwhite knew the policies as well as the issues faced by Latino/a families, she was able to justify the plan to develop a Latina mothers' group when other parents asked why the group was exclusive to Latina mothers. In another instance, when school buses were not available to transport students to perform the Flash Mob at the university, rather than shutting down the opportunity, Ms. Satterwhite used policy to figure out ways to legally transport students in cars. A third example involved the testing of English language learners. Concerned that the English language learners were being overly tested and that testing anxiety was excessively high for young students, Ms. Satterwhite followed policy (by ensuring that the tests were taken), but made sure that the children were in the company of teachers who not only knew them well but were perceived *by the children and their families* as supportive and loving. As she explained, "If they know the person and are comfortable and feel safe, they won't be afraid of the test and may do better."

Ms. Satterwhite believes that being a risk-taker is "a part of the [administrative] package; you have to be a risk-taker [if you are going to] make a difference in the lives of children," but she also believes that you must know policy to be able to take risks within it. At the end of the day, her goal is to ensure that students, families, and teachers have what they need in order to succeed.

Encourage Autonomy

Ms. Satterwhite knows that in some schools teachers have no voice. Programs are mandated and scripted to the point that teachers' wisdom and knowledge often are undervalued and underutilized. Ms. Satterwhite's approach is quite different. If a teacher presents an idea, Ms. Satterwhite's first question is, "How will it help the children academically and/or socially?" She wants teachers to feel empowered to go beyond the textbooks but to take responsibility for doing so in ways that clearly benefit the children most marginalized. Then she encourages them to "try it!" This is how the Flash Mob became a reality and also how the school developed and sponsored an Inaugural Ball after the first election of United States President Obama. It is also how university courses came to be taught on-site at Horrell Hill, giving university students opportunities to understand the importance of getting to know and value children and families in their communities.

Another powerful example of how Ms. Satterwhite provides teachers' autonomy is her support for the development of a summer program, Camp Discovery. Teachers were keenly aware the school could play an important role in sustaining and deepening the children's reading proficiency during the summer. So, several years ago one of the teachers suggested a 2-week summer camp to be held at the school, at no cost to the families. To ensure that it would be supported at the district level, Ms. Satterwhite read and reread policies regarding summer programs and found a way to actualize the idea within district guidelines: An academic camp not only met the needs of families and children at Horrell Hill, but addressed a school district policy that provided summer support for students at risk of retention. Ms. Satterwhite took steps to fully support the idea and make necessary arrangements for the development of Literacy Alive Camp Discovery.

Under Ms. Satterwhite's leadership, Literacy Alive Camp Discovery became an extension of the school's partnership with the University of South Carolina. During the academic year, early childhood education courses sometimes are taught on-site at the school, and preservice teachers engage in practicum and internship experiences there. Literacy Alive Camp Discovery was an opportunity for university students enrolled in summer education courses to continue their learning with Horrell Hill children. Camp Discovery has been in operation for 4 years, and regardless of her administrative demands, Ms. Satterwhite always takes time to stop by and involve herself in the activities of the day, whether the children are engaged in science experiments (Figure 9.1), book discussions, poetry readings, or Flash Mob performances.

Were it not for Ms. Satterwhite's trust in her teachers and in their ability to teach and lead, the camp would not have come to life. As she demonstrates, a courageous leader is someone who recognizes leadership abilities in others and supports them in ways that allow them to lead. As one teacher explained:

> You can [learn new ideas through] professional development all day but if the principal does not allow you to take that and work with it, then everything stops. So that's why when I work here, I'm not stuck. [Here] you know you can do this for the children. She doesn't shut you down. A lot of times things get Common Cored [a reference to national standards called the Common Core] out and everything that's really rich goes away; who does it take away from? The children.

Figure 9.1. Parthenia Satterwhite.

A LEGACY OF COURAGE, WISDOM, AND LOVE

If we are not careful about reminding ourselves why we are leading a school, we will miss valuable opportunities for teaching and learning that can last a lifetime. —Parthenia Satterwhite

Ms. Satterwhite does not like calling attention to herself. She feels very strongly that the school's accomplishments are not hers alone; they reflect work done in partnership with the children, teachers, and families: "It is all possible because of the relationship that we have with each other. . . . I don't do it alone." However, we call attention to her because we see stark contrasts between Ms. Satterwhite and administrators who do not possess her courageous characteristics. Everyone who knows Ms. Satterwhite recognizes that her courageous leadership is not of a moment; it remains constant.

Ms. Satterwhite works consistently with faculty, children, and families to help them become "effective agents for social change" (Banks & Banks, 1995, p. 157). She views them as her extended family and goes far beyond rhetoric to demonstrate that every day. She uses policies and mandates but is *not used by them*. She invests time with the belief that "the hearts of the children are built through relationships, and relationship-building takes time and a little effort." These commitments are clear in the kindness you feel as she looks into your eyes, in children's faces as she engages them, and in families' trust. This loving focus comes from a genuine belief in the beauty within each child, family member, and teacher, which she cherishes as a privilege of her work. As Ms. Satterwhite says:

> We can never get too busy to allow the mandates, high-stakes testing, and other educational political issues to cause us to miss the beauty of seeing the teachers and the children we serve. If we are not careful about reminding ourselves why we are leading a school, we will miss valuable opportunities for teaching and learning that can last a lifetime.

CHAPTER 10

Social Justice and the Principled Principal

All Children Are Gifted

Alfredo Celedón Luján

Isabelle Medina Sandoval was the principal at two schools in northern New Mexico. When she arrived at the first school, where 98% of the students were Latino/a, none of the students had been identified as "gifted." That's right—zero. At the other school, it appeared that there was an abundance of *giftedness*. Many students were designated with that label in a school where almost half of the student population was White, half Latino/a, and 2% American Indian. Isabelle knew that there were problems with these numbers. Committed to her belief in the brilliance of all children, she entered each school insisting, "*Every* child is gifted."

As I began to write this chapter, I knew that Isabelle's story was one that needed to be told. I wanted to communicate the importance of her social justice convictions to inspire reflection and change. To do so, it was important to find time for my own reflection about her assertion that every child is gifted. So I sought a place for quiet reflection.

The silence that allowed me to reflect on Isabelle's words was found at a campsite, a few miles from my home. I often come to this campsite in the foothills of the Sangre de Cristo Mountains for solitude. It's perfect for contemplation. I wish I could share the aroma and sound of coffee percolating on the stove inside the pop-up camper (Figure 10.1). This is neither Starbucks ambiance nor Keurig convenience; no, this is burble, gurgle, ahhh, the fresh scent of nature and caffeine, a bouquet that helps make this morning unique. I wish I could transport the olfactory warmth and plume of the campfire as I sit, sipping my ritual Clamato then OJ, waiting for the java, thinking about Isabelle, a principal who spent her career working to right injustices in schools. If I could transport an image of

Figure 10.1. New Mexico solitude: Perfect for reflecting on the work of Isabelle Sandoval.

the clouds being painted pink beyond the mountains at dawn, I would. If I could convey the silence beneath the rooster's crow, I would, because this is northern New Mexico, where Hernandez Elementary School, Atalaya Elementary School, and Isabelle Medina Sandoval live. It was here that I began to write.

HERNANDEZ IN ESPAÑOLA

Hernandez Elementary School is in the Española District. The people of Hernandez are *buena gente*—good people, humble people, genuine people. They are the real thing. While Rio Arriba often is defined in popular media by incidents of heroin addiction and poverty, that is *not* "El Norte." No, the beautiful landscape and the humility of *la gente* mark its essence. People here care about their land, their farming, their hunting, and especially their children. Great administrators like Isabelle know that there is so much more to the people and their children than media and stereotypes portray.

Hernandez Elementary School is situated among authentic adobe homes and affordable mobile homes adjacent to nearby arroyos and near Socorro's restaurant where the real thing, red and green *chile, frijoles*, and *chicharrones* are served—the authentic cuisine of this region. The school is a stone's throw from Highway 84/285, the road that branches north. One might consider this landscape a transition to Colorado. Abiquiú, Georgia O'Keeffe country, is just up the road from Hernandez. Abiquiú's red, rust, yellow, orange, and brown cliffside hues blend with the majestic wide blue sky. Some call this God's country. In this niche, the median individual income is $15,500; the median household income is $24,375. At Hernandez Elementary School, math proficiency is currently 17%; reading proficiency is 22%. Ninety-eight percent of the students are Hispanic, and 2% are White; 77.6% qualify for free or reduced-price lunch.

ATALAYA IN SANTA FE

Atalaya Elementary School is a public school in Santa Fe, the capital of New Mexico since 1608. Atalaya (English translation: Watchtower) serves students from the communities of Cerro Gordo, Apodaca Hill, and artsy Canyon Road in the affluent northeast sector of the city. Atalaya is within walking distance of St. John's—the "Great Books" liberal arts college—and two private schools: the K–6 Rio Grande and grades 7–12 Santa Fe Prep.

Atalaya Elementary School is nestled among million-dollar condos and multimillion-dollar faux adobe homes. In this neighborhood, even among the rich and famous, the median individual income is $26,360; the median household income is $49,564. Fifty-seven percent of the students are proficient in math and 62% are proficient in reading. The ethnic makeup of the students is 45.9% White, 45.9% Hispanic, 3.1% Native American, 3.1 % Asian, and 2.0% African American. Of the total number of students, 37.4% qualify for free or reduced-price lunch. The Santa Fe Public Schools (SFPS) serve K–12 students in "The City Different," a city with the markings of a cosmopolitan city but with a small-town feel.

Isabelle was principal at both Hernandez and Atalaya Elementary Schools. Later in her career, she became bilingual coordinator for the SFPS. Both schools and the District's bilingual program were successful under her tenure; students in both schools scored well on the standards-based assessments (SBAs). But Isabelle knew that while test results provide some measures of success, they are only part of the story and, in fact, fail to bring to the surface the full extent of children's knowledge and abilities.

Isabelle advocated for excellence in education throughout her career. Dr. Morgan, former associate superintendent at SFPS, described the essence of her success:

> Dr. Sandoval, simply put, is a great leader. While I have valued Dr. Sando-val's competence in all areas, I especially admire her keen understanding of teaching and learning and the application thereof for all students and their individual situations. Her high expectations never change with regard to all students performing well and the need to deliver appropriate, sound instruction for all.

MEETING ISABELLE

I first met Isabelle one morning in our neighborhood—Nava Adé—in Santa Fe. We lived in the same cul de sac, and by chance that morning we were outside working in our gardens. I was new to the "hood," so I went over and introduced myself. We got to talking about who we were and what we did, the small-town litany: "*Buenos dias*; hi, how are ya; where you from; *dime con quien andas y te dire quien eres*." I stumbled on the fact that her roots are in Mora, NM, one of the most beautiful yet one of the poorest counties in the United States. I discovered that she is related to one of my cousins on his father's side—the Medinas. She's cousin to my *Primo* Ramos and Uncle Eddie and *Primas* Stella, Anna, Medina, and Claudette. It figures. This is small-world northern New Mexican stuff. My family is from Nambé; family lore has it that a branch of our ancestors came from Mora over the pass; some settled in the mountainous village of Truchas and others dropped into the valley to make Nambé their home.

Isabelle grew up in Wyoming and was educated in a public school system imbued with deficit assumptions about children who spoke English as a second language. There, she was considered "retarded." This horrific experience led to her interest in supporting K–3 students, especially from communities negatively profiled because of uninformed, degrading, and destructive biases. She said:

> I'll never forget. I was in the 3rd grade . . . my dad worked for the post office. My mother was a cook. I come from a very humble background. The school I went to was mostly Hispanic . . . it was the poor side of town. The 3rd-grade teacher called my mother one day, and she said, "Isabelle is having problems," so my mother went in her [cook's] uniform to talk to the teacher . . . and then my mother came home, and I remember my mother talking to my father in English and Spanish: "The teacher says Isabelle is retarded and they want to move her to the retarded school . . . she can take a bus to Washington School." [This pronouncement] almost killed my spirit. And then my mother—and I can remember it to this day—she walked into the school and talked to the principal and said, "I will not give my permission." I remember that teacher because she was a White lady, and she was very discriminatory. I used to go through the basal [reading books] because they were very easy, and she thought I was just talking and fooling around.

As Isabelle told this story, she described the impact of her parents' actions to challenge this injustice:

> When I look at social justice, I look at my parents turning down the school to say [to me], "You will make a difference." Later, I realized that I probably

was gifted. I graduated with many honors—Phi Kappa Phi among them, but it was a struggle. I'm a very firm believer that *all* children are gifted.

HERNANDEZ SCHOOL: STEPS TOWARD CHANGE

After working in Colorado Springs as a teacher and administrator, then teaching in the Education Department at the College of Santa Fe, Isabelle missed working with children. So she found a position with the Española Public Schools. She interviewed with Superintendent Jaramillo and was offered the position of principal at Hernandez, a school under corrective action. "That's how I ended up there," she said. "It had been designated as a corrective action school. . . . It was really in a poor state."

Isabelle wanted the Hernandez job because she felt Hernandez was a place where someone needed to work toward social justice for the students and the community. She was familiar with the challenges faced when people are not appreciated for the richness of their culture, language, and the contributions of their communities:

I have a love for northern New Mexico [but] I know the injustices that take place when, one, you're rural, and, two, you have a Hispanic population. When I looked at the [testing] numbers, I could see how low the scores were, and because my background happens to be in literacy, Spanish, and English as a Second Language, that's where I wanted to be. . . . I loved the community, and I really felt, after I looked at the scores, it would be very much like teaching at the school where I went, and teaching [at Hernandez] would be like giving back to the community—making a difference for children.

Isabelle's challenge was to increase the literacy levels of young children in an economically depressed community where assumptions were rampant that they would not succeed. Isabelle has a different view:

When I see scores such as I did at Hernandez, I find it statistically impossible that students would be performing that poorly. So one of the first questions I have is, what is the communication like between home and school? And then I wonder, what about the delivery of instruction by the teachers? And thirdly, what professional preparation do the teachers have? I looked at those scores, and I thought, this is impossible. I just know from my own life. I would have been one of those students.

Becoming a Member of the Community

Isabelle's approach was to demonstrate that she was a genuine member of the community. She went to her roots to prove that she was a *Norteña* (from northern New Mexico) "straight up" (among other northern New Mexicans). It's an old school philosophy: Be a ballplayer among ballplayers, be an educator among educators, birds of a feather flock together, be authentic. She explained:

> As a newcomer to Hernandez, I was related to many persons in the community through genealogy. This connection established a genuine bonding. Speaking northern New Mexico Spanish and having "inside" knowledge of cultural elements added to the bond. [While] I was unaware of the geography and towns within the community, I [soon] learned about the richness of culture and languages near Hernandez. . . . I relied on the expertise of staff and their ties to the community [to teach me].

In spite of her northern New Mexico roots and commitment to learning about Hernandez, Isabelle initially found meeting with the staff to be difficult. They did not want an outsider coming in to change things. "But," she said, "one of the teachers was one of my former students at the College of Santa Fe, so she knew my background and what my expectations would be."

Isabelle involved the teachers in working with her to develop clear goals for the school: (a) improve student literacy and numeracy achievement; (b) engage parents in school activities, promoting a partnership; and (c) integrate technology into the classroom. She explained: "About 40% of the teachers were involved in collaborating and writing the schoolwide plan posted in the school. Weekly staff meetings were held to ensure progress of delivery of the goals and school plan."

"We're here," she told the faculty, "for the children." Isabelle's desire "was to have students maximize personal and academic potential. [She] wanted children to enjoy coming to school and finding treasures at the school as well as the treasures in their inner selves."

Getting to Know Children and Their Families

Isabelle knew how important it was to get to know the children and their families to become part of the community. To accomplish this, she greeted students and their parents at the front door before and after school. She was present for lunch duty and went outside with the students after lunch: "These opportunities provided me with social times to observe students with their peers as well as becoming familiar with parents and family."

Isabelle also attended family meetings each month after school and met with parents of emerging bilinguals in the mornings to discuss concerns over a cup of coffee. She created a Parent Room where parents could meet and take reading/language/math materials home to work on with their children. She ensured that the monthly newsletter was written in both Spanish and English and communicated directly with parents in Spanish. Isabelle credited her success in building relationships with children and families to her open-door policy and the fact that families knew they were valued.

A Team Effort

To effect academic change, Isabelle engaged the faculty in reviewing test scores to understand the position from which they would move forward: "This is where we are." She spent time regularly in classrooms observing, so she could plan for appropriate support. For example, Isabelle noticed a need for support in the teaching of writing, which led her to collaborate with the teachers to develop a plan to improve the teaching of writing:

> We met along with other district schools, to write our *Schoolwide Plan for Educational Success.* . . . It was a cooperative-learning group. . . . It wasn't just that we worked on Saturdays; we also analyzed data and scores during staff meetings and figured out how we could help students. I also provided a lot of professional development. Once they got into it, it really was a team effort.

Every Child *Is* Gifted

While working on the teaching of writing, Isabelle found something more troubling than the low scores. She asked the staff how many gifted children they had in their classrooms.

"I'll probably cry in a minute," she said as she told this story, "because it really bothers me." One of the teachers responded, "You must be kidding [to think] that we would have a gifted student at Hernandez!"

"Well," said Isabelle, "that [was] enough to get me going. I asked, 'How can you have a school without *any* gifted children?'" Isabelle explained her stance:

> My personal belief is that every child is gifted one way or another. . . . The greater communities of Hernandez, Española, New Mexico, and the United States are enriched by developing a caring student group aspiring to learn more. I expected teachers to model this in the classroom.

Another step Isabelle took to show that students were gifted was to start a MESA program (mesa.ucop.edu/about-us/) in the school. She identified a large group of students who were not otherwise seen as "gifted." Through that program, students worked with a teacher after school to develop scientific inquiry strategies. Parents and students were invited to monthly meetings to plan for and engage in science projects. Isabelle talked about the impact: "It was great to watch students increase their confidence and display scientific vocabulary."

Isabelle also began purchasing more materials for the classrooms:

> Because I came from a poor family that did not have books at home, I wanted my children to have books in the classroom. We bought not just leveled readers, but to ensure that children were always challenged, we also bought books that were three to four levels above.

Teacher Buy-In: Faculty Who Care About Latino/a Children

One thing nagged at me while conducting my interview with Isabelle, so I asked: "How in the world did you get teachers in on Saturday mornings?"

"They got paid real money [through Title I funds]," she said, and then laughed. "It really was a *small amount* of money." Isabelle emphasized that the *real* reason for buy-in was that the teachers were part of the community.

But the most important element that led to buy-in was the authentic caring of the teachers themselves. Most members of Isabelle's staff were Latino/a. They lived not just in Hernandez, but also in nearby La Mesilla and Ojo Caliente. In many schools, faculty demographics do not reflect those of the student population, but at Hernandez, they did. This turned the typical minority–majority status upside down as the Latino/a teachers were actually the majority. Many of the teachers had firsthand knowledge of the educational biases Latino/a and Native American students were facing; they were committed to changing that status quo. Thus, a strong foundation for teacher buy-in was teachers' deep personal investment in the success of children.

As a result, Isabelle did not find opposition to her belief in the giftedness of Latino/a children. For the most part, the staff and faculty were knowledgeable about the children, cared about them, and believed in them. Isabelle said, "Honestly, I've never worked with more professional teachers in my life." She found that those who did not buy into the school's philosophy eventually moved on. She said, "We're here for children. That, to me, is number one: how we work with our children and how we move them forward."

High Test Scores but So Much More

Eventually, Hernandez met the adequate yearly progress (AYP) requirements set by the state of New Mexico, and Isabelle received a letter from the Española School Board congratulating her and thanking her for her hard work. Isabelle's original assessment that it is *statistically impossible for students to perform so poorly* proved to be correct. She explained:

As I began to know my children, I realized that the teacher who said there were no gifted children in Hernandez was wrong. And it wasn't just the scores. It was the confidence I saw in the children. What's important is children saying, "I can do this," and that can't be calibrated on some test.

"What makes your accomplishment and that of your students [at Hernandez] *social justice* rather than simple educational success?" I asked. Isabelle explained:

Social justice means to me when you look at a school that's 98% Hispanic with students meeting AYP, feeling confident about what they are reading, and knowing that they are gifted. And their parents, too. . . . Social justice means that we are looking at all members of the community to say we are viable members of Hernandez. I really want people to respect each other.

SOCIAL JUSTICE AT ATALAYA:
HOW DO WE MAKE A FAIR SCHOOL FOR EVERYONE?

Isabelle left Hernandez to become principal at Atalaya Elementary School. Why? Her daughter-in-law became pregnant and she wanted to be closer to her grandkids. I asked what it was like moving from a high-poverty area to a school in an affluent area of Santa Fe:

To be honest, I thought Atalaya would be an easy transition compared to other schools. I had been an administrator for Academy District up north . . . these were some of the nicest people, and I mean, talk about affluence. It was a Carnegie Award–winning school. So I thought, "I bet Atalaya has some of the same components in its community." However, the Academy [experience] did not begin to prep me for what I found at Atalaya School. Many Anglo students had been zoned into Atalaya because their previous schools had not made AYP. And the staff, I'm not sure I had even one Hispanic teacher. I had a half-time Hispanic counselor and a Hispanic teaching assistant. . . . It was very, very different.

"So how did you deliver social justice at Atalaya?" I asked. Isabelle said she began by looking at test scores: "Again I found that Hispanics [30% of the students] were the lowest performing." She shared the demographic breakdown of scores with the teachers and asked, "How do we make it a fair school so that everyone is performing at grade level?" While observing teachers in their classrooms, she shared formative test data regarding the progress of Latino/a students and gender subgroups to help teachers recognize the inequities in their teaching and their teaching outcomes. While doing this, she realized that the school had no provisions for English language learners, so she instituted programs to support their success.

"TOO HISPANIC": INSISTING ON EQUITABLE TEACHING FOR *ALL* CHILDREN

Asking teachers to focus on disparities experienced by Latino/a children meant that Isabelle was deviating from tradition at Atalaya. The staff resisted when asked to look at scores across the board. Isabelle explained:

> I had walked into a tough situation at Hernandez, but there at least [the teachers, students, families, and I] shared some common cultural traits. At Atalaya it was different because there was no one [on the faculty] who looked like me, yet I was talking about Hispanic students and their performance. The nonverbal messages I heard were like, "Is she for real?" I didn't feel any sense of warmth. Even though people came to meetings and workshops, it was more perfunctory.

Isabelle added, "It wasn't all negative at Atalaya; I had some support from some really good teachers, too," but there was a clear split within the staff. Some of the older teachers did not agree with or understand the concept of social justice. They did not recognize that some styles of teaching might privilege some children over others. At one point, a staff member approached her and said, "Isabelle, you wouldn't believe what's out there."

"What do you hear?" Isabelle asked.

"I'm hearing there's a group of teachers and a group of parents who are bonding together to say you are too Hispanic for this school." Isabelle began to think about how to deal with this discriminatory stance against her and against children who looked and sounded like her:

> As a Brown Hispanic female, I have been subjected to educational discrimination at elementary, middle, high school, and university levels. To me, this was another level of discrimination. I felt bad for my students and staff. [However, while] these words mirrored obvious sentiments and communications among some teachers and parents, . . . I was warmed by the support of many staff members and community persons.

The Solution Is to Persevere

Isabelle's solution was to persevere and hold onto her convictions. She knew that it was necessary to disrupt teachers' negative attitudes about Latino/a students by helping them see the richness, wisdom, and knowledge of the children they taught and of their families. Doing would help them become more comfortable in those worlds. This comfort developed as Isabelle worked to build her own relationships with the teachers. In addition, Isabelle learned to draw energy and inspiration from staff members who already had a positive belief in and an appreciation for Latina/o children and families. Finally, she brought supportive programs into the school, similar to those she had initiated at Hernandez. The end result was that:

> We did make AYP, the Hispanic students were feeling more confident about their performance, and there was awareness among the staff that they had to be teaching for all students. But it was tough because the nonverbal messages I was receiving from some of the staff members were like, "Why are you doing this?" and "Why are you upsetting our day?"

Isabelle Sandoval continued working to do "what was right for all of the Atalaya students." This included writing two historical fiction children's books situated in New Mexico, focusing on student identity (Sandoval, 2009, 2012), thereby helping all students understand the rich heritage of the Latino/a and Native American students.

NEVER BREAK A CHILD'S SPIRIT

When I told Isabelle that I wanted to concentrate on her courageous leadership in early childhood education, she said, "That's the age that my grandson is." So it is for children like her grandson and all of her students past and present that Isabelle takes a courageous stand to ensure that children of Color, children learning English, and children from low-income households are no longer viewed as anything less than gifted (Figure 10.2). I wondered how Isabelle felt about her commitment in light of a recent proclamation from New Mexico's governor that any student who is not reading at grade level should be retained in 3rd grade. Encapsulating the core of her social justice commitment, Isabelle said: "I don't feel students should be retained. . . . If I feel *every* student is gifted, why would I break a child's spirit?"

SOCIAL JUSTICE AND DIGNITY: HONORING THE CODE

Isabelle sees social justice as part of the old Spanish honor code in New Mexico: "It means my word is as good as gold. . . . [The Superintendent] entrusted me with the children. I was going to do my best." She continued:

> [Social justice] is not a new term that has just been invented by researchers and school people. . . . All I have to do is look at the [1848] Treaty of

Figure 10.2. Isabelle Sandoval, advocate for young children's bilingual expertise.

Guadalupe Hidalgo [which validates everyone's right to dignity]. So when you think about social justice, you have to wonder, like I did when I was 8 or 9 years old, asking my grandfather, "*¿Quiénes somos . . . de dónde viene la familia Medina?*" And he would say, "Pues nosotros siempre hemos vivido aquí." And I would say, "Grandpa, tell me more." He would go to a shelf and pull down a little journal all handwritten by his father in Spanish.

In Spanish, Isabelle's great-grandfather had written stories of a rich family heritage, providing a strong contradiction to the label of "retarded" given to her in school. It is this dignity of all human beings that Isabelle sees as foundational to social justice, giving her energy and courage to take steps toward change.

CHAPTER 11

Creating Spaces for Critical Literacy and Technology to Cultivate a Social Justice Focus

Sarah Vander Zanden

> She's new. . . . What's she like? Well, new to us but not new to Bailey's [Elementary School]. . . . Former reading teacher. Smart. I hear she's a firecracker.

As with new administration in any school, questions were circulating about fit and impending changes when Jean Frey took on the role of principal at Bailey's Elementary School. Would she support teacher knowledge and inquiry? What does she understand about emergent literacy and inquiry as fundamental aspects in the education of young children? Would she understand the "Bailey's Way"? In hindsight, the staff would have been better off contemplating other things. Jean was dynamic, intellectual, and a constant source of energy—qualities recognized as foundational to supporting equitable educational experiences for young children.

LOGISTICS, STRENGTHS, AND CHALLENGES

In early 2001, with the passage of the No Child Left Behind Act, high-stakes testing was on the rise. The staff at Bailey's was concerned about the impact of testing on their programs, as were so many other educators across the United States. Virginia, where the school is located, had a series of tests labeled Standards of Learning that became increasingly more important. However, in the tangle of needs pulling on the school staff and administration, the pressure to increase achievement scores and to meet unrealistic benchmarks seemed to ignore actual student learning and progress.

School Logistics

Located just outside Washington, DC, the neighborhood included public housing and half-a-million-dollar homes, churches, a mosque, restaurants and shops with owners speaking many different languages, a check-cashing shop, and a new drugstore (which, despite community protest, replaced a much-loved soccer field). Some regarded the area as vibrant, and others might say congested; either way it was a busy and richly diverse community. The school housed approximately 800 students during the time referred to in this chapter; however, its population skyrocketed recently to 1,300 and Bailey's is now divided into a primary and an upper school.

Bailey's was the first public magnet school for arts and sciences in the district. It was designed to support the multilingual students in the neighborhood with rigorous programming and also was intended to attract English speakers to those same programs to serve as "language models." A small percentage of students who lived outside the school's boundaries attended through a lottery system. Typically, twice the number of families applied each year for available slots. Many parents were drawn to the school's Spanish immersion program, the reading/writing workshop model in the general education classrooms, and the focus on arts integration across the curriculum. Approximately 75% of the students received free or reduced-price lunch. The student population continues to be economically and culturally diverse.

Strengths

Under Jean's leadership, the school had an open door to the community—families, educators, politicians, and university partners. Neighborhood families often came to the school for English and computer classes, advice about community needs, and family learning nights. A small boutique housed in the school basement offered, at reduced cost, job support, and materials for new immigrant families. Bailey's staff members—teaching assistants, reading specialists, and classroom teachers—were knowledgeable and proud practitioners. They were dedicated to understanding the contexts of the population and deeply invested their time and commitment to teaching and learning.

Magnet programs such as Spanish immersion, arts integration, and science inquiry attracted observers. The students' linguistic and cultural variation was seen as an enviable privilege, and often TESOL teachers from other districts came to observe. Educators also came to see arts integration in action; focus groups met after observations to discuss pedagogical decisions with the teachers. Jean, like her predecessor Carol Franz, supported all of these initiatives with an eye on transparency and educational gains of the whole school. She was well aware that reflection via focus groups ultimately would impact both the observed within the school and the observers from outside.

Challenges

Regardless of the school's many strengths, there seemed to be a lingering perception of negativity grounded in deficit profiling of the Bailey's community and its students. This external perception often was made clear to teachers at district events. For example, upon learning that she worked at Bailey's, a new teacher at a district orientation meeting was asked, "Why would you ever want to teach *there*, with those kids? Nobody speaks English and that area is awful." Bailey's was a highly regarded model school, but that status could not remove the impact of deeply held beliefs and biases sitting just below the surface of decades of unequal economic structures, social division, and discrimination.

Students represented over 40 cultures, and many new immigrant families experienced significant constraints, including limited resources and unfamiliarity with the school culture. While it was a complex student population, Jean saw it as a resource rather than a hindrance. However, the small portion of affluent families and a mainly White middle-class staff of relatively new teachers were not always as appreciative of the opportunities that such a community offered. This cultivated a need for an increased professional development focus on cultural understanding and diversity. It is important to note that Jean *returned to* Bailey's after years in administrative positions at better-resourced schools. Her choice to lead and to address challenges was deliberate, and the staff and students benefited from that choice.

ESTABLISHING A CULTURE OF PROFESSIONAL LEARNING

Because of my admiration for Jean Frey and memories of my own growth and learning at Bailey's Elementary School, I reference the school with great enthusiasm as I talk with friends and family. Soon they look at me with glazed-over eyes and say things like, "Are you talking about that cult school again?" or "Hello? Come back to reality." Clearly, the school had a profound impact on who I am as a teacher today. One reason is that, under Jean's leadership, the school's culture generated what might be considered collective thinking. I believe this was done intentionally as Jean put pieces into place to develop a professional community of practice. Groups of teachers-as-learners were plentiful. Teachers-as-readers, teachers-as-researchers, teachers-as-artists, and critical literacy study groups met regularly and voluntarily. Together, teachers engaged in learning how to support the needs of diverse learners. Jean created the ethos in which learning together was the norm; she even provided food at times, so that staff could meet over dinner. During the day, multi-age classroom exchanges, such as a weekly kinder-garten to 5th-grade learning buddies program, supported learning across grade levels and fostered collaboration.

These kinds of opportunities resulted in various public projects and gener-ated knowledge from many perspectives. For example, several colleagues wrote professional books while I taught there (Fay & Whaley, 2004; Johnson, 2006; Parker & Pardini, 2006) and after I left (Johnson & Keier, 2010; Vasquez & Felderman, 2013). The critical literacy group contributed to a special issue of the journal *School Talk* focused on our study group (Vasquez & Egawa, 2002). Many teachers attended conferences with school-sponsored funding, supported student teachers, and taught courses for educators in the large district. The breadth and depth of these activities were part of the intellectual work of teaching, and it was energizing for novice and veteran teachers alike.

Each first-year teacher at Bailey's participated in a weekly professional devel-opment workshop. Often these workshop sessions were focused on developing assessments for learning and fostering reading and writing workshop knowledge, in particular for emergent readers and writers. Each session was geared toward supporting rigorous instruction for the culturally and linguistically diverse stu-dent population. Jean attended many of these sessions, drawing on expertise from her past role as a reading specialist.

During one session focused on developing communicative skills with English language learners, Jean role-played in a simulation to help the novice teachers un-derstand what it might feel like for students to navigate lessons in a new language. Seeing the principal learning and talking with them felt collegial and supportive to brand-new teachers. Her time could have been dedicated to numerous other responsibilities, yet she chose to be involved in the development of new teachers. Visibility, rather than surveillance, was one of Jean's means to foster collegiality.

LEADERSHIP AS A RHIZOME OF POTENTIAL

The metaphorical rhizome (Deleuze & Guattari, 1987) has long been applied in educational theory and research, particularly in early childhood education. It is interwoven here to offer a concrete image for Jean's approach. A rhizome is a root system that supports plants, such as couch grass and lilies, beneath the sur-face horizontally and in what might appear as haphazard strands. This structure enables new shoots to sprout up when the conditions are conducive to growth. A network spreads and interweaves below the sprout, ensuring a viable plant system. It is an apt metaphor for a leader whose choices supported a thriving and divergent educational community. Jean's administrative legacy is rhizomatic, unwavering, and, at times, reminiscent of a gnarly survivor. Deleuze and Guattari (1987) describe the rhizome as:

An uncentered growth, a multiplicity, characterized by connection and heterogeneity. It is constantly producing new shoots and rootlets. The rhizome as subterranean stem can be attributed to bulbs and tubers, but also to pack forms of animals such as rats and burrows. Viruses are also rhizomes, in all of their functions of shelter, supply, movement, evasion, and breakout. The rhizome includes the best and the worst, potato and couchgrass. (p. 7)

Often a rhizome is thought of somewhat negatively, like an unwanted plant that won't perish (such as a weed). However, this persistence also can be seen as highly prized tenacity, much like a leader's commitment to a school. Bailey's School, under Jean's administration, was a *rhizome of potential*.

Jean in the Classroom

Each first-year teacher was assigned an additional on-site mentor at Bailey's beyond the district's mentor program. This school-based mentor relationship typically involved a reading specialist, who supported new teachers as they set up reading and writing workshop protocols or instructional routines. Jean filled the role of reading specialist in my classroom during my first year of teaching. I observed her interact with my students, honoring their questions while keeping them on point. She modeled lessons to help me figure out how to identify literacy strengths of my students. She led book discussions and modeled dialogic conversation development (Johnston, 2004). She treated me as a knowledgeable peer despite my brief experience in the classroom and limited knowledge regarding reading instruction.

For the second series of lessons, Jean planned and conferred with me before and after each session. During one lesson she demonstrated how teaching syntax or language structures with the social studies textbook could both scaffold comprehension and support developing content knowledge. Jean, wearing her reading specialist hat, helped me see that social studies content mattered and the textbook could be useful. I can hear her explaining to me, "You can't read and write about nothing. Give them a starting point." Her lesson integrated content and modeled maintaining high standards. She firmly believed that students should have access to grade-level content in all subjects, from community studies to ancient civilizations.

Jean's Role Throughout the School

While Jean could not have a formal role in all teachers' classrooms, she was ever-present. She attended grade-level meetings, kept her office door open whenever possible, and was very approachable. She greeted students in the hallways and seemed to know everyone by name. She delivered birthday pencils, a long-held tradition in the school, and once explained that doing so allowed her to visit classrooms and offer a positive connection to each child—something that principals rarely get to do while seated behind desks in their offices.

Supporting Spaces for Critical Literacy

Jean's presence in the school, interacting warmly with children and families, was an essential element in her rhizomatic work as an administrator. However, it was her support of our critical literacy study group that had the most indelible effect on our lives as teachers, then and now.

Bailey's critical literacy study group was developed in conjunction with the National Council of Teachers of English (NCTE) Reading Initiative. Its impetus was our meeting Dr. Vivian Maria Vasquez at a literacy conference and being inspired by her work in early childhood critical literacies. Jean immediately supported our request to invite her to spend time in our school. That relationship, initiated over 15 years ago, continues to support those who remained at Bailey's and those who have moved on to new spaces. Through this collaboration, a group of approximately 12 staff members met monthly for 3-hour sessions to discuss theory and practice linked to critical literacy.

I joined the group 6 months after it began and immediately felt both intimidated and excited about the conversations. We examined everyday texts, poetry, children's books; we explored positioning and perspectives even when some of these ideas disrupted practices at our school. The group read articles and discussed complexities presented by scholars such as Hilary Janks, James Gee, and Barbara Comber. In fact, I recall several extensive discussions about big 'D' and little 'd' discourses (Gee, 1996) that left us gasping for air as we laughed and cried our way through figuring what this meant for our teaching.

We linked theory to our teaching lives, became a community, and began to understand how a critical literacy stance could be a part of our identities as teachers. It guided our planning much more than any unit plans. The conversations were not always easy, but difficult dialogues were necessary to our growth. As one teacher wrote:

> It was hard not to get defensive—it was difficult to get called on our assumptions. But I noticed we took the time to ask, "What made you say that?" "Can you talk more about that?" We had created a safe place to talk about sensitive issues. Lately our thoughts turn to how we are positioning our students. (Vasquez & Egawa, 2002, p. 2)

Jean supported us on multiple levels. She worked with her budget to make sure funds were available for us to buy resource books and materials and so that study group members could present our work at NCTE's national conventions and the Literacies for All conference of the Whole Language Umbrella. Jean was an active member of the group, and she attended most sessions. While I can't say with certainty, I suspect she was instrumental in inviting participation of the two vice principals. I was a very new teacher when I joined the group, and the administrative team's participation heightened the value of our work.

Jean seemed to enjoy the intellectual space and the collegiality of the group. She engaged with us, exploring ideas and demonstrating a teacher-as-thinker mentality as we envisioned and effected change in classrooms. With us, Jean engaged in the messy work of democratic discussion. In the process, she also supported the development of many teacher leaders.

ROOTLETS

Rhizomes are hard to eradicate because of the many rootlets that survive undetected below the surface. This organic structure is daunting and can be unwieldy because it offers potential for new, uncontrolled growth as conditions are met for development. From a social justice standpoint, the rootlets that were cultivated through Jean Frey's leadership became forces for good in the world both within and beyond Bailey's School. Other rootlets were the possibilities for public and curricular engagement and change that were nurtured because of the administrative support, which allowed them to take on lives of their own. There were many projects that were possible because of Jean's courageous support for independent and critical thinking. Some of the rootlets that made their way into the world beyond Bailey's are described in the following sections.

Community Support: Building Multicultural Respect

Bailey's School is located just outside of the Washington, DC, metropolitan area, near the Pentagon. After the 9/11 attacks on the World Trade Center and the Pentagon, the school faced many situations requiring emotional support and time to heal. Several young Muslim students, including a 2nd-grader named Osama, were bullied by other children. Osama's 2nd-grade teacher, like so many other educators, felt unprepared to manage classroom discussions about the terrorist attack and repercussions felt by some of her students. Jean immediately called teachers together with counselors to formulate plans to support students and prevent bullying in the future.

A Public Voice: Taking a Stand Against Testing Injustice

A significant challenge Jean faced was that while she deeply respected students and teachers, the external accountability measures increasingly seemed to indicate that the folks who pushed that agenda did not. She wrote a letter to families explaining the ramifications of not meeting target achievement goals laid out in the directives of the No Child Left Behind legislation. This letter created quite a stir in the local community, generating multiple newspaper articles (M. Fisher, 2004; Mathews, 2004a, 2004b). Jean explained in this letter that the staff would still teach students to think like scientists and historians, even though this was not measured on standardized tests. Loudly, she shared the horrors that these accountability measures unleashed for new students, and her words were highlighted in *The Washington Post*: "'Right now, we're judged by our attendance rate and English and math scores,' Frey says. 'How about parent satisfaction? Student progress?'" (M. Fisher, 2004, p. B01).

Also reported were Jean's words describing her frustration that children who had just arrived from other countries were required to sit down and fill out bubbles on a test. The *Washington Post* article continued:

> "I would love to hear what they said at home that night," she says. "They were totally mystified. One child could say 'Hello' and another just waved; they'd been here one week and 10 days. But I had to make them sit here for two hours, three days a week, filling in circles so we could hit the 95 percent participation target. What a waste." (M. Fisher, 2004, p. B01)

Jean's public outcry was well received, especially by families and staff members, but it was also highly controversial. As teachers, we were protected from what I imagine must have been a political nightmare for any administrator. Shortly after the articles were published, Jean, spurred by district pressure to control the public's perception of the county's schools, begrudgingly held a discussion with the staff about appropriate media etiquette. However, I do not recall her apologizing or retracting her stance as she advocated for real learning over test preparation. Her outreach to the public sphere raised awareness of the ramifications of testing for many students, just as it invited critique. This model for educators reinforced our pedagogical pride and supported our fierce advocacy for children as inquirers and for taking a stand against injustices.

A Global Presence: Support for Experimentation with New Ideas

The final example describes a slice of a larger project produced the year after Jean retired. In this section, teacher Carol Felderman explains how the work of the critical literacy group created space for her to advocate for a podcasting project with her 2nd-graders. This is importantly linked to Jean, whose work to establish and sustain the critical literacy study group and to stand up to injustices was so strong that it did not die when she left; rather, it lived on as one of the strongest rootlets from her work.

Carol's story. Grappling with the unruly ideas and tenets of critical literacy required support. Especially welcome was the reassurance that it was okay to try again. I felt fortunate to be part of an environment where having the time to wonder, consider triumphs, and reflect upon mistakes without criticism was valued by our administration. This support developed my pedagogical confidence, which continued well after Jean's retirement. In my work, it meant having the confidence to explain to a new administrator what was happening in my classroom in a manner that was backed with theory and expansive definitions of best practices. What I needed to explain to our new principal did not directly follow the grade-level standards but rather integrated them in new and authentic ways.

Given the pressure to meet mandated achievement gains, I knew that explaining our critical literacy curriculum as one that came from the children might not be easily accepted. Our new principal took a chance in supporting the continuation of the critical work he inherited upon entering Bailey's.

In co-constructing the school year's curriculum with the children—or as we consider them, future rootlets—the class uncovered new layers to critical literacy and social justice work. The greatest discoveries came from the podcasting project, supported by Vivian Maria Vasquez. Critical conversations during our class meetings raised topics that soon became part of the *100% Kids* podcast (Figure 11.1). There was often uncertainty and messiness. For example, we began with the question, "Can we make a podcast?" which simultaneously carried the responses, "Yes!" and "No! We're just kids!"

Time went on, and the children discovered how the topics they presented on the show could attract a sizeable global online audience. The conversations, script writing, rehearsals, and production of the podcast allowed the class to extend their conversations beyond the four walls of our classroom. The public responses to questions addressing animal rights, the environment, and bullying generated further discussion. We created a space in our 2nd-grade classroom for globalized problem-solving, which went beyond the curriculum standards.

The discoveries and accomplishments that came with such work were more than Vivian and I could have ever imagined. In the final days of the project, we learned from a family about extended effects of the podcast. Part of the podcast was a comments section and map (via clustrmaps.com) where folks who were listening could indicate their locations (Figure 11.2). A dot often appeared in Colombia, South America.

Two students, Scarlett and Martha, were excited, as their families were from Colombia. Martha, who was a quiet student, began to talk about her grandparents who lived in Colombia and how she could not go there to see them. She talked about how much she loved her grandparents and how much she knew they

Figure 11.1. *100% Kids* **banner.**

Figure 11.2. Cluster Map.

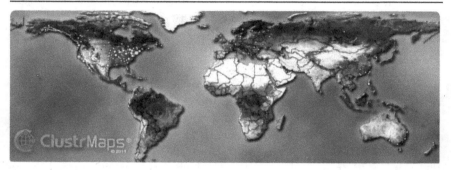

loved her. She shared that they were her mom's parents and that her mom did not get to see them often.

At the end of the year, Martha's mother explained that her parents listened to the podcast from Colombia. They subscribed each week so they could hear their granddaughter's voice and learn about what she was learning in school. Martha's mother thanked us for providing their family with a link between grandparents and granddaughter.

The impact of the podcast was both immediate and asynchronous as it crossed geographic and cultural boundaries. From the onset of the project, I expected the children would develop literacy skills and reach a new audience through the use of technology, but I did not realize that the podcast also would assist in connecting families who otherwise might not be accessible. The podcast provided a means for the children to express their concerns and opinions to a greater audience and also became a vehicle for demonstrating student learning. When Martha's mother proudly explained that her parents could hear their granddaughter speaking Spanish and talking about what she was doing in her American school, she provided Vivian and me with a view of the familial affordances of the podcast that were beyond what we considered when we initiated the project.

While Jean was not the administrator on site during the podcasting project, Carol was able to justify the work theoretically and practically to the new administrator (many schools were limiting technological inquiry as a means of ensuring security) in large part because Jean had cultivated an environment of possibilities, even when they disrupted dominant practices. This illustrates how Jean's support and encouragement of collective intellectual thinking and doing promoted educational change in new settings even beyond her presence.

CONCLUSION: RHIZOME OF POTENTIAL

While some leaders may view the questioning of normative practices as undercutting their authority, Jean encouraged us to think in new ways and try out new ideas that pushed the norm to new levels. The dilemma of mandated testing did not stop her from supporting our work. And, because she articulated the injustices of forcing students to take standardized tests when they had attended the school for only 1 or 2 weeks, some of the marginalization of students became visible beyond the school walls.

Stories from Jean's leadership provide important examples of how foundations of independence and inquiry can be fostered under an administration that pushes and pulls back as needed. Creating spaces for critical literacies shattered preconceived assumptions about literacy, particularly with diverse populations. Under Jean's leadership, teachers expected students to shape the instruction rather than teachers forcing curriculum based on district scope and sequence onto students. In many ways this expectation was negotiated through the events described as Carol's class engaged locally and globally, privately and publicly.

Jean was not perfect as a principal. Like the rest of us, there were decisions and situations that could have been managed differently. Perhaps the media surrounding the testing dilemma could have been encouraged to interview families and/or students to bring their voices directly to the issues. Perhaps the door that felt open to many of us did not feel as open to everyone. However, her unyielding commitment to countering injustices and attention to inquiry as a tool for literate problem-solving served the Bailey's community well. Jean expected meaningful discussion, questioned assumptions, and respected student and family knowledge.

Jean's convictions, the tenets of teaching and learning she held dear, impacted me significantly. The critical literacy group offered a sanctioned space for us to engage as inquirers—to reveal our vulnerabilities, raise questions, and plan actions to address those questions. Cochran-Smith and Lytle (2009) theorize inquiry in a way that describes the work we were able to accomplish:

In educational settings, where teachers, students, and other stakeholders are engaged in inquiry and mutual deliberations, common assumptions about the roles and outcomes of teaching, learning, and schooling are debated and transformed. So too are ideas about teachers as leaders. (p. 148)

We were, indeed, becoming teachers-as-leaders engaged together in the situated intellectual work of building knowledge and effecting change. The independent thinking and collective growth of our educational community are due in part to Jean's courageous administrative persistence and the space she created for so many rootlets to grow and prosper.

CHAPTER 12

Intentional Practices

One Administrator's Path Toward Equity

Meir Muller

The students of Rabbi Zusha, hearing that he was dying, came to pay him one last visit. To their surprise, they found him trembling with fear.

"Why are you afraid?" they asked. "You have been as righteous as Moses!"

"When I stand before the heavenly throne," Zusha answered, "I am unafraid of being asked: 'Zusha, why were you not like Moses?' Or 'Zusha, why were you not like King David?' I am afraid to be asked, 'Zusha, why were you not like Zusha?'"

Similar to Rabbi Zusha, Dr. Sabina Mosso-Taylor's approach to courageous leadership is to continually outgrow herself, holding herself accountable for that growth. This means that, as an early childhood administrator and as a human being, she never settles into the complacent view that her current understandings and efforts to promote educational equity are good enough. As Sabina said, "Many people are marginalized every day; who am I to say that it was a good day? Maybe I made good decisions but maybe I missed or misinterpreted something; I can do even better tomorrow."

"It is all about the pillow," explained Sabina. "I have to be able to put my head on the pillow at night and reflect on the decisions I made that day." So each night, Sabina asks herself: Is each child's family, heritage, and home language equitably represented, valued, and actively drawn upon in the classroom? Does each family feel welcomed with access to their children's classrooms and decision-making processes of the program? Do staff members feel that their backgrounds

Courageous Leadership in Early Childhood Education, edited by Susi Long, Mariana Souto-Manning, and Vivian Maria Vasquez. Copyright © 2016 by Teachers College, Columbia University. All rights reserved.

are valued? Are they able to enact equity for all children and families? In this way, Sabina constantly pushes herself to study, reflect, grow, and use her knowledge to take action—tomorrow.

For 8 years, Sabina's professional tomorrows centered on her position as the administrator of a public child development program in the Southeastern United States. The program, for 3- to 5-year-olds, was located in 13 classrooms in schools throughout the district. As a result of Sabina's leadership, the program is widely known as offering education of the highest quality for young children. Sabina's role in the program's development and her daily and genuine involvement with children and families (Figure 12.1) does not go unnoticed by teachers, families, and district administrators. The district assistant superintendent gives her high praise: "Sabina is passionate about what her program provides. Sabina's success rate and families that return to her program speaks for itself." Similarly, parents greatly respect and admire Sabina, as one parent wrote:

> Sabina sets the bar high. . . . I want the administrator in the next program to be as enthusiastic as she is. I want them to have the same open-door policy that she does. I want them to be as loving to my children as Sabina is. . . . [She is] a visionary, a great gift.

Because of this high regard for her work, Sabina recently was asked to serve as principal of an elementary school set up specifically to "take struggling students and produce satisfaction and achievement rather than frustration and failure" (www.richland2.org/cfa/pages/about-.aspx). This chapter, however, focuses on Sabina's 8 years with teachers of very young children, drawing on a 3-year period when she engaged the teaching staff in the study of discrimination and privileging in schools and society.

SABINA'S LEADERSHIP

Sabina's office was housed in one of five modest portable buildings grouped behind a large elementary school. Connections to children and convictions about equity were immediately visible to anyone entering her office—in the books on her shelf, drawings and notes from children, and quotes displayed around the office that undergirded her foundational beliefs.

This focus on relationships and equity was felt again upon entering classrooms. On any given morning one could see multilingual morning messages and multicultural artifacts from families and the community. Visitors might hear English, Spanish, Hindi, Hebrew, Tamil, Russian, Urdu, Chinese, and/or Mandarin spoken as teachers, children, and families interacted with and taught

Figure 12.1. Dr. Sabina Mosso–Taylor.

one another. These were just a few of many ways that Sabina's commitment to social justice was evidenced through her leadership. As teacher Tammy Frierson explained:

> Some people say they are committed [to equity] but [Sabina] really *is* passionate. She's committed to our school being diverse and treating all of our families with a great deal of respect. . . . It's like the tip of the typical pyramid; you see the top doing it and it makes you want to aspire to be more open and more willing get to know someone outside your own box 'cause she's putting herself out there.

GUIDING PRINCIPLES

I've never seen a principal [who] liked diversity like her. . . . It's not just in words, it's in acts. —Rocio Heron, teacher

Sabina's clearly communicated beliefs drove her program's equity focus. Nothing happened by accident. She intentionally built a diverse student population and engaged teachers in the ongoing study of what it means to educate equitably in a multicultural society. She acted on her conviction that administrators must have a deliberate plan to facilitate this focus and the courage to sustain the work.

Sabina's administrative plan was built on a set of principles or commitments that she developed through study and experience. These commitments are described in the following sections of this chapter. They communicate the complexities of a process that must be faced if administrators are to make the decision to take a stand for schools that are truly multilingual, multicultural places that support *all* students.

Commitment to a Focus on Equity

Directing the child development program, Sabina was very clear that a focus on broadening the norm to genuinely embrace multiculturalism, multilingualism, and equity for all students would not just be a *part* of her expectation, but would be *foundational* to the work of leading and teaching. She understands that helping teachers recognize how institutions drive inequities is essential to a focus on equity. These inequities come to life when curriculum, testing, teaching styles, and identification of students for special education and gifted programs privilege children who are White, middle-class, and monolingual speakers of so-called Standard English (Delpit, 2012; Nieto, 2013). Overturning these realities was non-negotiable. This was clearly articulated in Sabina's day-to-day interactions with families, colleagues, and district administrators, and in her hiring decisions and professional development program planning.

Commitment to Ensuring a Diverse Student Population

Intentionality in ensuring that the families in her program reflected a diverse society was a key commitment in Sabina's work. This was grounded in her understanding that if children are to appreciate a diverse world and contribute to building a more equitable one, they need to be in the company of those who represent a range of nationalities, ethnicities, races, incomes, family structures, and languages. For this reason, Sabina used a variety of strategies to actively seek a diverse student population and to hire a diverse staff.

Sabina knows that diversifying educational settings does not happen by accident. Rocio Heron, the program's Spanish-language teacher, provided one example of how Sabina worked to ensure diversity by fighting for children and their families to enroll in and remain in the program. Although this was a public program, fees were required because preschool programs are not universal or mandatory in South Carolina and therefore were not fully funded by the state. Rocio explained:

Sabina told José's mother, "Don't go away; don't go to another school; stay here!" And for a month, we helped her with the tuition payments and other things because Sabina really realizes the importance that José and his mother make for us. It's not just in words; it's in acts. I've never seen somebody like that.

Commitment to Multilingualism

Merely recruiting a diverse population does not, of course, guarantee equity. Other commitments are critical to normalizing diversity in ways that do not privilege one group over another. One way Sabina did this was by embracing multilingualism. Over and over, family members and teachers commented on her dedication to fostering a program that genuinely valued multiple languages. Rocio described her perspective, contrasting Sabina and other administrators:

> Many administrators don't like Latinos because they think we are poor or ignorant or we are not going to give anything [to the school]. . . . If everyone was like her, [it would be different]. She led me and the parents to value our Spanish.

Rocio first realized that Sabina held this unwavering commitment when she asked Sabina about creating a school announcement board written in Spanish:

> I came here not really knowing what [Sabina] liked, what was her philosophy. . . . I [Rocio] made a board for the school [with announcements in Spanish] and said, "Can I put it in your office?" And she said, "I don't want Spanish just in a corner; Spanish should be everywhere."

Another way Sabina enacted this commitment was by encouraging teachers and family members to share their languages and/or teach language lessons in the classroom. This became a regular occurrence (Figure 12.2).

Sabina also advocated for children who needed support to maintain their home languages. For example, she realized that one of the students was not speaking Spanish at home or at school even though it was the primary language in his home. Prior to coming into Sabina's program, the child had attended an English-only day care and, as a result, stopped speaking Spanish. When Sabina learned this, she and Rocio developed a plan whereby Rocio would speak Spanish with him at school and Tammy (the child's classroom teacher) would intentionally incorporate Spanish in daily classroom routines. Although Tammy had already embraced Spanish in her classroom, this deliberate action to make Spanish part of the classroom's normalized practice signified a shift: The morning read-aloud

Figure 12.2. Parent Ms. Avali teaching a song in Tamil (left) and the Urdu language chart created for the children by parent Dr. Siddiqui (right).

was conducted in both Spanish and English, Spanish was used in the morning message, the children sang Spanish songs during gathering time, and the children were addressed in both Spanish and English. In addition, Tammy began joining the children as a participant in the Spanish lessons taught by Rocio. Within a month, the child was using both languages at home and in school.

Commitment to an Open-Door Policy, to Listening

Families knew they were always welcome in the classrooms and in Sabina's office. She never positioned herself as unreachable. A story told by a parent about their first meeting captures the down-to-earth nature of Sabina's relationships with families:

> The first time I met her, I was bringing the twins' application and she was covered from head to toe with dirt because she was working in the school garden. She was like, "Give me a second; I just have to clean up." And I was like, "You're the principal?" It was very disarming. I was very okay with that.

Another parent explained how much she valued Sabina as a listener: "She's nonjudgmental [and] a great listener. Even when I figured she could probably complete my sentences, she didn't." When asked about advice they had for other administrators based on what they valued about Sabina, one parent captured the views of many: "Listen to your parents. Really hear your parents. . . . Nobody knows our child better than we do . . . just hear us."

Commitment to Your Own Growth

Sabina believes that the facilitation of equity work cannot happen without commitment from administrators to the ongoing development of their own professional knowledge. She described this as being *theoretically connected*, meaning that in order to promote more equitable practices, administrators must continue to develop and refine their own theoretical and pedagogical knowledge base.

Sabina acknowledged that this can be frustrating: "There is so much that I don't know and there are just so many hours in a day to read, reflect, discuss, and learn." But she perseveres as a learner, knowing how important it is to stay current so she can guide the teachers with whom she works accordingly.

Commitment to Supporting Teachers' Professional Study

While continuing to build her own knowledge, Sabina made teachers' ongoing professional growth foundational to her program. Her goal was to create a culture in which educator-as-learner was a way of life.

Study group strategies. One of the most effective ways Sabina found to build this culture was to engage her staff in regular, focused study groups. Sometimes they met in locations outside of school—at a restaurant, at Sabina's house. She often started these biweekly after-school sessions with 15 minutes of written reflection so that teachers could jot down thoughts, classroom connections, and questions from articles or books they were reading. With this opportunity to reflect, discussions tended to be more productive and focused.

Another approach was to begin sessions with 30 minutes for quiet reading, recognizing that it was difficult for teachers to otherwise find time for professional reading. This also served as a time for teachers to decompress and refocus at the end of the school day.

During their study group experience, Sabina chose texts to support reflection, discussion, and deepened insights by focusing on topics such as critical literacies in early childhood (Cowhey, 2006; Vasquez, 2004), race and racism (Delpit, 1988; Howard, 2006; Tatum, 2007), home and community literacies (Long, Anderson, Clark, & McCraw, 2008), and critical multicultural education

(Compton-Lilly, 2004; Souto-Manning, 2013). Sabina sometimes provided guiding questions to trigger discussions that followed quiet reading or reflective writing. For example:

- What key ideas do you glean from this reading?
- What connections do you make to your own experiences?
- How does this knowledge enhance or challenge your current understanding?
- What might this mean for your classroom?

Sabina also encouraged teachers to keep a journal, always having it nearby to record their own and others' thoughts, feelings, observations, and assumptions about race, ethnicity, and language. These journals become another impetus for discussion and self-reflection.

At the end of each study group session, Sabina engaged staff in discussing how the session challenged, affirmed, or altered their thinking. She asked teachers to *name* their growth and their questions as they considered ways to apply new insights to their teaching.

Accessing resources. In support of teachers' professional study, Sabina actively sought opportunities to engage with speakers who could provide further perspectives regarding the work. She prioritized funding to make this possible, as when she supported teachers' attendance at local, state, and national workshops and conferences that bolstered their equity focus.

Creating safe spaces for self-examination. Sabina feels that professional study can be successful only when the school's climate provides a safe environment for educators' self-examination and honest dialogue, particularly when engaged in conversations about racial, ethnic, and linguistic power, privilege, and prejudice.

Teachers who worked with Sabina commented on the trust and comfort they gained with her over time, seeing it as essential to discussing issues that otherwise might make them feel uncomfortable or vulnerable. As one teacher said after a particularly intimate discussion about race: "I can't believe I am telling you this, as usually this is not something I talk about [outside my own racial/ cultural group]." Sabina emphasized that this comment did not reflect a feeling that existed early in their relationship, but occurred after "3 years of weekly conversations about equity, race, and trust-building."

One strategy that Sabina used to build this safe place was to share her own vulnerabilities as she worked through new understandings. For example, she shared one of the first times she came head-to-head with biases she did not think she possessed. Having prided herself on valuing diversity, she described her prior views:

I was born in Brooklyn. I am an Italian-German American, lived in a diverse neighborhood, had Jewish friends, friends of Color, I thought I knew about diversity. It was true that I had diverse experiences and many friends of Color, but I was completely oblivious to the racism, oppression, and language marginalization that existed.

Sabina went on to explain that it was in a graduate course that she first acknowledged issues of White privilege; she described the defensiveness she felt when required to engage in self-examination. The class read Peggy McIntosh's (1995) famous article about White privilege. In response to a section on unearned White privileges, Sabina wrote in the margins: "Is that fair?" She felt that McIntosh's statement was unfair, initially denying that White people were disproportionately privileged—thus protecting her White privilege. She told this story in a faculty study group hoping that, by revealing her own initial defensiveness, she would position herself vulnerably and could better support critical and honest dialogue. She demonstrated that for those who have enjoyed unearned racial, linguistic, and ethnic privileges, it takes hard work and constant reflection to acknowledge those realities and choose to interrupt them. Sabina explained the courage required to make herself vulnerable:

Perhaps the most courageous act is facing up to my own shortcomings and making them visible for teachers, parents, and students to see. That can be very hard to do. Particularly when I [have to admit to] ways I contribute to racist thinking and the ways in which I stereotype or do not interrupt deficit thinking.

In this way, Sabina communicated her belief that educators must be vigilant in constantly identifying and confronting our own biases as they emerge in day-to-day life. She sees this as foundational to creating safe spaces for others to engage in self-examination (Irvine, 2003; McIntyre, 1997).

Commitment to Getting to Know Families Outside of School

Another commitment that Sabina asked of teachers and of herself was to spend time in homes and communities of children from backgrounds different from their own. The purpose was for teachers to build relationships, overturn stereotypes, and challenge misperceptions that they and others might hold about the children they teach, their families, and their communities. As a result, staff members spent time in places of worship, homes, and other community spaces *with* children and families. Prior to these experiences, Sabina engaged staff members in foregrounding their own and others' assumptions and stereotypes. Later, they discussed how those assumptions had been challenged and how their teaching might reflect more informed views of children and their families. Families seemed appreciative of this turning of the tables to get to know them on their own turf. As one parent explained, "It means so much to me that you took the time to visit us and that you care about my child's identity."

Commitment to Interrupting Discriminatory Comments and Actions

Much of Sabina's work was focused on supporting teachers in identifying discriminatory beliefs, comments, and actions. But she also knew that they needed strategies for interrupting bias. Through study group discussions, they were able to share experiences to help one another develop this ability. In one such discussion, teacher Tammy Frierson described an incident that occurred in her classroom when the students were learning about Chanukah. One of the parents brought dreidels for the children. Another parent, picking up his son that day, commented that his child did not need the information about Chanukah nor did he need the dreidel. Tammy explained her reaction:

> I reminded [the parent] that if he wanted the students to listen to him and respect him when he comes to the class to talk about being Hindu, he had to give respect to our Jewish friends in their religious practice. He agreed and asked [his son] about the [dreidel] game Thom taught him and took the information home with him.

In a similar story of interruption, Sabina told the staff about having dinner at a student's home. During the meal, the father mentioned that he was considering pulling his older child out of another school because the school's test scores were low, attributing the low scores to the number of Black students at the school. Sabina described her attempt to counter this narrative by explaining (to the father) that low test scores often reflect the bias of the tests and narrow instructional methods but do not indicate that children of Color are less intelligent or capable.

Sometimes learning to interrupt meant challenging teachers' own misperceptions. In one instance, Sabina shared that a teacher, learning that an African American parent had not paid for his child's lunch program, commented, "Well they *obviously* cannot afford to pay." Sabina asked the teacher to consider why she felt this was "obvious," and it was soon apparent to the teacher and to Sabina that the comment came from unacknowledged bias about race and income. This led to discussions about the ease with which negative profiling occurs and how destructive it is to our ability to teach equitably.

In another example, Sabina and one of the teachers visited a local mosque having been invited by two Muslim families from the school's community. After the visit, the teacher explained (to the faculty study group) that her own embedded misperceptions and biases had come to the surface when they pulled up to the mosque: "When we pulled up and walked in, I was like, oh my, they don't want us here." This prompted another teacher to acknowledge her bias: "Yes, it's the image of seeing somebody that looks like somebody you associate with something negative and . . . you just assume that they're not good."

Sabina described these as "negative visceral reactions." Rather than demeaning teachers for them, she was grateful for a space where they could come to the surface so the group could talk through them. The group discussed how fears and biases are often the result of misinformation and societal bombardment of negative stereotypes. This led to discussions about why such biases existed, why they were ill-founded, how those fears constituted obstacles for teaching equitably, and how teachers could be alert to, identify, and disrupt such biases in the future.

Commitment to Countering Color-Blindness as a Virtuous Stance

Building a climate where honest talk could occur also provided openings for important discussions about color-blindness. In one study group meeting, for instance, a teacher announced, "I just don't get it. I want to, but I just don't understand how our students are really all that different from one another" (Mosso-Taylor, 2013, p. 114). An African American staff member replied, "You wouldn't feel it because you've never had to think that way" (p. 114). Understanding that many people claim color-blindness because they believe it communicates an antibias stance (Sue, 2015) helped Sabina engage the group in further discussion about how a color-blind mentality devalues the very histories, languages, and contributions that make us a rich multilingual and multicultural society; assumes Whiteness as normalcy; and eliminates the possibility of talking about issues of racial discrimination and inequity.

Commitment to Building Relationships with District Administrators

Sabina knew that to succeed in doing social justice work, it was important to be respected by and have the support of district officials. She made a point of talking with them during principals' meetings, attending district book studies, and regularly inviting them to visit the program's classrooms. Each interaction created an opening for sharing her philosophy and commitments. Sabina explained:

It was important that the district administrators and the superintendent knew me and my intentions for our program. An example of this occurred when the district announced that part of our program would be changed to a Montessori model. I was concerned that the curriculum would be restrictive, given the multicultural model I embraced. I met with the superintendent to share my concerns. After listening, he responded by saying that he trusted me to do what was right for our students and used my name to coin a new model—"Mosso-ssori"—indicating his trust in my ability to use the model, but expand on and alter it.

Commitment to Persevere

Sabina believes that the ability to persevere in this work requires first recognizing that inequities exist and then coming to the conclusion that you have no choice but to work to overturn them. She explained: "Once you start operating through an equity lens, you never see anything the same way."

Sabina knows, however, that perseverance comes with challenges, one of them being the ability to sustain confidence in one's capacity to do the work. She admits to fighting dips in confidence, constantly working to convince herself: "You can do this. You can do this. This is the stance you are going to have to take."

Another challenge was finding patience and trust in the potential for change. She recounts:

> [At first] I was distraught because I wasn't seeing great changes [right away]. . . . But now I see it differently. Equity work is in the successful actions [I see every day]: speaking to a student in Spanish, reading a book about a child's culture, challenging a colleague to think deeply. . . . These actions add up; they hopefully are part of the process of shifting the balance.

Voicing a final challenge to perseverance, Sabina talked about losing friends who were not comfortable with changes they saw in her, friends who commented that "she doesn't laugh at jokes or approve of our conversations." While Sabina is usually able to "let them go," she acknowledged that "there's a part of me that is depressed because I am losing my friends and I feel alone" (Mosso-Taylor, 2013, p. 283). But then she described how feelings of aloneness can be overcome by seeking "like-minded individuals/friends [who can help you] build stamina to sustain this work" (p. 284).

CONCLUSION

For Sabina, the bottom line is that "we have no option; we are nothing if we are not true to our beliefs." This conviction is foundational to her response when asked how she hopes people will remember her career:

When I lay my head down on the pillow for the last time, I hope people say, "She made a difference for the children and families who she encountered and had the privilege to work with. She cared, she was passionate; she was committed to the work."

Like Rabbi Zusha, Sabina says, "I really want people to think, 'Sabina did everything Sabina could have done.'"

CHAPTER 13

Humanity, Heart, and Praxis

FOUNDATIONS OF COURAGEOUS LEADERSHIP

Sabina Mosso-Taylor

It is often said that it takes a village to raise a child. But who runs the village? Who sets the tone in the village? Before the village can raise a child, they need a leader to plan the village. A leader to consider . . . how to care and provide for the villagers, and a leader who creates an environment that facilitates future leaders.

These are the words of Rabbi Meir Muller, PhD. He is principal of the Cutler Jewish Day School (CJDS) in Columbia, SC. The quote is from a presentation given by Rabbi Meir at the Jewish Early Childhood Education Leadership Institute in New York City. As Morah Sheindal (Meir's wife and colleague at CJDS) shared, his words "illustrate the importance of courageous leadership and the role administrators play in their schools."

Key to Meir's courage is his dedication to doing what is right for children and for the world at large. While he ensures the school's excellence in many areas, his commitment to social justice allows him to take an unequivocal stand to support a more equitable society, which includes his work to help young children understand their role in that process. The CJDS website (www.cjdssc.com/#!our-mission) explains this commitment to justice as one of four pillars of the school's philosophy, which are: (1) active nurturing of child and family, (2) academic rigor with an emphasis on inquiry, (3) praxis/social justice, and (4) Jewish life and living. The website defines praxis as:

> The translating of an idea into practical action [spanning] from having children doing acts of kindness to having children work on root issues of injustice. . . . Facilitating the children's recognition of these opportunities affords the highest goals of learning.

Through Rabbi Meir's leadership, the school acknowledges this conviction as one of the *highest goals of learning*. To ensure the enactment of these goals, Morah Sheindal explained that Meir "refuses to sacrifice the education of the children over the anxiety of adults." The child and the future of our society are at the center of all his decisions. As Sheindal pointed out, "This is who Meir is; he is a *mensch*, a person of integrity." This is the characteristic that is at the foundation of Meir's courageous leadership.

THE CUTLER JEWISH DAY SCHOOL

Meir and Sheindal moved to the Southeastern United States from New York in 1991. They were hired by the Chabad of South Carolina to bring the "joy of Judaism to the Jewish people of South Carolina," a state that even today is only 0.3% Jewish (approximately 3,000 people). The following year, Meir was asked to direct a small preschool being planned for Jewish children in Columbia, SC. In 1992, CJDS opened its doors with 12 Jewish children, housed in the local Jewish Community Center. Now, 22 years later, the school serves 146 children and, thanks to the generosity of the Cutler family and others, will soon expand its structure by 10,000 square feet. The student population also has expanded to become richly diverse, with children who are African American, White, Asian, and Latino/a, and who represent Jewish, Hindu, Muslim, and Christian faiths as well as children whose families do not affiliate with organized religions. Although the school is tuition-based, scholarships are provided for families who cannot afford the yearly cost; this helps to ensure economic diversity.

SO HEARTS AND MINDS CAN SOAR:
TEACHING AS LOVE, KNOWLEDGE, AND ACTION

It is impossible to teach without . . . [a] well-thought-out capacity to love. (Freire, 1998, p. 3)

The school's motto—"so hearts and minds can soar"—captures the philosophy that undergirds the practices at CJDS. Meir's commitment to social justice parallels this philosophy as he puts heart and humanity at the forefront. Drawing on the teachings of educators and Jewish scholars who wrote about true education as inconceivable without a profound commitment to humanity (Darder, 2008; Freire, 1998), Meir leads from the belief that "the only way you can teach love is by loving." Anyone who has met Meir knows this to be true. It begins when he greets each student on the first day of school, welcoming them into a community that creates safe and loving spaces for teaching and learning (Figure 13.1).

Parent of two CJDS students Angie Baum spoke about the school as a place where joy comes from the heart: "Kids are happy. . . . Everyone knows my children's names. It's fluid; feels like everyone is in this school together." Another parent explained, "There is a special feeling knowing that your child is so loved, protected, nurtured, and, not to mention, educated in all facets of life. I really feel that the children of CJDS are a step ahead in life." Parent Scott Smoak agreed:

> Rabbi Meir and the CJDS serve children of diverse backgrounds by nurturing, educating, and loving each child. As a United Methodist pastor and a parent of a 5th-grader, I experience this refreshing and essential aspect of living and working in a community. All persons are special all of the time at CJDS.

Rabbi Meir believes that this ethos lays the foundation for learning, in particular the kind of learning that will help children contribute to a more just world. However, he also recognizes that this kind of love—teaching toward humanity—necessitates the *insight to recognize injustice* and *willingness to take action against it*. Meir knows that creating an educational environment that embraces these ideals requires administrative intention and deliberate steps fueled by commitment, knowledge, heart, and courage.

Figure 13.1. Dr. Muller and children from the Cutler Jewish Day School.

BUILDING A SCHOOL:
THE COURAGE TO HONOR DIVERSITY

> It is Rabbi Meir's leadership that has made inclusiveness [in the school's student population] happen. Many families are knowledgeable in diversity and actually they are there because they believe that this should happen. —CJDS parent

Today CJDS attracts families who value a diverse, inclusive school, focused on issues of social justice as foundational to academic growth. They are drawn to CJDS practices that ensure a diverse student population and equity in education. However, building a school with that foundation did not happen overnight. Meir and Sheindal negotiated a variety of challenges, beginning with their arrival in South Carolina.

Facing Stereotypes Within and Beyond the Jewish Community

Before Meir and Sheindal left New York, some colleagues in the Jewish community worried about how they would be received in a Southern town like Columbia, SC. Given their Orthodox Jewish practice and appearance (Meir wears a yarmulke—a skullcap—and tzitzit, fringes worn by men on their clothing), friends were concerned about attitudes of stereotype and bias they would face without support from a larger orthodox Jewish community.

The need to contradict stereotype was definitely an issue when they arrived. The only exposure (if any) that many South Carolinians had to Jewish people was from movies like *Fiddler on the Roof*. These depictions provided the only portrait (and expectation) they had of anyone who was Jewish. Even some Jewish families expressed concern that, as orthodox Jews, Meir and Sheindal would ask their children to practice Judaism in ways inconsistent with their own family traditions. Mark Crawford, parent of a child at CJDS, described this initial tension:

> As a non-orthodox Jewish family we worried that if we attended the school we would be expected to practice in ways other than we did. It is unheard of in the Jewish community to see those practicing in orthodox ways to be accepting of non-orthodox practices. You just don't see that anywhere. So I was initially skeptical. However, that wasn't the case.

Meir and Sheindal were able to address these challenges because of their open and embracing personalities and also because of their education in Chabad schools. Chabad is an outreach organization that does not let labels (reform, conservative, or orthodox) separate people and aims to serve all within the Jewish community. Chabad schools are situated within the Chassidic group, which is dedicated to teaching how to find balance across differences, particularly within their Jewish faith. Consequently, as Meir explained, their goal "was to set up a school that valued every family regardless of how they expressed their Judaism or religious traditions."

Maintaining One's Own Beliefs While Valuing Others'

When the school first opened, a primary challenge was to stay true to the mission of educating Jewish children while considering whether to enroll children who were not Jewish. Meir described how, in the early days, "we just never thought that [the school's] role was to serve anyone other than the Jewish community." However, the question of admitting non-Jewish children became more visible when non-Jewish teachers were hired and wanted their children to attend the school. Initially, board members questioned this change, and, as Meir explained, "there were regular calls from Jewish colleagues, talking about intermarriage and not following the faith and fear that allowing non-Jewish students into the school would promote both."

Meir struggled not only with the constant questions but also with self-doubt about whether having non-Jewish children would decrease the focus on Judaism, particularly as this was the only Jewish school in the region. He wrestled with these issues, feeling intuitively that a diverse school would be good for everyone, but wondering how to reconcile that with his responsibility to create a space for the education of Jewish children in Columbia: "I worried that Jewish education would be decontextualized. . . . How would I keep the school open to those who want to come and not decrease attractiveness to Jewish families?"

Over and over, the wisdom of Jewish scholars pointed Meir toward an inclusive educational environment where the school's responsibility would be to help teachers and children understand and learn from one another. Among many scholars, Meir drew on the words of Rabbi Hillel, a famous religious leader, who wrote: "That which is hateful to you, do not do to another. That is the whole Law. The rest is commentary. Now go and learn" (*Babylonian Talmud, Tractate Shabbat, Folio 31, front (a) side*). Meir explained the quote:

> It might be interpreted as the golden rule; however, it actually means that it is not good enough just to love everyone . . . to love means to understand the other person, so one must go and learn about their culture, home life, language, lifestyle, etc.

As a result, CJDS broadened its outreach to all children and families. The school is now known for its commitment to valuing diverse experiences, knowledge, and traditions. Today, the impact of this commitment is clear when listening to families describe their experiences. For example, the parent of one of the school's first African American students recalled:

> Although my youngest son is now 18 years old, I can still recall how refreshing it was to find a school that was welcoming of all children . . . Rabbi Meir and his entire staff were . . . committed to include all the children and families as though we were part of an extended family. For the first time in my son's school career—he had attended two local public schools previously, with dire experiences . . . we felt as though we had found a friend and a home.

Similarly, another parent spoke about how CJDS welcomed her son who has Down syndrome:

> From the moment I contacted Rabbi Meir about the school, I felt welcomed. With my child having Down syndrome, there are certainly differences between him and his classmates. His team of educators took the time to meet with me to address specific goals . . . to ensure my son receives the best possible experience daily. Although he has special needs, they have created an environment that does not isolate him but broadens his learning experience. Finding a home here at CJDS has truly been a blessing and I have seen my son's development soar.

THE COURAGE TO LISTEN, LEARN, AND ASSIST

Meir is admired in all arenas in which he interacts for his commitment to listening first, asking thoughtful questions, and then engaging in discussion. Examples of those intentional yet genuine and heartfelt elements in his approach provide a window into this leadership style. Listening first means having the courage to trust others enough to validate what they have to say.

Complaints Are Stories That Need to Be Heard

One of Meir's greatest strengths is that he is a listener. Rather than passing immediate judgment, he listens to understand, seeking the stories behind the concerns. Encouraging families to express their thoughts about school issues takes courage, but Meir sees this approach as connected to attitudinal shifts:

> When an administrator stops looking at families' concerns as complaints but shifts to the position of hearing their stories as a fellow human being who wants the best for their child, one sees that a complaint is an opportunity to offer assistance and guidance.

To establish trust while seeking to understand the root of families' and/ or staff members' concerns, Meir is sure to ask enough questions so that other people have the opportunity to share their thoughts before he makes decisions. Meir asks: "Tell me more about that." "Why do you think that is?" "Can you tell me a little more?" When people are given the opportunity to re-explain and re-articulate, problems become much clearer and, often, the people voicing the problems come to solutions on their own. It is a powerful tool.

Getting the Facts

Another strategy that Meir uses is to seek information so that he can better address concerns. For example, at one point, some families complained because the school accepted Jamie (pseudonym), a child with Down syndrome. They worried that Jamie would take away resources and teaching efforts from the other children. Acknowledging the families' concern, but not giving in to them, Meir collected data by sitting in the classroom, counting the number of times the teacher and the teaching assistant interacted with Jamie. He found that Jamie required less or the same attention as any of the other students. This empirical evidence provided support for Meir's convictions and helped him allay families' concerns. As a result of Jamie's inclusion in the class, everyone benefited. The other children were better prepared to advocate for an inclusive society, and while they served as peer teachers, they were *also learners*, recognizing and benefiting from the skills, knowledge, and perspectives Jamie had to offer.

Willing to Disagree but Not Compromise Goals

One parent, looking back on his child's days at CJDS, remembered the expertise with which Meir balanced points of view:

> He was ever mindful of each concern, always trying to see it with fresh eyes and an open mind, but ultimately willing to disagree when it did not serve the best interest of a child or the school. He is willing to compromise when it is an appropriate thing to do. He does what he can to make everyone happy, but he will take a stand.

Staff members also comment on Meir's ability to validate viewpoints while holding onto his basic convictions. Kelly Stanton, the school's assistant principal, spoke about Meir's diplomatic approach:

> He always respects us for our knowledge but questions and challenges us, too. It's never him telling us what we should do. He always asks questions.

He may say, "I disagree," but it is always because he believes so strongly about something. He is very diplomatic.

PROFESSIONAL DEVELOPMENT:
THE COURAGE TO FOCUS ON EQUITY

Meir's approach to professional development embodies the words of Mukhopadhyay, Henze, and Moses (2013), who wrote that "it is especially critical . . . that proactive leaders create positive conditions for interaction and understanding among diverse groups" (p. 213). Meir creates these conditions through the choices he makes when engaging staff in professional study that focuses on equity issues.

Book Study

Reading and discussing professional literature are mainstays of professional development at CJDS. Over the years, Meir has led the faculty in exploring a range of professional books, most recently, *Multicultural Teaching in the Early Childhood Classroom: Approaches, Strategies, and Tools* (Souto-Manning, 2013). Not only did this book serve to generate a rich conversation about ways in which faculty and staff could further engage in critically multicultural teaching practices, support their students, and increase multicultural understanding, but Meir was able to invite the author to visit and lead a staff discussion.

Sometimes books are chosen to help staff talk to one another across racial, religious, and other differences; one particularly helpful text was *The Essential Conversation: What Parents and Teachers Can Learn from Each Other* (Lawrence-Lightfoot, 2004). Reading this book helped create a safe space for teachers to hear one another's perspectives, leading to new insights. In one of many examples, teachers discussed family involvement. The book created an opening for one teacher to explain that, just because a family may not express interest in school in the same way that teachers might expect, this does not mean there is a lack of family concern for the child's education. This is one of many conversations supported by carefully selected texts that helped teachers broaden their own lenses to be more culturally responsive to students and families.

Allocating Funds So That Students Can Benefit
from Insider Perspectives

Another way that Meir involves staff in learning about more equitable teaching is by allocating funding to prioritize visits by people who can provide insider perspectives about social justice issues and/or cultural awareness. As a result, the children at CJDS have had opportunities to learn from civil rights activists, people who are differently able, speakers of languages other than English, and African dancers and drummers. Although Meir is quick to explain that one person does not speak for an entire group, visitors provide rich opportunities for the students to engage in conversations that push their thinking in important ways.

Supporting Professional Growth While Respecting Teachers' Time

Meir provides opportunities for formal after-school professional development, but he understands that it is sometimes difficult to engage in professional learning after a long day of teaching. More often, he engages staff in conversations during the day and provides them with his undivided attention when they have questions or want to talk through an idea or issue.

One of Meir's most appreciated professional development strategies is his Monday memo. These weekly notes to staff are famous in the school's community for informing, urging, and sharing ideas in support of teachers' ongoing reflection and growth. Each memo highlights concepts that Meir would like the staff to consider, often focusing on issues related to social justice. Meir described a particular Monday memo in which he asked staff members to engage all students in critical discussions about civil rights. As a result, 3-year-olds to 5th-graders had deepened curricular experiences compared with previous years. When asked why the lessons were improved, one of the teachers told Meir, "Because you talked so much about it in the Monday memo, we knew it was something that we needed to do and do well."

ADAM'S STORY:
COURAGE TO USE ADMINISTRATIVE POWER WISELY

While Rabbi Meir practices justice as a way of life, one story is particularly helpful in illustrating the range of strategies he uses to listen, learn, inform, and take a stand. It is the story of Adam (pseudonym), an intersex child, who was born with both male and female genitalia and hormones. Adam was adopted as a toddler, but a few months prior to adoption (at 16 months of age), the Department of Social Services and a group of physicians decided that the child should undergo sex-assignment surgery, choosing the female gender (the Southern Poverty Law Center currently is representing the family in a lawsuit to contest this decision).

The family began to raise the child as a girl named Rachel (pseudonym), eventually enrolling her when she was 4 years old at CJDS. In the years that followed, as male hormones became more dominant, the child began to identify as a boy. His parents supported him when, at 10 years of age, he came to identify himself as Adam. This meant that, after knowing him for 6 years as Rachel, Adam's CJDS classmates were asked to regard him as a boy and call him Adam.

For Meir, the decision to support Adam and his family was non-negotiable. At the same time, he recognized that there might be families and staff members who would feel otherwise. He wrestled with the thought that families might leave the school because he supported Adam's transition, but ultimately he "was prepared to lose families should they not be satisfied with the decision." Meir said, "It was that clear to me. If [teachers and families] don't have the courage to stand up to something so basic, then there is a mismatch between what they believe and what the school stands for."

However, Meir did not come to this decision without doing his homework. It was important to obtain facts to understand the situation from medical and psychological perspectives. He and Sheindal (Adam's Judaic studies teacher) sought the insights of a doctor, who provided important information that would allow Meir to talk knowledgeably with others. Then Meir considered the concerns that families, children, and teachers might express. He knew that some families would want advice about how to discuss Adam's transition with their own children. So, in a letter to families (Figure 13.2), he provided language they could use when discussing the issue with their children. The letter illustrates the way Meir used knowledge, compassion, and the pillars of the school to educate families and put minds at ease.

In considering how to support Adam and the children at CJDS, Meir and Sheindal met with the students and invited their questions. They anticipated that some of the younger students would ask about hair and clothes, and older students would ask about anatomical differences. Meir recalled, "We were interested in the children's questions and looked forward to discussing this with the children and families."

As anticipated, the students were very respectful and asked excellent questions. They were more concerned with forgetting to call him Adam or that they would mix up gender pronouns: "What if I forget and call him Rachel?" "What if we say 'she' instead of 'he'?" Meir reminded the students that they might forget at times but that Adam would help remind them and that, as a school, they would all work to remember to honor his new name and identity.

As a result, there was an outpouring of support from the majority of the families. In fact, one of the only concerns expressed was about which bathroom Adam would use, but as Meir explained, "it was more curiosity and showed no disrespect or lack of support." One parent summed up the feelings of many:

I remember receiving the letter and thinking, this is exactly why I am so happy that I am here at CJDS. This is the kind of message I want my children to hear from their administrator. He took a stance that wasn't alienating,

Figure 13.2. Rabbi Meir's letter to parents: Building knowledge for families and children in support of Adam.

Dear Families,

I met with the _____ family this morning and they have shared information about their daughter Rachel. Rachel was born with both male and female hormones. In fact, one out of every 1,500 babies is born with anatomy or chromosomal patterns that don't fit typical definitions of male or female. After consultation with numerous noted health care professionals, input from Rachel, and much research, the family has decided to raise Rachel as a boy.

Rachel has chosen to be called Adam and should be treated as any other boy.

Many families often look for words to use with their children when new situations arise. Here are two possible ways to discuss this topic with your child:

1. You can explain to your child that this is a decision that the family has made and it is our job to do everything we can to support the family.

2. If in the past you have explained to your child that the distinction between boys and girls is the type of genitals they have, then you can add the following new language, which is more accurate. Hormones (a chemical) that a baby has even before they are born help form the person. Some hormones help with brain function, some with how we grow, and some determine if we will be a boy or girl. Some people are born with both girl and boy hormones and they must make a decision if they want to be treated as a boy or girl. When Adam was born, the doctors decided he should be a girl, when the _____ family adopted him, they continued to raise him as a girl, but now that he is older, it has become clear that he wants to be raised as a boy. From now on, we will call Rachel, Adam, and treat him as a boy.

As you know, one of the four pillars of our school is that of actively nurturing every child and family. This pillar is based on Jewish tradition and the NAEYC Code of Ethics. We look forward to welcoming Adam to school tomorrow and supporting him and his family in any way we can.

If you have any questions, please know that I am always available to assist in speaking to you or your child about this topic.

Rabbi Meir Muller

but rather influential. He helped everyone see why this was so important to do—to support [Adam] and his family. He appealed to the human side of the issue. This was an example of how he teaches through leadership.

Meir described how the school's *active nurturing* pillar guided him as he worked to safeguard Adam's transition:

I intentionally included the word "active" in this pillar because nurturing is not just accepting the status quo, giving a hug now and then, but active [nurturing] means doing something for people who need help. A school leader by definition has power and that power needs to be actively directed in providing the best for every child and family.

Adam's father believes that it was the socially just environment at CJDS that allowed Adam to feel comfortable enough to make the change. He appreciated Meir's recognition of the complexities connected to bias and misinformation and explained: "Adam was resilient enough to make this change because the CJDS was so comfortable for him." Through it all, Rabbi Meir did not compromise his support for Adam and his family, nor did he ignore the concerns of families in his school. The bottom line is that he had the courage and the wisdom to stand up knowledgeably against heteronormative views and create a space where Adam could be himself.

CONCLUDING THOUGHTS

Rabbi Meir's ability to take a courageous, unapologetic stand for justice is, in his words, "a lifelong process." In that quest, Meir *lives to become* (Freire, 1970), a process that has deep roots in his family and heritage. Morah Sheindal explained:

Meir comes from a very strong family. . . . He felt very, very loved and his grandparents were around. He's the grandchild of [Holocaust] survivors and I think that on some level does contribute to Meir's makeup. . . . He grew up in a climate of discussion about education overshadowed by one of the most gruesome periods in world history.

Insights gained as the grandchild of Holocaust survivors underscore Meir's conviction that injustices will continue unless we take a stand to stop them. Knowledge of this history sharpened the lens through which he recognizes injustices and considers his responsibility to effect change. Meir also attributes his rabbinical studies and graduate work to his commitment to caring, thoughtful reflection, and listening to others' stories in the interest of creating a more equitable world. Meir explained:

> I have a rabbinical degree; in my studies I was taught about listening and caring, and I knew about people being oppressed from Jewish history, but I had no idea about teaching. Through my lens of Jewish philosophy and history, topics such as equity pedagogy and inquiry-based learning impacted my work at the CJDS. These provided a theoretical base that helped bolster my ability to act in more courageous ways.

Rabbi Meir Muller's sense of responsibility regarding praxis (knowledge + action) is foundational as he uses the power entrusted to him. His goal is to guide teachers in helping young children develop as world citizens who can recognize, reflect on, and challenge oppression while embracing diversity in its many forms. At the heart of the work is his strong belief that humanity and mind must work together as the real work of praxis and the highest goal of learning.

CHAPTER 14

Vision, Voice, and Action

CREATING PATHWAYS TO SOCIAL JUSTICE

Nathaniel Bryan, Lamar Johnson, Dywanna Smith,
Brittany Garvin, and Anthony Broughton

Ms. Cecelia Gordon Rogers is the principal at Charleston Development Academy, a predominantly African American public school in Charleston, SC. In the face of opposition, Ms. Rogers (Figure 14.1) courageously advocated on behalf of Black children, convincing school district officials to support the academic needs of historically marginalized Charleston County students.

According to Michie (2009), education is a site of both struggle and hope. It is a site of struggle because of the pressure felt by educators as a result of biased information that permeates in- and out-of-school contexts. Education is a site of hope because it has the potential to enable educators to look toward a promising future that allows them to view the world from a newfound perspective. Many times, hope comes to life through the encouragement of those individuals we consider to be courageous leaders. Reverend Dr. Martin Luther King Jr. described such leaders as individuals who stand firm not only in moments of comfort and convenience, but also at times of challenge and controversy. This is an accurate description of Ms. Cecelia Gordon Rogers.

In this chapter, we share Ms. Rogers's story as a courageous school administrator who made a difference in the lives of young children from culturally and linguistically diverse backgrounds. We share examples from Principal Cecelia Rogers's personal and professional experiences that specifically highlight innovative administrative strategies in early childhood education. These strategies include her collaborative efforts and the social action networks she used to explicitly address issues of social and educational injustice.

One of the situated representations of how Ms. Rogers challenged such injustices was the social justice curriculum she put in place. Through this and other strategies, she widened the table so that many people could sit together. Ms.

Figure 14.1. Ms. Cecilia Rogers, dedicated to the children of Charleston.

Rogers emphasizes that these strategies are truly important if school administrators are serious about providing equitable learning experiences and safe, nurturing environments that encourage excellence and character building in order to promote the personal and social development of motivated, responsible, and caring students from historically marginalized communities.

INTRODUCING CHARLESTON DEVELOPMENT ACADEMY

During a 3-day visit to Charleston Development Academy (CDA), we had opportunities to interview Ms. Rogers and members of her staff about their roles in creating pathways to social justice. Based on those interviews, we organized this chapter around three broad themes that reflect deliberate strategies used by Ms. Rogers to address issues of race, class, and education through her administrative process:

- The establishment and enactment of a collective vision
- The activation of voice
- The execution of actions

ESTABLISHING AND ENACTING A VISION

To historically situate the courage of Ms. Rogers, we consider the actions of an important Charleston-based civil rights activist. Known to many as the

Mother of the Civil Rights Movement, Septima P. Clark, an educator and activist, was courageous during some of the most turbulent times in what was becoming the "desegregated" Charleston. Although *Brown v. Board of Education* (U.S. Supreme Court, 1954) recently had directed schools to integrate at deliberate speed, like most schools in Southern states, those in Charleston County were slow to adhere. Despite these slow responses, Black and White children often were bused to new sites and gradually forced to integrate. Unfortunately, while this was happening, Black teachers and administrators at the formerly segregated schools lost their jobs *en masse* as schools were closed down (Foster, 1997). In response, Clark fought to speed up the integration process for Black students and teachers in Charleston County School District (CCSD) (Foster, 1997). This courageous act and Clark's tireless commitment to educational equity resulted in death threats.

Ms. Cecelia Rogers

Ms. Cecelia Rogers embodies Clark's courageous spirit as she continues to carry out Clark's legacy to support the education of Black children in Charleston County. Ms. Rogers explained, "Having been a person of the [Civil Rights] Movement, it is hard to support the status quo." Responding to educational inequities as a result of her strong commitment to the Civil Rights Movement, Ms. Rogers led a team of educational stakeholders with a shared vision to ameliorate the schooling experiences of young children from Charleston's west side community. They did this through the establishment of a school that focused on providing a safe and nurturing environment that encouraged excellence and character-building initiatives in order to promote the personal and social development of motivated, responsible, and caring students.

What is interesting about Ms. Rogers's story is that she neither wanted to become an educator, nor did she see herself leading the charge to establish a school and serve as its administrator. She started her career as a stay-at-home mom who spent time volunteering in her children's classrooms. These classroom experiences became catalysts for her love and passion for working with children from culturally and linguistically diverse backgrounds and thereafter inspired her to pursue postsecondary education.

While attending the College of Charleston to pursue a degree in Elementary Education, Ms. Rogers worked as a teacher's assistant. Once she completed her degree, she became a full-time certified public elementary school teacher. Because of her commitment as a freedom fighter in schools, someone who worked against the oppression of the historically disadvantaged, many school administrators encouraged her to become a principal. Ms. Rogers explained, "I never wanted to become a principal. In fact, when I was encouraged by administrators who trained me, I always told them no." However, the word "no" that frequently came out of her mouth contradicted the courageous "yes" that was in her heart. As a result, she later pursued a master's degree in Educational Administration from the Citadel, South Carolina's military college. Ms. Rogers studied under Dr. Dilligard and Mr. Mack, district administrators in Charleston County. She said that these individuals taught her what it meant to be fully committed to working equitably for children, understanding the production of transformative knowledge, and recognizing that people need to rehumanize themselves by undoing oppressive structures that interrupt such knowledge (King, 2005). After finishing her degree, leading her church's education committee, and spending years imagining a vision to open a public school, Ms. Rogers was hired to serve as the school administrator for the Charleston Developmental Academy.

A School Where Minds Are Developed, Characters Built, and Futures Engineered

Established in 2003, CDA is now a high-performing school accredited by the National Association for the Education of Young Children. It is located in Charleston's west side in a building named in honor of Septima P. Clark. Ms. Rogers described CDA as a school where minds are developed, characters are built, and futures are engineered. According to South Carolina School Report Card data, CDA has maintained *above-average* to *good* school ratings since 2009, consistently exceeding the ratings of most schools with similar characteristics in the district and surrounding communities. Although established to address the educational needs of students from Charleston's west side, CDA attracts students from all over Charleston and its surrounding communities. Serving approximately 179 students in pre-K to 8th grade, CDA has become the little secret about which everyone is starting to talk.

Although the school has thrived under her leadership, Ms. Rogers insists that she could never take full credit for the establishment and success of the school, because the vision of CDA was the result of tremendous community collaboration. Clergy members, community leaders, and families came together to share ideas about ways to implement that vision. However, the courageous acts of Ms. Rogers continue to keep the school focused on its original mission and purpose: to improve the academic and social performance of children by decreasing student suspensions and expulsions.

Ms. Rogers insisted that "schools seemingly were neither meeting the academic nor social needs of the community children and as a result parents did not know what to do." She further admitted that the types of schooling children were experiencing at that time were connected to larger sociopolitical issues associated with the gentrification of low-income communities. Ms. Rogers reflected:

What was going on at that time was a paradigm shift in the community . . . a cultural shift in the community, a population shift. . . . The community, in 1999, when we began to entertain the idea of establishing a school, began to see shifts in community demographics, and we see more evidence of that today. Now, in 2014, there are so many high-rise buildings, so much property that has gone to other people who were not part of the community. There was so much property around the Ebenezer AME Church community area that we allowed to slip out of our hands. And all the suspensions and expulsions children were experiencing at that time were directly connected to this larger goal of gentrification.

Ms. Minnie Parker, a retired educator who taught in public schools for 47 years and now works at CDA, corroborated Ms. Rogers's assertions, suggesting the school was needed not only to disrupt the disproportional suspension and expulsion rates among Black children, but to decrease the number of Black students who were assigned to special education.

Current research suggests that Black (and Latino/a) students are suspended and expelled from schools at far greater rates than their White counterparts. Such removals from schools start as early as preschool (Elias, 2013; Howard, 2014). In addition, Ford (2013) documented that Black students are assigned to special education classrooms at disproportionately high rates. Combining excessive assignment to special education with excessive suspension and expulsion rates is the start of what many scholars have referred to as the school-to-prison pipeline (Elias, 2013; Ford, 2013; Noguera, 2003): the systematic funneling of students, mainly Black and Latino/a, out of public school settings into the criminal justice system (Alexander, 2010; Elias, 2013). For Black students, this is the beginning of the "New Jim Crow" or the mass incarceration of Black people in society writ large (Alexander, 2010).

Ms. Rogers remembered when teachers were part of the community; they knew all of the children and their families and had a vested interest in their well-being. Suspending and expelling children from schools and assigning them to special education were not valid options then. Ms. Rogers lamented that this is no longer the case in many Charleston communities. In her efforts to interrupt the suspension, expulsion, and special education pipeline, she chose to arm parents with strategies to advocate for their young children.

As we listened to Ms. Rogers reflect on her early experiences as a student, we were reminded of Foster's (1997) groundbreaking *Black Teachers on Teaching*, in which she documented how Black teachers, during segregation, were part of communities in such a way that left a lasting impact on Black communities. Foster (1997) explained that Black teachers had a strong concern for Black children and their families, which could not be replaced by any other group of teachers.

Black teachers were what Morrell (2004) called "community teachers," or individuals who become part of the community in which they teach. Black teachers invested their time in, and demonstrated their love and care for, not only Black students, but other children from a range of racial and ethnic backgrounds. These teachers helped to positively transform students in a way that allowed them to see the importance and value of their multiple identities and cultures.

Ms. Rogers was adamant about seeking avenues to better educate children from Charleston's west side. The solution she came to was the establishment of CDA as a beacon of educational justice for children who had been historically disenfranchised. In August 2003, CDA opened its door to roughly 75 students. Since then, its teachers have educated a population of students who are part of a community unjustly characterized by violence and illegal drug activities. Since its inception, the school has included additional grade levels enabling it to enroll more students. However, if Ms. Rogers and others had not fought laboriously—attending school board and district-level staff meetings and activating their voices to start and maintain CDA for the community—such a dream could never have been realized.

ACTIVATING VOICE

Although a well-established school, CDA still experiences challenges that are no different than those of other urban public schools, particularly schools working against educational inequities. Noguera (2003) suggested that public schools in urban centers still face challenges that hinder their abilities to meet the academic and social needs of the students they serve, mainly Black and Latino/a students. Ms. Rogers worked against such challenges by being vocal about her concerns at the district level and with community members who had the agency and/or power to support and effect change. For example, at the school district level, she advocated for a pre-K program not supported in the original school charter. She felt that the program was an essential component to the success of the school and its students. Such a program would enable her teachers to engage in early education with young children from the community. Researchers have long suggested that early childhood education fosters academic and social success in schools (Barnett, 2004; Souto-Manning, 2013).

Advocating for a pre-K program was an uphill battle for Ms. Rogers and her team. Promises made by district-level administrators relative to integrating pre-K into CDA were never kept. Similarly, meetings initiated by district-level administrators to discuss the possible integration of a pre-K program were often canceled. CDA was consistently excluded from federal grants that were designed to improve pre-K programs. When the district was awarded grant funding to support pre-K initiatives, CDA was not given any part of the funds to support its pre-K plans. Funds were often granted to schools serving more affluent populations as opposed to programs such as CDA's.

Maintaining her professionalism and grace under fire, Ms. Rogers regrouped and revisited her original plans to integrate a pre-K program. She placed parents on the front line of advocacy. Those parents' voices proved to be instrumental in CDA's finally being granted permission to integrate pre-K into its programming.

The courage and commitment it takes to persevere with actions such as these should not be understated. Traditionally, school administrators who worked against a biased status quo in this way were in danger of losing their positions in top-down organizational structures. Ms. Rogers knew and faced the realities that:

> Jobs will have to be sacrificed, positions of prestige and status given up, favors forfeited. . . . When one forcefully challenges the racist system, one cannot, at the same time, expect that system to reward [individuals] or even treat [individuals] comfortably. (Ture & Hamilton, 1967, p. 15)

Ms. Rogers's voice has encouraged Charleston's longest-serving mayor, Joseph P. Riley, to allot space on nearby city property to establish a new school building, since the school's current location is no longer conducive to meeting its needs. For example, more space is needed to increase the number of students admitted to the school, particularly at the early childhood level. Currently, there is an active waiting list of students, and the number of applicants continues to increase. Although the city has granted the land, Ms. Rogers and her staff still await funding to start the building process.

In his 2012 State of the City Address, Mayor Riley applauded Ms. Rogers for achieving national recognition for student academic achievement and also lauded her for her persistence and courage in approaching city officials to grant land to build a new school. Ms. Rogers admits that receiving the land was a great feat for the school. She noted:

> It took courage to meet with city officials and the Mayor to ask for such a large favor. However, I found out it became easy when I invited officials to the school to see what my staff and I were doing with the young children. It was also easy when I took my students to public events and [the officials] saw the potential they possessed.

School administrators are often not prepared in educational leadership programs to take courageous political steps to engage politicians in school-level business as Ms. Rogers did.

TAKING ACTION

As we toured the school, observed classrooms, and listened to shared narratives, we were particularly interested in initiatives in the newly integrated pre-K–3 programs. There were several notable actions that distinguished CDA from other schools. Ms. Rogers, her faculty, and staff clearly were working against the status quo as they spoke passionately about a culturally centered early childhood curriculum, positive redirection as a method of school discipline, and shared documents supporting what we considered *Ubuntu* leadership—their potential drawing from a Bantu term used to express the notion of a universal bond of sharing that connects all humanity (Boutte, López-Robertson, & Powers-Costello, 2011). Using this concept, every staff member is considered a part of the school's *Kondaa*, or leadership team (Carruthers, King, & Watkins, 2013). We were extremely impressed with Ms. Rogers's intentional hiring of individuals we refer to as "academic elders and eldresses," experienced veteran teachers who came out of retirement to teach and/or volunteer to assist CDA students.

Ubuntu Leadership

Ms. Rogers admitted that leading a school, particularly one that addresses educational inequity, requires the school administrator to take an approach where everyone in the building is humanized and/or seen as a leader, and where leadership roles are shared to support a thriving community. This is a highlight of *Ubuntu* leadership. Ms. Rogers explained that the only way to help teachers and staff members recognize the need for and join in the development of a vision that worked against the status quo was to help them recognize their potential and take ownership of their professional strengths to benefit the school community. With respect to fostering leaders who are agents of change, she noted:

> When you ask people to share, people will commit. I share my leadership role, because it is not about me. Everyone must be responsible and accountable for preparing students.

Ms. Minnie Parker praised Ms. Rogers's leadership style, explaining that when she first came to teach at CDA, Ms. Rogers encouraged every teacher to take on a leadership role by sharing their gifts and talents. Ms. Parker noted, "Ms. Rogers encouraged us to take the vision and run with it for the good of children and everyone we work with." Ms. Georgie Brown, a retired educator of 36 years who started at CDA in 2010, sees the benefit of Ms. Rogers's leadership style in classrooms because "teachers engage in teamwork and are not afraid to work together."

The spirit of *Ubuntu* leadership was evident throughout our tour of the school. Ms. Ardmease Cunningham-Mitchell, the school's parent liaison, provided explicit details regarding the curriculum used in classrooms across grade levels. In our experiences with traditional schools, most parental liaisons are unaware of specific classroom curricula. It is clear that *Ubuntu* leadership is the driving force at CDA and is foundational for not only creating a culturally centered school environment, but also for fostering a culturally centered curriculum.

Culturally Centered Early Childhood Curriculum

In 1933, Carter G. Woodson wrote:

> The educational system as it has developed both in Europe and America [is] an antiquated process which does not hit the mark even in the case of the needs of the White man himself. If the White man wants to hold on to it, let him do so; but [Black people] . . . should develop and carry out a program of [their] own. (p. 12)

Ms. Rogers sees CDA and its culturally centered curriculum as such a program because, like Woodson, she feels Black students need a schooling experience different from the schooling experiences of other children, so that they will value their culture. This culturally centered perspective aligns with the notion of culturally relevant pedagogy (Ladson-Billings, 1995a, 1995b) through which teachers are expected to ensure student academic success, use cultural referents to encourage cultural competencies, and ensure students' sociopolitical awareness.

While observing in a kindergarten classroom, we watched the teacher use images of Black professionals from magazines to engage students in critical conversations about who could serve in professional capacities. Students began to make cultural connections, sharing information relative to family members. Ms. Parker explained that before children can progress in school and life, they must know from where they came; their histories and heritages must be present throughout all aspects of their schooling experience. Furthermore, several researchers (Ladson-Billings, 2009; Milner, 2010, 2014; Souto-Manning, 2013) have asserted that when teachers use such culturally relevant and transformative teaching methods, they provide students with counternarratives that debunk traditional and mainstream ideologies regarding whose culture counts in classrooms and in society. This is an important consideration for young Black children who often are taught to devalue and decenter their culture in traditional early childhood classrooms (Boutte et al., 2011).

Ms. Rogers added that to ensure cultural balance, she constantly adjusts the curriculum to ensure that school experiences value and honor students' cultural experiences. Ms. Rogers provided an example from her analyses of writing test score data, which she used to justify curricular adjustments:

> You know children start testing in 3rd grade and each year I got test scores back I noticed students were not scoring as well as they could in writing. Some were scoring at the exemplary mark, others at the proficient, and some at the basic/below-basic category. They were receiving low scores in voice. . . . This data was suggesting that Black children cannot write, but what people do not understand is that Black children are inundated with so many writing voices; they cannot hear and develop their own writing voice. We don't teach in a way that they can develop their voices. So, I hired a teacher, Dr. Kaye, to help our children develop their writing voice by using cultural notions they understand and about which they can write. Dr. Kaye allows the children to use photography to capture their cultural experiences and then she allows them to write about them.

Further, Ms. Rogers spoke about cultural experiences in which CDA students participate that continue to offer opportunities that build on the notion of a culturally centered curriculum, such as partaking in African drumming conducted by an African drummer from the Charleston community. The students also have opportunities to attend many of the local Black cultural events, including the Moja Arts Festival, an annual cultural celebration highlighting Black and Caribbean art.

Positive Redirection as a Method for School Discipline

Ms. Rogers does not believe that suspension and expulsion are effective options. Instead she believes in positive redirection whereby school administrators show students love and care from the outset. When serious disciplinary issues arise among students, she involves teachers, parents, and administrators. This perspective echoes what Milner and Tenore (2010) consider culturally relevant school and classroom management practices, useful in helping school administrators and teachers understand issues of equity where "a caring community of family members is created" (p. 560).

The Academic Elders as Teachers and Volunteers

In the Afrocentric tradition, elders and eldresses are respected in the community for the wisdom they possess (King, 2005). For Ms. Rogers, drawing on this source of community wisdom is a vital part of CDA. She observed that "to have veteran [teachers] collaborate with less experienced [teachers] is both biblical and

Afrocentric. It's biblical and Afrocentric because the elders know the way and they are responsible for teaching the way to the younger generations."

Ms. Brown, a veteran teacher, also sees the benefits of having veteran teachers at CDA:

> When the children who attend school here see veteran Black teachers, particularly those who come from the same background they do, it encourages them to excel. When they see them in front of the classroom and they have poise, professionalism, and education, they [students] want to do the same things. I love it because when the children see me read, they want to read. When they see me take interest in books, they want to purchase the books.

She even recalls the impact Black elders and eldresses had on her life when she attended public schools:

> I know this may sound funny, but I remember how my former Black teachers impacted me. When I was a small child, I wanted to become a teacher because my teacher smelled good. When my students enter the classroom and say, "Oh Ms. Brown, you smell good," it reminds me of my childhood days when I would say I wanted to be like my teacher.

At the time of this writing, few research studies have explored the impact that having elders and eldresses in school classrooms might have on students' academic and social achievement. Currently, there are 11 elders and eldresses at CDA, and most of them teach at the early childhood level.

For teacher recruitment, Ms. Rogers used nontraditional strategies: hearsay and word of mouth. For example, she listened to the stories of parents in the communities who spoke of impactful teachers. Additionally, Ms. Rogers drew from a pool of exceptional teachers from the community whom she knew well. She suggested that this is essential to meeting the needs of the community, to the education of children, and to carrying out the goal of building on the cultural heritage in Black communities. She noted:

> Black children need to see people who look like them in classrooms . . . people who are conscientious and genuinely have their interest at heart. That is why recruiting veteran teachers is important. Furthermore, we have lost the talents of effective Black teachers throughout generations and we need to hold on to those who embody those talents as long as we can.

Recruiting teachers in such a way is a courageous act, which defies one-dimensional traditional teacher recruitment methods. While teachers can be considered highly qualified based on credentials, Ms. Rogers proposed that they also must be highly qualified based on classroom practice and knowledge of children's cultures.

CONCLUSION

The strategies presented in this chapter are not exhaustive, and there is a plethora of other examples where Ms. Rogers demonstrated courage by implementing a vision, activating her voice, and taking socially just actions. In this chapter, we simply offer a glimpse into the administrative practices employed by a courageous leader to make schooling more equitable for young children who have been historically left out of or marginalized from opportunities for educational success.

CHAPTER 15

The Courage to Lead

STRATEGIES FOR ACTION

Vivian Maria Vasquez, Susi Long, and Mariana Souto-Manning

> The classroom with all its limitations remains a location of possibility. In that field of possibility we have the opportunity to labor for freedom, to demand of ourselves and our comrades, an openness of mind and heart that allows us to face reality even as we collectively imagine ways to move beyond boundaries, to transgress. This is education as the practice of freedom.
>
> —hooks, 1994, p. 207

The leaders whose practices are shared in this book see early childhood education as a location of possibility in the practice of freedom. They demand of themselves and others an openness of mind and heart as they work to support colleagues in facing realities and moving beyond boundaries. They focus on negotiating spaces for teachers to "make it possible for students to become themselves" (Horton & Freire, 1990, p. 181), for students to know that they and their communities represent a rich past and a dynamic present, and that they can look toward a hopeful future. At the same time, they insist that multicultural education goes beyond mere "tropes for policies and practices" (Castagno, 2014, p. 4), recognizing that hopeful futures will not be realized without addressing injustices that prevail in schools and society. They are very aware that open hearts must be anchored in firm commitments to call out inequities and move deliberately to disrupt and dismantle them.

While it seems obvious that these actions would be obligations of any educational administrator in a democratic society, the reality is that they are not. For such actions to become fundamental to schooling everywhere, we need courageous leaders who can identify places where our democracy fails and lead others to question enculturated views of rightness as associated primarily with English-only, White, middle-class, heterosexual, Christian ways of being. Even though we live in a richly diverse country, these deeply embedded views provide some of the most significant barriers to meeting the needs of our nation's students and humanizing the world in which we live (Ingersoll & Strong, 2011; Lazar, 2011; Sue, 2015).

This distressing reality is punctuated by the fact that culturally relevant, social justice, and humanizing pedagogies have long been identified as educational pathways to promoting a critical consciousness in all children and to fostering greater academic achievement (Baldwin, 1963; Banks, 1995; Blackburn, 2011; Du Bois, 1903; Freire, 1970; Gay, 2010; Ladson-Billings, 1995a; Nieto, 1999; Paris, 2012; Woodson, 1933). This is especially important for children who are stereotyped, degraded, or made invisible by curricula and teaching practices, but ultimately enriches the educational experiences of *all* children. And yet, in educational institutions throughout the country, these practices are the exception rather than the rule. In the words of anti-bias early childhood educators Louise Derman-Sparks, Debbie LeeKeenan, and John Nimmo (2015), "too many early childhood programs [continue to] ground their environment, curriculum, teaching styles, and language in the dominant culture" (p. 11), and too few teachers and administrators have supported opportunities for critical self- and institutional examination, questioning privilege, and challenging disprivilege.

The persistence of this standard can create further blinders that may keep us from recognizing inequities, such as the over-referral of African American boys to special education (Kunjufu, 2005), the under-referral of students of Color to talented and gifted programs (Ford, 2013), the eradication of home languages and literacies when they could be valued as essential assets (Martínez, 2010), curricula that focus primarily on European American histories and contributions (Gay, 2014; Ladson-Billings, 1994; King & Swartz, 2014), texts and practices that focus on heteronormative beliefs about gender and sexual orientation (Cowhey, 2005; Hermann-Wilmarth & Ryan, 2013), and the imposition of systemwide school reforms based on standardized testing rather than on countering curricular and pedagogical privileging.

The administrators whose leadership practices are featured here have a strong sense of responsibility to use the power entrusted in them to challenge these practices and policies. They are committed to building their own and their colleagues' insights in ways that remove the blinders that mask inequities. Recognizing that the young children of today will become adults who ultimately will make decisions that will guide every institution within our society, they urge us to understand that this is not only possible, but it is imperative if we are serious in our professed desire to create a more equitable world.

BEING COURAGEOUS:
PRINCIPLES, STRATEGIES, AND ACTION

Whether it is putting their own vulnerability on the line to join teachers in examining beliefs, practices, and policies; insisting on the rights of children and families who have historically been marginalized, ignored, stereotyped, and/ or disparaged; publishing rebuttals highlighting the inequities of standardized tests; refusing to rigidly interpret mandates; or informing themselves to more knowledgeably support others, the administrators in this book stand up for the rights of diverse learners and their families. Their acts of courage reverberate through their stories. Each chapter makes clear that these leaders do the work because of clearly articulated principles that guide them. We offer a compilation of these principles as interrelated elements in a toolkit for social justice leadership (Table 15.1).

To enact the principles outlined in Table 15.1, the leaders in this book use a range of strategies grounded in focused goals. They do so recognizing that change does not happen overnight; that the process is rife with tensions, frustrations, and self-doubt; that mistakes made along the way require careful and critical reflection; and that patience and respite are necessary in order to reboot and rebuild. The goals to which these administrators are committed help them focus, define, and sustain socially just and culturally relevant leadership in their own settings. Their goals are foundational to everyday practices in which they engage as courageous leaders committed to equity. The goals and strategies they employ to reach them are outlined in Table 15.2.

AN INVITATION TO STAND UP AND STEP OUT

One isn't necessarily born with courage but one is born with potential. Without courage, we cannot practice any other virtue with consistency. We can't be kind, true, merciful, generous, or honest.
—Maya Angelou (1988)

This collection of stories began with the legacy of early childhood leader Bessie Gray, whose courage allowed her to practice kindness, truthfulness, mercy, generosity, and honesty. Ms. Gray defined courage as "stepping out of the box . . . when you don't know what the end result will be." Like Ms. Gray, each of the administrators in this book stood up and stepped out even when uncertain where their steps might lead. They stepped out because they believe in children, families, and teachers, because they know that there is much we must do to challenge and conquer the biases that histories have so carefully taught. They stepped out in respectful and resourceful ways, taking seriously their responsibility to play a key role in embracing "the practice of freedom" (hooks, 1994, p. 207) through education.

We know, however, that the real courage to stand up and step out comes when administrators admit to, understand, and speak out against practices and policies that have become so normalized in educational systems that those not negatively impacted by them often walk right by without notice, enacting their privilege. Real courage is shown when leaders help others acknowledge that educational structures continue to ensure success for some at the expense of others. The administrators in this book show this courage in insightful, fallible, and thoughtful ways. We urge you to join them. Our children deserve no less.

Table 15.1. A Toolkit of Principles for Social Justice Leadership

Principles for Social Justice Leadership	Requiring Courage to:
Recognize injustices; acknowledge their stronghold in educational institutions; commit to disrupting and dismantling them.	• Identify biases (your own, others', institutional) based on race, language, nationality, ethnicity, sexual orientation, gender identification, income, dis/ability, religion, etc.; understand how those biases perpetuate educational inequities; take action to change them. • Inform yourself to understand the sociopolitical contexts of early childhood education, including histories that led to the "education debt" (Ladson-Billings, 2006) owed today. • Refuse common justifications and descriptors that sort children, such as the "achievement gap" and "limited English proficiency"; reject deficit ideologies. • Educate yourself about myths that promote stereotypes and discriminatory practices (racist, classist, linguistic, homophobic, etc.); actively seek to understand and document children's and families' infinite capacity. • Use strategies in Table 15.2 to take action regarding this and every other principle.
Live life with humility, humanity, and love.	• Recognize and challenge rhetorical definitions of humanity and love. That is, move from talk to praxis (talk + reflection + action). Live the credo that love and humanity require high expectations, caring, and action against injustice. • Position love and humanity within relationships deemed authentic by all participants in the relationships. • Position self as learner, genuinely recognizing that "no one knows it all; no one is ignorant of everything" (Freire, 1998, p. 39). • Create spaces where injustices that impede authentic caring are recognized, challenged, and changed.

Table 15.1. A Toolkit of Principles for Social Justice Leadership (continued)

Principles for Social Justice Leadership	Requiring Courage to:
Define a clear vision and focus for your social justice leadership.	• Have a clear vision and sustained purpose for fostering socially just education. • Develop the ability to articulate your vision and back it up (with research, demographics, etc.). • Stay focused; be alert to how easily distractions (paperwork, deadlines, newly mandated assessments, etc.) can become excuses used to deflect from the work at hand. • Keep equity at the center of every decision, particularly when faced with mandates, compliance issues, negative attitudes, and naysayers. • Position children's, families', and communities' expertise, histories, and heritages at the core of curricula, teaching practices, and institutional decision making.
Constantly work to understand in/justice issues.	• Ask critical questions to understand others' (children, families, teachers, community members) perspectives regarding (in)justice and (in)equity in your school; use their truths to inform your decision making. • Lead teachers and staff in self-examination and institutional examination as you deepen knowledge about racism/antiracism, equity/inequity, and privilege/disprivilege through reading, discussion, attending conferences, inviting speakers, sharing weblinks and TED talks; use growing knowledge to disrupt traditions of inequity. • Lead teachers and staff in (re)learning histories to understand the power structures that continue to influence policies, pedagogies, and perceptions today. • Make your own learning journey visible, including the vulnerabilities you experience; set an example for consistent study, critical reflection, and turning reflection into action.
Seek allies and engage in critical and productive collaborations.	• Surround yourself with critical others—family members, community members, like-minded colleagues—for support, energy, sustenance, and respite; have the courage to let go of toxic or counterproductive relationships. • Access (or establish) critical professional learning communities to inform decision making and devise ways to collectively move forward. • Make clear that power does not reside with one individual, but that an educational community committed to equity requires collaborative efforts in which multiple voices are heard and power is distributed.

Table 15.1. A Toolkit of Principles for Social Justice Leadership (continued)

Principles for Social Justice Leadership	Requiring Courage to:
Engage in ongoing and informed advocacy.	• Identify and speak out against unjust practices and policies that impede success for all learners. • Advocate for and with students who have been traditionally marginalized, made invisible, and failed by schools and preschools; pay particular attention to race, ethnicity, language, religion, sexual orientation, gender identification, and dis/abilities. • Take an informed stand by getting the facts on any issue and using them to make and articulate decisions (for example, the disproportionality of school suspensions and special education referrals by race and gender; and/or immigration and challenges faced by families). • Know that advocacy can take many forms as you stand up for the rights of children, families, and teachers by making public statements, writing letters, dismantling and replacing unjust curricula and practices, and working with (and informing) policymakers to change inequitable policies. • Cultivate others' advocacy and leadership (colleagues', families', students', community members').

Table 15.2. Goals and Strategies for Taking Action

Goals	Strategies/Actions

Position families as vital to the operation of the school/preschool; ensure that their voices are sought and validated through joint action.	• Find out about social justice issues *from* families; conduct interviews, develop questionnaires, engage in conversations as you get to know families within contexts and communities familiar and comfortable to them.
	• Move beyond rhetoric ("I value your opinion") to action defined by humility, validation, genuine partnership, and respect.
	• Collaborate with families to (re)define policies, practices, and attitudes; work with families to take action *together*.
	• Make *all* school events bilingual or multilingual to include and foreground families in respectful ways; go the extra mile to make this happen—your community is full of language resources.
	• Advocate for and ensure child care, transportation, and meals to increase family participation during school meetings and events.
	• Work with families as co-researchers of their children's learning; listen to families and validate (give credence to) their words.
	• Expand services to include the needs and interests of adult learners who are a part of the school community: host GED classes, citizenship test study groups, college informational sessions, legal aid, assistance meetings, etc.
	• Engage families as allies for equity by:
	  – discussing injustices fostered by the educational system and by society, learning and problem-solving together;
	  – meeting with families to ensure they know their rights (what educational institutions can and cannot require; recognizing and calling out discriminatory practices);
	  – working with parents to help them understand and negotiate the culture of power in U.S. schooling—how to access gifted and talented programs, how to enroll their children in kindergarten, how to access quality and low-cost after-school programs, etc.;
	  – supporting families to value their own cultural, linguistic, and social knowledge as assets for themselves, their children, and the school;
	  – cultivating and engaging family members as school leaders.

Table 15.2. Goals and Strategies for Taking Action (continued)

Goals	Strategies/Actions
Demonstrate an authentic commitment to students' communities.	• From a strengths-based stance, involve yourself and teachers with families in students' communities; learn from families and community members (not as voyeurs, drive-by observers or evaluators) as you foster respectful and supportive relationships. • Spend time in students' homes and communities to learn about practices that support their learning out of school; lead teachers in utilizing that knowledge to inform and transform in-school practices. • Make time for home/community visits during professional development days, take teachers' classes so they can engage in family and/or community visits, and/or find ways to compensate teachers' time for doing so on evenings and/or weekends. • Ensure that families feel comfortable with home and community visits, asking them to define where, how, and when those visits will take place.
Understand and embrace bilingualism and multilingualism as the norm; insist on language equity.	• Educate yourself and the teachers with whom you work about (a) bi/multilingualism as an indication of cognitive, cultural, and linguistic knowledge and ability—as a local and global asset and (b) strategies for supporting bi/multilingualism through classroom and community resources and practices. • Help teachers understand code-switching as a skill to be valued as children use it every day, as well as linguistic variation as an enviable resource. • Engage in bi/multilingual communicative practices with children and families as you learn and honor the multiple languages of the school community. • Ensure that linguistic resources (bi/multilingual programs, translators, multiple-language texts) support/validate *all* of the languages spoken in the school community (not only the most common ones). • Be aware of linguistic hierarchies (the idea that some language forms are better than others—for example, Spanish from Spain being positioned as better than Spanish from the Dominican Republic) and work to challenge and dismantle such hierarchies in your educational setting. • Provide translation support during testing or select tests in children's home languages; educate families about their rights regarding standardized testing, particularly when only provided in English (such as their right to opt out).

Table 15.2. Goals and Strategies for Taking Action (continued)

Goals	Strategies/Actions
Hire, respect, and support a richly diverse body of teachers as knowledgeable partners who are willing to move beyond rhetorical expressions to grow and take action for equity and justice	• Hire a diverse teaching and support staff—rich with teachers of Color, teachers who are bilingual/multilingual, and teachers who are LGBTQIA. Include members of the community as teachers and staff. This is especially important during a time when more than three-quarters of all early childhood teachers in the United States are White and monolingual. • Make sure that *all* the teachers you hire are able to see, understand, and respect the brilliance in every child, and regard each child as capable and worthy; don't take their word for it—*watch them interact with children and families*; ask them to share ways they demonstrate respect for all families. • Engage teachers as co-researchers with you in the quest to understand inequities and develop equitable pedagogical and institutional practices. • Know that bias is often anchored in fear of many things; help teachers acknowledge their fears and work to turn fear into opportunities for learning. • Provide ongoing opportunities for teachers to engage in critically focused professional study on site in your school and for attending equity-focused conferences; invite guest scholars to support faculty in (re)learning histories and recognizing oppression and privilege. • Provide supported, consistent spaces for teachers to use their growing knowledge to examine all aspects of schooling and then rethink, re-envision, and replace unjust practices and policies systematically. • Build relationships with teachers without deficit assumptions of them, just as you want them to develop deficit-free relationships with children/families. • Spend daily time in classrooms as a teaching partner, modeling just practices and dispositions; collaborate, don't threaten; participate, don't merely observe. • Approach teacher evaluations from a collaborative stance. As you meet with teachers to discuss lessons and other practices, help them develop and use a critical eye to recognize, dismantle, and replace deficit-based attitudes and inequitable pedagogies. • Support teachers in positioning children's linguistic, social, and cultural knowledge centrally in the curriculum, broadening sociolinguistic/sociocultural awareness for *all* students. • Make your own vulnerabilities visible; share your growth experiences; model your own self-directed learning. • Cultivate teachers as leaders; establish an environment in which teachers become empowered to carry on the work of social justice.

Table 15.2. Goals and Strategies for Taking Action (continued)

Goals	Strategies/Actions
Keep mandates and testing in perspective.	• Do not use mandates and compliance measures as an excuse for inaction. Action within mandates *is* possible. Make it your business to know policies so that you can support teachers in working within and beyond them. • Interpret mandates *with* families and teachers in ways that are empowering, productive, and supportive of your vision. • Empower teachers with the knowledge and skills to teach within and beyond constraints; help teachers build skills in articulating how equity teaching addresses mandates. • Help teachers support students' success within existing systems while remaining true to the goals of a culturally relevant and socially just education.

Generate and use funding creatively to make socially just teaching possible; avoid funding-based deflections from the work.	• Through grants, collaborations with agencies and institutions, partnerships with the community, and reallocation of budgetary funds, commit to supporting and/or securing:
	  – classroom and professional development materials to support teaching grounded in social justice commitments;
	  – time and resources for teachers to visit classrooms where educators are engaged in social justice work;
	  – time and resources for teachers and families to attend social justice–focused conferences and meetings;
	  – materials for families to use at home as identified through interactions with families and teachers;
	  – time for teachers to study/collaborate with one another and with families outside of school hours;
	  – before- and/or after-school programs;
	  – a family space within the school with relevant materials;
	  – opportunities to learn from community members and other guests who bring a range of worldviews to the school.

Table 15.2. Goals and Strategies for Taking Action (continued)

Goals	Strategies/Actions
Lead from an activist stance.	• Demonstrate your life as an educational activist by making your stance clear—in words and actions—to children, teachers, families, and policymakers. • Share the definition of an activist, a person who advocates and campaigns for social change, (re)defining it not only within the context of your school community but in the wider community and society at large by identifying injustices, engaging in dialogue, and devising ways to foster transformative action together. Remember that justice is not just an imperative for the children in your care, but for children everywhere. • Regularly communicate information about and opportunities for engaging in activism and advocacy to teachers, staff, families, and community members through weekly emails, regular notes, social media, and other forms of communication. • Find out the facts; educate yourself thoroughly about the equity issues experienced within and beyond your school community; use that knowledge to address concerns, fears, discomfort, and ignorance. • Take public stances to challenge injustice by writing Op-Eds and blogs, and participating in marches and protests. Invite the school community to join you. • Establish partnerships with agencies and organizations known to foster activism—for example, Rethinking Schools (rethinkingschools.org), Welcoming Schools (welcomingschools.org), and the New York Collective of Radical Educators (nycore.org). • Critically reflect with your school community on the effects of media portrayals of activists and social movements. For example, the #BlackLivesMatter movement, immigration, and charter schools. Engage colleagues and families in discussions about your responsibility to communities beyond your school. • When you find yourself faltering or backing down, remember those who have come before you, the sacrifices they made, the legacy and example left for you, and the inequities you are working to dismantle. Stand up and step out!

References

Note: Many of these references were used by leaders in this book to inform their work. Thus, this can also serve as a resource list to support self-study and professional development.

Alexander, M. (2010). *The new Jim Crow: Mass incarceration in the age of colorblindness.* New York, NY: New Press.

Allen, J. (2007). *Creating welcoming schools: A practical guide to home–school partnerships with diverse families.* New York, NY: Teachers College Press.

Allen, J. (2010). *Literacy in the welcoming classroom: Creating family–school partnerships that support student learning.* New York, NY: Teachers College Press.

Angelou, M. (1988, March 5). Interview with Maya Angelou. *USA Today.* Available at http://www.usatoday.com/story/news/nation-now/2014/05/28/maya-angelou-quotes/9663257/

Anzaldúa, G. (2002). (Un)natural bridges, (un)safe spaces. In G. Anzaldúa & A. L. Keating (Eds.), *This bridge we call home: Radical visions for transformation* (pp. 1–5). New York, NY: Routledge.

Baldwin, J. (1963, December 21). A talk to teachers. *The Saturday Review, 45*(51), 42–44.

Banks, C. A. M., & Banks, J. A. (1995). Equity pedagogy: An essential component of multicultural education. *Theory into Practice, 34*(3), 152–158.

Banks, J. A. (1995). Multicultural education: Historical development, dimensions, and practice. In J. A. Banks & C. M. Banks (Eds.), *Handbook of research on multicultural education* (pp. 3–24). New York, NY: Macmillan.

Barnett, W. S. (2004). *Better teachers, better preschools: Student achievement linked to teacher qualifications* (Policy Brief No. 2). New Brunswick, NJ: National Institute for Early Education Research.

Beachum, F. D., White, G., FitzGerald, A. M, & Austin, A. L. (2013, Spring). Urban schools: Poverty, plight, and potential. *UCEA Review, 54*(2), 9–10.

Blackburn, M. (2011). *Interrupting hate: Homophobia in schools and what literacy can do about it.* New York, NY: Teachers College Press.

Blanchett, W. J., Mumford, V., & Beachum, F. (2005). Urban school failure and disproportionality in a post-Brown era: Benign neglect of the constitutional rights of students of color. *Remedial and Special Education, 26*(2), 70–81.

Bloomingdale Family Program. (2013). *Education plan.* New York, NY: The Bloomingdale Family Program.

Bonilla-Silva, E. (2000). This is a White country: The racial ideology of the Western nations of the world system. *Sociological Inquiry, 70*(2), 188–214.

Boske, C. (November 2009). *It begins from within: Conceptualizing a "catalytic perspective" for school leaders*. Paper presented at The University Council for Educational Administration Annual Conference, Anaheim, CA.

Boutte, G. S., & Hill, E. L. (2006). African American communities: Implications for culturally relevant teaching. *The New Educator, 2*, 311–329.

Boutte, G. S., & Johnson, G. L. (2013). Do educators see and honor biliteracy and bidialectalism in African American language speakers? Apprehensions and reflections of two grandparents/professional educators. *Early Childhood Education Journal, 41*, 133–141.

Boutte, G., López-Robertson, J., & Powers-Costello, B. (2011). Moving beyond colorblindness in early childhood classrooms. *Early Childhood Education Journal, 39*(5), 335–342.

Bredekamp, S. (1987). *Developmentally appropriate practice in early childhood programs serving children from birth through age 8*. Washington, DC: NAEYC.

Bredekamp, S., & Copple, C. (Eds.). (1997). *Developmentally appropriate practice in early childhood programs serving children from birth through age 8* (2nd ed.). Washington, DC: NAEYC.

Byrne-Jiménez, M., & Orr, M. (2007). *Developing effective principals through collaborative inquiry*. New York, NY: Teachers College Press.

Cannella, G. (1997). *Deconstructing early childhood education: Social justice and revolution*. New York, NY: Peter Lang.

Carruthers, I., King, J., & Watkins, D. (2013, October). *Reclaiming and celebrating what works: Passing the torch* [Brochure for A Black Education Congress].

Castagno, A. (2014). *Educated in Whiteness: Good intentions and diversity in schools*. Minneapolis, MN: University of Minnesota Press.

Cheruvu, R., Souto-Manning, M., Lencl, T., & Chin-Calubaquib, M. (2014). Race, isolation, and exclusion: What early childhood teacher educators need to know about the experiences of pre-service teachers of color. *The Urban Review, 47*, 237–265.

Clark, K. B., & Clark, M. P. (1947). Racial identification and preference in Negro children. In T. M. Newcomb & E. L. Hartley (Eds.), *Readings in social psychology* (pp. 169–178). New York, NY: Holt, Rinehart & Winston.

Clyne, M., Isaakidis, T., Liem, I., & Rossi Hunt, C. (2004). Developing and sharing community language resources through secondary school programmes. *International Journal of Bilingual Education and Bilingualism, 7*(4), 255–278.

Coates, T. (2015). *Between the world and me*. New York, NY: Spiegel & Grau.

Cochran-Smith, M., & Lytle, S. L. (2009). *Inquiry as stance: Practitioner research for the next generation*. New York, NY: Teachers College Press.

Coelho, E. (2004). *Adding English: A guide to teaching in multilingual classrooms*. Toronto, ON, Canada: Pippin.

Compton-Lilly, C. (2004). *Confronting racism, poverty, and power: Classroom strategies to change the world*. Portsmouth, NH: Heinemann.

Copple, C., & Bredekamp, S. (2009). *Developmentally appropriate practice in early childhood programs serving children from birth through age 8* (3rd ed.). Washington, DC: NAEYC.

Copple, C., Bredekamp, S., Koralek, D., & Charner, K. (2013). *Developmentally appropriate practice: Focus on preschoolers.* Washington, DC: NAEYC.

Cowhey, M. (2005). Heather's moms got married: Second graders talk about gay marriage. *Rethinking Schools, 19*(3), 10–12.

Cowhey, M. (2006). *Black ants and Buddhists: Thinking critically and teaching differently in primary grades.* Portland, ME: Stenhouse.

Dantas, M. L., & Manyak, P. C. (Eds.). (2010). *Home–school connections in a multicultural society: Learning from and with culturally and linguistically diverse families.* New York, NY: Routledge.

Darder, A. (Ed.). (2008). *The critical pedagogy reader* (2nd ed.). New York, NY: Routledge.

Darder, A. (2015). *Freire and education.* New York, NY: Routledge.

Darling-Hammond, L. (2013). *The flat world and education: How America's commitment to equity will determine our future.* New York, NY: Teachers College Press.

Darling-Hammond, L., & Bransford, J. (Eds.). (2005). *Preparing teachers for a changing world: What teachers should learn and be able to do.* San Francisco, CA: Jossey-Bass.

Davis, K. (2007). *A girl like me* [Documentary film]. Available at www.youtube.com/watch?v=z0BxFRu_SOw

Deleuze, G., & Guattari, F. (1987). *A thousand plateaus: Capitalism and schizophrenia.* Minneapolis, MN: University of Minnesota Press.

Delpit, L. (1988). The silenced dialogue: Power and pedagogy in educating other people's children. *Harvard Educational Review, 58*(3), 280–299.

Delpit, L. (2012). *Multiplication is for White people: Raising expectations for other people's children.* New York, NY: New Press.

Derman-Sparks, L., & Edwards, J. O. (2012). *Anti-bias education for young children and ourselves.* Washington, DC: NAEYC.

Derman-Sparks, L., & Ramsey, P. (2011). *What if all the kids are White? Anti-bias multicultural education with young children and families* (2nd ed.). New York, NY: Teachers College Press.

Derman-Sparks, L., LeeKeenan, D., & Nimmo, J. (2015). *Leading anti-bias early childhood programs: A guide for change.* New York, NY: Teachers College Press.

Donnelly, A., Morgan, D. N., Deford, D. E., Files, J., Long, S., Mills, H., . . . Styslinger, M. (2005). Transformative professional development: Negotiating knowledge with an inquiry stance. *Language Arts, 82*(5), 336–346.

Du Bois, W. E. B. (1903). *The souls of Black folk.* Greenwich, CT: Fawcett.

Duncan-Andrade, J., & Morrell, E. (2008). *The art of pedagogy: Possibilities for moving from theory to practice in urban schools.* New York, NY: Peter Lang.

Durán, L., Roseth, C., & Hoffman, P. (2010). An experimental study comparing English-only and transitional bilingual education on Spanish-speaking preschoolers' early literacy development. *Early Childhood Research Quarterly, 25*(2), 207–217.

Edwards, P. A., McMillon, G. T., & Turner, J. D. (2010). *Change is gonna come: Transforming literacy education for African American students.* New York, NY: Teachers College Press.

Elias, M. (2013). The school to prison pipeline: Policies and practices that favor incarceration over education do us all a grave injustice. *Teaching Tolerance, 43*, 39–40.

Espinosa, L. M. (2008). *Challenging common myths about young English language learners.* New York, NY: Foundation for Child Development.

Fanon, F. (1952). *Black skin, White masks.* New York, NY: Grove Press.

Fay, K., & Whaley, S. (2004). *Becoming one community: Reading and writing with English language learners.* Portland, ME: Stenhouse.

Fergus, E., Noguera, P., & Martin, M. (2014). *Schooling for resilience: Improving the life trajectory of Black and Latino boys.* Cambridge, MA: Harvard Education Press.

First Nations Studies Program. (2009). *The residential school system.* Available at http://indigenousfoundations.arts.ubc.ca/home/government-policy/the-residential-school-system.html

Fisher, M. (2004, October, 12). Falls Church school won't teach to the test. *The Washington Post,* p. B01.

Fisher, M. T. (2007). *Writing in rhythm: Spoken word poetry in urban classrooms.* New York, NY: Teachers College Press.

Ford, D. Y. (2013). *Recruiting and retaining culturally different students in gifted education.* Waco, TX: Prufrock Press.

Foster, M. (1997). *Black teachers on teaching.* New York, NY: New Press.

Freire, P. (1970). *Pedagogy of the oppressed.* New York, NY: Continuum.

Freire, P. (1998). *Teachers as cultural workers: Letters to those who dare teach.* Boulder, CO: Westview Press.

Fu, D. (2009). *Writing between languages: How English language learners make the transition to fluency.* Portsmouth, NH: Heinemann.

García, E. E. (2012, October). *Teaching young English language learners.* Paper presented at Quality Universally Inclusive Early Responsive Education (QUIERE) Seminar Series, New York, NY.

García, E. E., & Frede, E. C. (Eds.). (2010). *Young English language learners: Current research and emerging directions for practice and policy.* New York, NY: Teachers College Press.

García, E. E., & García, E. H. (2012). *Understanding the language development and early education of Hispanic children.* New York, NY: Teachers College Press.

García, O., & Kleifgen, J. (2010). *Educating emergent bilinguals: Policies, programs, and practices for English language learners.* New York, NY: Teachers College Press.

Gay, G. (2010). *Culturally responsive teaching: Theory, research, and practice* (2nd ed.). New York, NY: Teachers College Press.

Gay, G. (2014). Race and ethnicity in U.S. education. In R. Race & V. Lander (Eds.,), *Advancing race and ethnicity in education* (pp. 63–81). New York, NY: Palgrave Macmillan.

Gee, J. P. (1996). *Social linguistics and literacies: Ideology in discourses* (2nd ed.). London, UK: Taylor & Francis.

Genishi, C., & Dyson, A. H. (2009). *Children, language, and literacy: Diverse learners in diverse times.* New York, NY: Teachers College Press.

Genishi, C., & Dyson, A. H. (2012). Racing to the top: Who's accounting for the children? *Bank Street Occasional Papers, 27,* 18–20.

Giago, T., & Giago, D. (2006). *Children left behind: The dark legacy of Indian mission boarding schools.* Santa Fe, NM: Clear Light.

Gillborn, D. (2005). Education policy as an act of White supremacy: Whiteness, critical race theory and education reform. *Journal of Education Policy, 20*, 485–505.

González, N., Moll, L., & Amanti, C. (Eds.). (2005). *Funds of knowledge: Theorizing practices in households, communities and classrooms*. New York, NY: Routledge.

Goodlad, J. I. (2004). *Romances with schools: A life of education*. New York, NY: McGraw-Hill.

Goodwin, A. L., Cheruvu, R., & Genishi, C. (2008). Responding to multiple diversities in early childhood education. In C. Genishi & A. L. Goodwin (Eds.), *Diversities in early childhood education: Rethinking and doing* (pp. 3–10). New York, NY: Routledge.

Gregory, E., Long, S., & Volk, D. (Eds.). (2004). *Many pathways to literacy: Young children learning with siblings, peers, grandparents, and communities*. London, UK: RoutledgeFalmer.

Gutiérrez, K. D., Morales, P. L., & Martínez, D. (2009). Re-mediating literacy: Culture, difference, and learning for students from non-dominant communities. *Review of Research in Education, 33*(1), 212–245.

Haitana, T., Pitama, S., & Rucklidge, J. J. (2010). Cultural biases in the Peabody Picture Vocabulary Test-III: Testing Tamariki in a New Zealand sample. *New Zealand Journal of Psychology, 39*, 24–34.

Hayes, H., & Juárez, B. (2012). There is no culturally responsive teaching spoken here: A critical race perspective. *Democracy in Education, 20*(1), 1–14.

Hermann-Wilmarth, J., & Ryan, C. (2013). Interrupting the single story: LGBT issues in the language arts classroom. *Language Arts, 90*(3), 226–231.

Heron, J. (2008). *The complete facilitator's handbook*. London, UK: Kagan.

hooks, b. (1994). *Teaching to transgress: Education as the practice of freedom*. New York, NY: Routledge.

Hoover-Dempsey, K., & Sandler, H. M. (2005). Why do parents become involved: Research findings and implications. *The Elementary School Journal, 106*(2), 105–130.

Horton, M., & Freire, P. (1990). *We make the road by walking: Conversations on education and social change*. Philadelphia, PA: Temple University Press.

Howard, G. (2006). *We can't teach what we don't know: White teachers, multiracial schools* (2nd ed.). New York, NY: Teachers College Press.

Howard, T. (2010). *Why race and culture matter in schools: Closing the achievement gap in America's classrooms*. New York, NY: Teachers College Press.

Howard, T. (2014). *Black maled: Perils and promises in the education of African American males*. New York, NY: Teacher College Press.

Ingersoll, R., & Strong, M. (2011, June). The impact of induction and mentoring programs for beginning teachers: A critical review of the research. *Review of Educational Research, 81*(2), 201–233.

Irvine, J. J. (2003). *Educating teachers for diversity: Seeing with a cultural eye*. New York, NY: Teachers College Press.

Jensen, R. (2005). *The heart of Whiteness: Confronting race, racism, and White privilege*. Santa Fe, NM: City Lights.

Johnson, P. (2006). *One child at a time: Making the most of your time with struggling readers, K–6*. Portland, ME: Stenhouse.

Johnson, P., & Keier, K. (2010). *Catching readers before they fall: Supporting readers who struggle, K–4.* Portland, ME: Stenhouse.

Johnston, P. (2004). *Choice words: How our language affects children's learning.* Portland, ME: Stenhouse.

Jordan, P., & Hernandez-Reif, M. (2009). Reexamination of young children's racial attitudes and skin tone preferences. *Journal of Black Psychology, 35*(3), 388–403.

King, J. (2005). *Black education: A transformative research and action agenda for the new century.* New York, NY: Routledge.

King, J., & Swartz, E. (2014). *"Re-membering" history in student and teacher learning: An Afrocentric culturally informed praxis.* New York, NY: Routledge.

Kirkland, D. (2013). *A search past silence: The literacy of Black males.* New York, NY: Teachers College Press.

Kohli, R. (2009). Critical race reflections: Valuing the experiences of teachers of color in teacher education. *Race, Ethnicity and Education, 12*(2), 235–251.

Kumashiro, K. (2012). *Bad teacher! How blaming teachers distorts the bigger picture.* New York, NY: Teachers College Press.

Kunjufu, J. (2005). *Keeping Black boys out of special education.* Chicago, IL: African American Images.

Ladson-Billings, G. (1994). *The dreamkeepers: Successful teachers of African American children.* San Francisco, CA: Jossey-Bass.

Ladson-Billings, G. (1995a). But that's just good teaching! The case for culturally relevant pedagogy. *Theory Into Practice, 34*(3), 159–165.

Ladson-Billings, G. (1995b). Toward a theory of culturally relevant pedagogy. *American Education Research Journal 32*(3), 465–491.

Ladson-Billings, G. (2006). From the achievement gap to the education debt: Understanding achievement in U.S. schools. *Educational Researcher, 35*(7), 3–12.

Ladson-Billings, G. (2009). *The dreamkeepers: Successful teachers of African American children* (2nd ed.). San Francisco, CA: Jossey-Bass.

Ladson-Billings, G. (2015, April). *Justice . . . just, justice!* Social Justice in Education Award Lecture. American Educational Research Association Annual Meeting. Chicago, IL. Available at http://www.aera.net/EventsMeetings/AnnualMeeting/PreviousAnnualMeetings/2015AnnualMeeting/2015AnnualMeetingWebcasts/SocialJusticeinEducationAward(2015)LectureGloriaJLadson-Billings/tabid/15943/Default.aspx

Laman, T. (2013). *From ideas to words: Writing strategies for English language learners.* Portsmouth, NH: Heinemann.

Lawrence-Lightfoot, S. (2004). *The essential conversation: What parents and teachers can learn from each other.* New York, NY: Ballantine.

Lazar, A. (2011). Access to excellence: Serving today's students through culturally responsive literacy teaching. In P. Schmidt & A. Lazar (Eds.), *Practicing what we teach: How culturally responsive literacy classrooms make a difference* (pp. 3–26). New York, NY: Teachers College Press.

Leahy, T., & Wilson, R. (2008). *Historical dictionary of Native American movements.* Lanham, MD: Scarecrow Press.

Lewis, A. E. (2001). There is no "race" in the schoolyard: Color-blind ideology in an (almost) all-White school. *American Education Research Journal, 38*(4), 781–811.

Long, S., Anderson, C., Clark, M., & McCraw, B. (2008). Going beyond our own worlds: A first step in envisioning equitable practice. In C. Genishi & A. L. Goodwin (Eds.), *Diversities in early childhood education: Rethinking and doing* (pp. 253–269). New York, NY: Routledge.

Long, S., Volk, D., López-Robertson, J., & Haney, M. J. (2014). "Diversity as a verb" in preservice teacher education: Creating spaces to challenge the profiling of young children. *Contemporary Issues in Early Childhood, 15*(2), 152–164.

López-Robertson, J., Long, S., & Turner-Nash, K. (2010). First steps in constructing counter narratives of young children and their families. *Language Arts, 88*(2), 93–103.

Lyiscott, J. (2014, February). *3 ways to speak English* [Video file]. Available at https://www.ted.com/talks/jamila_lyiscott_3_ways_to_speak_english?language=en

Madhlangobe, L., & Gordon, S. (2012). Culturally responsive leadership in a diverse school: A case study of a high school leader. *NASSP Bulletin, 96*(3), 177–202.

Martínez, R. (2010). Spanglish as literacy tool: Toward an understanding of the potential role of Spanish-English code-switching in the development of academic literacy. *Research in the Teaching of English, 45*(2), 124–145.

Mathews, J. (2004a, October 19). How No Child Left Behind helps principals. *The Washington Post*, p. VA08.

Mathews, J. (2004b, November 4). No one need feel left behind by federal education mandate. *The Washington Post*, p. VA08.

McIntosh, P. (1995). White privilege and male privilege: A personal account of coming to see correspondences through work in women's studies. In M. Anderson & P. Collins (Eds.), *Race, class and gender: An anthology* (2nd ed., pp. 70–80). Belmont, CA: Wadsworth.

McIntyre, A. (1997). *Making meaning of Whiteness: Exploring racial identity with White teachers.* Albany, NY: State University of New York Press.

Michie, G. (2009). *Holler if you hear me: The education of a teacher and his students.* New York, NY: Teachers College Press.

Miller, E. (2015). Discourses of Whiteness and Blackness: An ethnographic study of three young children learning to be White. *Ethnography and Education, 10*(2), 137–153.

Milner, H. R. (2010). Disrupting deficit notions of difference: Counter-narratives of teachers and community in urban education. *Teaching and Teacher Education, 24*(6), 1573–1598.

Milner, H. R. (2014). Culturally relevant, purpose-driven teaching and learning in a middle school social studies classroom. *Multicultural Education, 21*(2), 9–17.

Milner, H. R. (2015). *Race(ing) to class: Confronting poverty and race in schools and classrooms.* Cambridge, MA: Harvard Education Press.

Milner, H. R., & Tenore, F. (2010). Classroom management in diverse classrooms. *Urban Education, 45*(5), 560–603.

Moll, L., Amanti, C., Neff, D., & González, N. (1992). Funds of knowledge for teaching: Using a qualitative approach to connecting homes and classrooms. *Theory Into Practice, 31*, 132–141.

Morrell, E. (2004). *Linking literacy and popular culture: Finding connections for lifelong learning.* Norwood, MA: Christopher-Gordon.

Mosso-Taylor, S. (2013). *Professional conversations about race, culture and language in early childhood literacy education: An administrator's journey* (Unpublished doctoral dissertation). University of South Carolina, Columbia.

Mukhopadhyay, C. C., Henze, R., & Moses, Y. T. (2013). *How real is race? A sourcebook on race, culture and biology.* Lanham, MD: AltaMira Press.

Myers, M. (2013). Finding common concerns for the children we share. *Phi Delta Kappan, 94*(8), 40–44.

National Association for the Education of Young Children. (2009). *Position statement: Developmentally appropriate practice in early childhood programs serving children from birth through age 8.* Washington DC: NAEYC. Available at https://www.naeyc.org/files/naeyc/file/positions/position%20statement%20Web.pdf

Nieto, S. (1999). *The light in their eyes: Creating multicultural learning communities.* New York, NY: Teachers College Press.

Nieto, S. (2013). *Finding joy in teaching students of diverse backgrounds: Culturally responsive and socially just practices in U.S. classrooms.* Portsmouth, NH: Heinemann.

Nieto, S., & Bode, P. (2011). *Affirming diversity: The sociopolitical context of multicultural education* (6th ed.). New York, NY: Allyn & Bacon.

Noguera, P. (2003). Schools, prisons, and social implications of punishment: Rethinking disciplinary practices. *Theory Into Practice, 42*(4), 341–350.

Noguera, P. (2009). *The trouble with Black boys: . . . And other reflections on race, equity, and the future of public education.* San Francisco, CA: Jossey-Bass.

North, G. (2008). *Spoken word.* Available at www.nelsonatkins.org/images/PDF/Calendar/PoetrySlam_SpokenWord.pdf

Ntelioglou, B. Y., Fannin, J., Montanera, M., & Cummins, J. (2014). A multilingual and multimodal approach to literacy teaching and learning in urban education: A collaborative inquiry project in an inner city elementary school. *Frontiers in Psychology, 5*(533), 1–10. Available at www.ncbi.nlm.nih.gov/pubmed/24994986

Obama, B. (2015). *Remarks by the President at the 50th anniversary of the Selma to Montgomery marches.* Available at www.whitehouse.gov/the-press-office/2015/03/07/remarks-president-50th-anniversary-selma-montgomery-marches

Paris, D. (2012). Culturally sustaining pedagogy: A needed change in stance, terminology, and practice. *Educational Researcher, 41*(3), 93–97.

Parker, E., & Pardini, T. (2006). *The words came down! English language learners read, write, and talk across the curriculum, K–2.* Portland, ME: Stenhouse.

Perry, T., Moses, R. P., Wynne, J. T., Cortés, E., & Delpit, L. (Eds.). (2010). *Quality education as a constitutional right: Creating a grassroots movement to transform public schools.* Boston, MA: Beacon Press.

Pilkington, D., & Garimara, N. (2013). *Follow the rabbit-proof fence.* Brisbane, Australia: University of Queensland Press.

Razfar, A., & Gutiérrez, K. (2013). Reconceptualizing early childhood literacy: The sociocultural influence and new directions in digital and hybrid mediation. In J.

Larson & J. Marsh (Eds.), *The SAGE handbook of early childhood literacy* (2nd ed., pp. 52–79). London, UK: SAGE.

Rodney, W. (1972). *How Europe underdeveloped Africa.* Baltimore, MD: Black Classic Press.

Ruíz, R. (1984). Orientations in language planning. *National Association for Bilingual Education Journal, 8*(2), 15–34.

Sandoval, I. M. (2009). *Guardians of hidden traditions.* Santa Fe, NM: Gaon Books.

Sandoval, I. M. (2012). *Hidden Shabbat: The secret lives of Crypto-Jews.* Santa Fe, NM: Gaon Books.

Shapon-Shevin, M. (2010). *Because we can change the world: A practical guide to building cooperative, inclusive classroom communities.* Thousand Oaks, CA: Corwin.

Shulman, L. (2004). *The wisdom of practice: Essays on teaching, learning, and learning to teach.* San Francisco, CA: Jossey-Bass.

Siddle Walker, V. (1996). *Their highest potential: An African American school community in the segregated South.* Chapel Hill, NC: University of North Carolina Press.

Siegel, M., & Lukas, S. (2008). Room to move: How kindergarteners negotiate literacies and identities in a mandated balanced literacy curriculum. In C. Genishi & A. L. Goodwin (Eds.), *Diversities in early childhood education: Rethinking and doing* (pp. 29–47). New York, NY: Routledge.

Skutnabb-Kangas, T. (2002). Marvelous human rights rhetoric and grim realities: Language rights in education. *Journal of Language, Identity, and Education, 1*(3), 179–205.

Smith, L. T. (2012). *Decolonizing methodologies: Research and indigenous peoples* (2nd ed.). London, UK: Zed Books.

Souto-Manning, M. (2010a). Challenging ethnocentric literacy practices: (Re)positioning home literacies in a Head Start classroom. *Research in the Teaching of English, 45*(2), 150–178.

Souto-Manning, M. (2010b). *Freire, teaching, and learning: Culture circles across contexts.* New York, NY: Peter Lang.

Souto-Manning, M. (2010c). Teaching English learners: Building on cultural and linguistic strengths. *English Education, 42*(3), 249–263.

Souto-Manning, M. (2013). *Multicultural teaching in the early childhood classroom: Approaches, strategies, and tools, preschool–2nd grade.* New York, NY, & Washington, DC: Teachers College Press & ACEI.

Sue, D. W. (2015). *Race talk and the conspiracy of silence: Understanding and facilitating difficult dialogues on race.* Hoboken, NJ: John Wiley & Sons.

Tabors, P. O. (2008). *One child, two languages: A guide for preschool educators of children learning English as a second language.* Baltimore, MD: Brookes.

Tatum, A. (2009). *Reading for their life: (Re)building the textual lineages of African American adolescent males.* Portsmouth, NH: Heinemann.

Tatum, B. D. (2007). *Can we talk about race? And other conversations in the era of school resegregation.* Boston, MA: Beacon Press.

Theoharis, G. (2009). *The school leaders our children deserve: Seven keys to equity, social justice, and school reform.* New York, NY: Teachers College Press.

Ture, K., & Hamilton, C. V. (1967). *Black power: The politics of liberation*. New York, NY: Vintage Books.

U.S. Department of Education. (2014). *Early reading first program*. Available at www2. ed.gov/programs/earlyreading/index.html

U.S. Supreme Court. (1954). *Brown v. Board of Education of Topeka, 347 U.S. 483*. Available at https://supreme.justia.com/cases/federal/us/347/483/

Valdés, G. (1996). *Con respeto: Bridging the distances between culturally diverse families and schools*. New York, NY: Teachers College Press.

Valdés, G. (1997). Dual-language immersion programs: A cautionary note concerning the education of language-minority students. *Harvard Educational Review, 67*(3), 391-430.

Valdés, G. (2001). *Learning and not learning English: Latino students in American schools*. New York, NY: Teachers College Press.

Valenzuela, A. (1999). *Subtractive schooling: U.S. Mexican youth and the politics of caring*. Albany, NY: State University of New York Press.

Vasquez, V. (2004). *Negotiating critical literacies with young children*. New York, NY: Routledge.

Vasquez, V., & Egawa, K. (Eds.). (2002). Rethinking the literacy curriculum: The Bailey's elementary school reading initiative study group. *School Talk, 8*(1), 1–6.

Vasquez, V., & Felderman, C. (2013). *Technology and critical literacy in early childhood*. New York, NY: Routledge.

Walker, A. (2006). *We are the ones we have been waiting for: Inner light in a time of darkness*. New York, NY: The New Press.

Wheeler, R., & Swords, R. (2004). Codeswitching: Tools of language and culture transform the dialectically diverse classroom. *Language Arts, 81*(6), 470–480.

Whitehead, J., McFadden, G., & Carstarphen, V. (1975). Wake up everybody [Recorded by Harold Melvin & the Blue Notes featuring T. Pendergrass]. On *Wake up everybody* [Record]. Philadelphia International Records.

Woodson, C. (1933). *The mis-education of the Negro*. New York, NY: Associated Press.

Yelland, N. (2010). *Contemporary perspectives on early childhood education*. Maidenhead, UK: Open University Press.

Young, V. A., Barrett, R., Young-Rivera, Y., & Lovejoy, K. B. (Eds.). (2013). Appendix. In *Other people's English: Code-meshing, code-switching, and African American literacy* (pp. 1–19). New York, NY: Teachers College Press. Available at http://www.tcpress.com/pdfs/9780807755556_app.pdf

Zentella, A. C. (Ed.). (2005). *Building on strengths: Language and literacy in Latino families and communities*. New York, NY: Teachers College Press.

About the Contributors

Anthony Broughton is an education associate at the South Carolina State Department of Education and *Call Me Mister* Site Coordinator at Benedict College. He is pursuing a PhD in Early Childhood Education from the University of South Carolina (USC) with scholarly interests that include the use of hip-hop pedagogy in early childhood. He is an author of children's books, including *Wishes of Wisdom* and *Lesson by Nature*.

Nathaniel Bryan is a clinical assistant professor at the University of South Carolina in Columbia. He received his doctorate in Educational Leadership and is pursuing a PhD in Early Childhood Education at USC. His research explores the constructed identities and pedagogical styles of Black male kindergarten teachers and is featured in *Gifted Child Today* and the *Interdisciplinary Journal of Teaching and Learning*.

Mónica Byrne-Jiménez is an associate professor in Educational and Policy Leadership at Hofstra University. Her interests include the intersection of ethnicity/identity in leadership and professional development and the role of facilitators in adult learning. She is coauthor of *Developing Effective Principals Through Collaborative Inquiry*. Her other work appears in the journals *Leadership and Policy in Schools* and *Voices in Urban Education* and in *Handbook of Research on Educational Leadership for Diversity and Equity*.

Brittany Garvin is a teaching assistant in the College of Education at the University of South Carolina. She is completing her PhD in Teaching and Learning, with an emphasis on culturally relevant science education. Her scholarly interests include STEM education in urban classrooms. Awards include the Southern Regional Education Board Doctoral Scholar Fellowship and the National Association for Research in Science Teaching European Science Education Research Association Fellowship Award.

Marcelle M. Haddix is a Dean's Associate Professor in English Education at Syracuse University. She earned her PhD from Boston College with scholarly interests in the literacy experiences of students of Color, English teaching, and teacher education. Dr. Haddix's work is featured in *Research in the Teaching of English, English Education, Linguistics and Education*, and *Journal of Adolescent* *and Adult Literacy.* Recognitions include the AERA K Early Career Award and NCTE's Promising Researcher Award.

Mary Jade Haney holds an MEd in Curriculum and Instruction from and is pursuing a doctorate at the University of South Carolina. She has been a public school educator for 18 years. Her greatest joy is inspiring children to develop voices that challenge inequities in educational spaces. She advocates for students and families at Horrell Hill Elementary School in Columbia, SC. She believes all children have the ability and potential to make positive contributions to the world.

Lamar Johnson is a faculty member at Miami University, OH. He received his EdD in Curriculum and Instruction from the University of South Carolina. His research investigates intersections of race, literacy, and education and is featured in the *Journal of African American Males in Education* and *The National Journal of Urban Education.* He is a Cultivating New Voices Among Scholars of Color (NCTE) Fellow and an AERA Research Institute participant.

Susi Long is a professor of Early Childhood Education at the University of South Carolina. She received her PhD from The Ohio State University. Her articles and books focus on home and community literacies, new teachers, and cross-cultural and culturally responsive literacy practices. Dr. Long received NCTE's 2013 Early Literacy Educator Award and served in leadership roles, most recently as Chair of Trustees of NCTE's Research Foundation and co-director of NCTE's Professional Dyads and Culturally Relevant Teaching program.

Julia López-Robertson is an associate professor of Language and Literacy Education at the University of South Carolina. She spent 17 years as a bilingual primary teacher in Boston and Tucson, completing her PhD at the University of Arizona. Her scholarly agenda advances understandings about emerging bilingual/multilingual students and their families, and also focuses on the transformation of teacher education to support equitable teaching for all children.

Alfredo Celedón Luján is a middle school teacher norteño (raised in northern New Mexico). He graduated from New Mexico State University and Bread Loaf School of English. He was writer-in-residence (Alaska's Multicultural Artists in the Schools) and three-time NEH Fellow, and his Monte del Sol School students were featured in Annenberg's *The Expanding Canon.* His writing appears in multiple journals and *Santa Fe Nativa: A Collection of Nuevomexicano Writing.* He was awarded New Mexico's 2014 Golden Apple Award for teaching.

Rebeca Madrigal is a dual-language teacher at Dos Puentes Elementary School in New York City. She received her master's degree in Bilingual/Bicultural Education from Teachers College, Columbia University, and has been a dual-language teacher for over 15 years. She is one of the founding teachers of Dos Puentes Elementary and, prior to teaching there, was a bilingual 1st-grade teacher at P.S.

165 in New York. She is vested in fostering bilingualism, biliteracy, and multi-culturalism in young children.

Karina Malik received her MA from Teachers College, Columbia University, and is a 1st-grade, dual-language special education teacher at Dos Puentes Elementary School in New York City. She is certified in early childhood education, special education, and bilingual education; 2014–2015 was her first teaching year. She was awarded a Quality Universally Inclusive Early Responsive Education (QUIERE) scholarship from the U.S. Office of Special Education Programs. She is especially vested in equitable education.

Jessica Martell is a public school teacher in New York City and an instructor at Teachers College, Columbia University. Jessica holds a master's degree from CUNY's Hunter College. She has 20 years of experience teaching dual-language (Spanish/English) kindergarten, 1st and 2nd grades. She is a trustee of the NCTE Research Foundation and a charter member of NCTE's Professional Dyads and Culturally Relevant Teaching program. She received NCTE's 2014 Early Childhood Educator of the Year Award.

Yandra Mordan-Delgadillo has been an early childhood teacher at the Bloomingdale Family Program in New York City since 1999. Yandra's association with Bloomingdale started when her children entered the program as students. She is currently pursuing a master's degree in early childhood education/special education from Teachers College, Columbia University, and was awarded a QUIERE scholarship from the U.S. Office of Special Education Programs. She is committed to culturally relevant bilingual teaching and to creating authentic partnerships with families.

Sabina Mosso-Taylor is principal of the Center for Achievement in Columbia, SC. She earned her PhD from the University of South Carolina, where she is an adjunct instructor. Her research interests include professional development around race, culture, and language, as well as nurturing students' literate identities in early childhood language and literacy education. She received National Board Certification as an Early Childhood Generalist in 2002 and again in 2012.

Meir Muller earned rabbinical ordination as well as a PhD in Early Childhood Education from the University of South Carolina. He is a clinical assistant professor at USC and principal of the Cutler Jewish Day School. His research interests include constructivist theory informed by equity pedagogies. Dr. Muller lectures widely on early childhood education. In 2014, he presented a paper in Israel for the International Research Group on Jewish Education in the Early Years.

Michele Myers holds an EdS and PhD from the University of South Carolina, where she is a clinical assistant professor. Her interests focus on the literacy practices of rural children and families of Color and the preparation of teachers to appreciate diverse models of familial caring and academic support. Her work is featured in *Phi Delta Kappan.* She was recognized in 2010 as a Cultivating New Voices Among Scholars of Color Fellow (NCTE).

Kindel Nash is an assistant professor of Urban Teacher Education and Language and Literacy at the University of Missouri, Kansas City. Her scholarly interests center on critical race theory, critical sociocultural theory, and early literacy teacher preparation. Dr. Nash's work has been published in *Language Arts, The Urban Review, Journal of Curriculum Theorizing, Journal of Transformative Education, African American Learners*, and other national journals.

Bilal Polson is an assistant principal at Northern Parkway Elementary School in Uniondale, New York. He graduated from the LaGuardia High School of the Performing Arts and received his BA from New York University and doctorate in Educational Leadership from Hofstra University. He has presented his work at AERA, the University Council for Educational Administration, and NCTE national conferences. He serves on the Governing Board of NCTE's Early Childhood Education Assembly (ECEA) and is a participant in the NCTE's Professional Dyads and Culturally Relevant Teaching program.

Detra Price-Dennis is an assistant professor at Teachers College, Columbia University. She received her PhD from The Ohio State University. Price-Dennis's research focuses on digital literacy pedagogies to create equitable learning environments, sociopolitical and sociocultural aspects of literacy learning, and critical perspectives on children's and young adult literature. Her work can be found in the *Journal of Negro Education, Journal of Writing Teacher Education,* and *English Education,* among others.

Dywanna Smith is a middle-level English/language arts specialist in Richland School District Two in Columbia, SC, and a doctoral candidate in Language and Literacy Education. Her research explores the intersections of race, literacy, and body size. She has worked in middle-level education for 12 years. As an English/language arts researcher and teacher, she has presented both nationally and internationally.

Geralyn Sosinski is Director of Early Education at El Centro Academy in Kansas City, KS, a dual-language preschool program focusing on curriculum in Spanish and English. She earned her master's and bachelor's degrees in Early Childhood/Elementary Education from the University of Kansas. Ms. Sosinski has over 20 years of classroom experience. Her interests and passions include bilingualism, dual-language learners, and family literacy.

Mariana Souto-Manning is an associate professor at Teachers College, Columbia University. She received her PhD from the University of Georgia. Her research is grounded in critical perspectives on early language and literacy, multicultural education, and teacher education. She has published many articles and books, including the award-winning *Multicultural Teaching in the Early Childhood Classroom*. She has received multiple research awards, including AERA's Division K Innovations in Research on Diversity in Teacher Education Award. She has held appointive and elected positions with professional organizations such as ACEI, AERA, and NCTE. She is chair of the NCTE Research Foundation.

Sarah Vander Zanden is an assistant professor at the University of Northern Iowa. She earned her PhD at Indiana University. She is a former elementary classroom teacher. Her interests include teacher education, critical literacy, and discourse analysis. Her work has been published in *Language Arts*, *Critical Literacy: Theories and Practice*, and *Journal of Early Childhood Literacy*. She is the current cohost of the *Voice of Literacy* podcast.

Vivian Maria Vasquez is a professor of education at American University. She was a preschool and elementary school teacher for 14 years. She received her doctorate from Indiana University, Bloomington. Her work focuses on critical literacies and the use of digital tools in ECE. She has published nine books, including the award-winning *Negotiating Critical Literacies with Young Children*, and received honors and awards from major professional organizations, including NCTE and AERA, where she has held appointive and elected positions.

Index